FICTION AND THE FICTION INDUSTRY

Bloomsbury Academic Collections: English Literary Criticism

This carefully chosen selection of 56 classic works of literary criticism comes from the archives of Athlone Press, one of the most distinguished publishers of English criticism in the period 1950–2000.

The volumes in the collection cover all periods and styles of literary criticism, from Beowulf to Pinter, and include works of literary theory as well as studies of specific periods, writers or works. Authors include Herbert Grierson, Barbara Hardy, Christopher Norris, George Kane, EMW Tillyard, Patricia Ball, Geoffrey Tillotson, David Holbrook, and John Sutherland.

All titles are issued in cased bindings as complete facsimile editions; ebook versions are also available.

Titles in English Literary Criticism are available in the following subsets:

English Literary Criticism: General Theory and History

English Literary Criticism: Pre-1700

English Literary Criticism: 18th-19th Centuries

English Literary Criticism: 20th Century

Other titles available in English Literary Criticism: General Theory and History include:

A Critical History of English Poetry, Herbert Grierson and J. C. Smith

Boccaccio in England: From Chaucer to Tennyson, Herbert G. Wright.

Fiction and the Fiction Industry, J. A. Sutherland

Librarianship and Literature: Essays in Honour of Jack Pafford, Edited by A. T. Milne

Suggestion and Statement in Poetry, Krishna Rayan

Tellers and Listeners: The Narrative Imagination, Barbara Hardy

The Advantage of Lyric: Essays on Feeling in Poetry, Barbara Hardy

The Fable as Literature, H. J. Blackham

The Making of the Modern Canon: Genesis and Crisis of a Literary Idea, Jan Gorak

The Story-shaped World: Fiction and Metaphysics, Some Variations on a Theme, Brian Wicker

William Empson and the Philosophy of Literary Criticism, C. C. Norris

FICTION AND THE FICTION INDUSTRY

J. A. Sutherland

BLOOMSBURY ACADEMIC COLLECTIONS
English Literary Criticism – General Theory and History

B L O O M S B U R Y
LONDON • NEW DELHI • NEW YORK • SYDNEY

Bloomsbury Academic
An imprint of Bloomsbury Publishing Plc

50 Bedford Square
London
WC1B 3DP
UK

1385 Broadway
New York
NY 10018
USA

www.bloomsbury.com

Bloomsbury is a registered trade mark of Bloomsbury Publishing Plc

First published in 1978
This edition published in 2013 by Bloomsbury Publishing plc

Bloomsbury Academic Collections
ISSN 2051-0012

British Library Cataloguing-in-Publication Data
A catalogue record for this book is available from the British Library.

ISBN: 9781472513151 (Hardback)
ISBN: 9781472511713 (ePDF)
ISBN: 9781472536129 (Bloomsbury Academic Collections: English Literary Criticism – General Theory and History)
Entire Collection ISBN: 9781472535412 (Bloomsbury Academic Collections: English Literary Criticism)

Library of Congress Cataloging-in-Publication Data
A catalog record for this book is available from the Library of Congress

Fiction and the Fiction Industry

Fiction and the Fiction Industry

J. A. SUTHERLAND

UNIVERSITY OF LONDON
THE ATHLONE PRESS
1978

Published by
THE ATHLONE PRESS
UNIVERSITY OF LONDON
at 4 Gower Street, London WC1

Distributed by
Tiptree Book Services Ltd
Tiptree, Essex

U.S.A. and Canada
Humanities Press Inc
New Jersey

British Library Cataloguing in Publication Data

Fiction and the fiction industry.
1. Publishers and publishing—Great Britain
I. Title
338.4'7'070573 Z323

ISBN 0 485 11177 2

Printed in Great Britain by
WESTERN PRINTING SERVICES LTD
BRISTOL

Acknowledgements

Part of the work for this book was done at Dartmouth College, New Hampshire, and I am grateful to the College and the Baker Library for the facilities they provided me. I would like to thank Nicholas Dyson and Karl Miller for much constructive criticism.

Contents

Abbreviations used in the text

AC	Arts Council Annual Report
Aut	The Author
Ban	Bananas
BB	Books and Bookmen
Bk	The Bookseller
DT	The Daily Telegraph
ES	The Evening Standard
FSF	Fantasy and Science Fiction
Grd	The Guardian
HW	The Human World
IHT	International Herald Tribune
LAR	Library Association Record
List	The Listener
Marg	Margins
NF	New Fiction
NR	The New Review
NS	The New Statesman
NSoc	New Society
NYRB	The New York Review of Books
NYT	The New York Times
NYTBR	The New York Times Book Review
Obs	The Observer
PE	Private Eye
PP	Plays and Players
PW	Publishers' Weekly
RT	Radio Times
S	Screen International
ScotI	Scottish International
Sp	The Spectator
SR	The Saturday Review
SS	Sight and Sound
ST	The Sunday Times
STel	The Sunday Telegraph
T	The Times
THES	The Times Higher Education Supplement
Time	Time Magazine
TLS	The Times Literary Supplement
TO	Time Out
VV	Village Voice

Introduction

Books are not ordinary merchandise.
Publishers' Association, 1962

The twentieth century is commonly taken as the era of inexorably rising production and as inexorably falling standards. Kingsley Amis's 'more will mean worse' has acquired a proverbial currency and an accepted truth extending far beyond the original debate on higher education and whether undergraduates more resemble finite bottles of hock or infinite tins of salmon. We fear the plentifulness of our age and the restless energy of its industry; Amis's law sums up what is for most people an instinctive response. As regards literature it is not simply instinct; there is a substantial case that mass literacy, mass-production and mass-consumption has lowered quality and standardised achievement. This view was given an authoritative statement in Q. D. Leavis's *Fiction and the Reading Public* (1932). Leavis's study drew in part on I. A. Richards's early work and the assertion was given other restatements of more or less intense pessimism, in *Scrutiny*, for whom *Fiction and the Reading Public* was the necessary 'New Realisation'; in T. S. Eliot's *Notes towards the Definition of Culture* and the proposed cultural hierarchy with its governing elites and docile mass for whom learning is less necessary than 'a respect for learning'; and in Richard Hoggart's *The Uses of Literacy* which argued, as the allusion in the title suggests, that cultural achievement must be earned by adversity in the face of shortage.

These influential critics would persuade us that the plenitude and convenience of twentieth-century reading matter is not riches but evidence of mechanical exploitation verging, at its most efficient, on cultural totalitarianism. Indeed, writing of the state of English fiction in 1932 Mrs Leavis uses language which historical hindsight might regard as appropriately applied to the emergence of European fascism:

I have here isolated [she wrote] and shown the workings of a number of tendencies which, having assumed the form of commercial and economic machinery, are now so firmly established that they run on their own and whither they choose; they have assumed such a monstrous impersonality that individual effort towards controlling or checking them seems ridiculously futile. This is probably the most terrifying feature of our civilisation. (*Fiction and the Reading Public*, London, 1932, p. 270)

Leavis wrote as a detached critic and 'literary anthropologist'—a borrowed term recording her apprehension of a new cultural savagery which must be scientifically understood before it can be properly combated. Publishers, from their commercially involved position in the book-making process, have often been inclined to agree that mass-production of books had reached the point where alarms must be sounded. Two years after *Fiction and the Reading Public* Geoffrey Faber put forward his professional opinion as to the cause of present troubles and a short, purgative remedy:

The market is glutted. General publishing is therefore fast degenerating into a gambling competition for potential best-sellers. This is a profoundly unsatisfactory state of affairs which may have—will have—very evil effects on the future of English letters. . . . But in so far as over-production is a cause of the evil, we have the remedy in our own hands. We have only to agree to reduce our output in order to restore the book trade to a healthy condition. (*A Publisher Speaking*, London, 1934, p. 136)

'Fewer and better'; the call has been echoed by a minority of thoughtful publishers throughout the century. One can juxtapose with Faber's the following comment by J. P. Dessauer, writing in *Publishers' Weekly*, 7 October 1974:

Surfeit and mediocrity are luxuries we can no longer afford. Unless we are prepared to suffer internal strangulation, to suffocate under the weight of millions of unwanted and unsaleable books ground out yearly, we shall have to find ways to curtail the industry's over-production.

But what, one may ask, constitutes over-production? The glut which Faber contemplated amounted to under 10,000 titles a year in Britain and the US; Dessauer's 'surfeit' is 30,000 and more in each market. Clearly the terminology here is less flexible than the figures which inspire it.

In other ways one can score fairly easy opening points against the pessimistic view that more has inevitably meant and will inevitably mean worse. In the case of *Fiction and the Reading Public* one can compare prophecy with what happened. The book was published in 1932 and records, as we have seen, 'terror' at the changes wrought in English civilisation by commercialism, urban centralisation and the mass-market for literature. But it was only three years afterwards that, via the High Street chain of Woolworth's, Penguins were launched. This was one of the more culturally welcome events of the century. Yet Penguins needed the most aggressive and Americanised of the multiple stores to break into the market. They needed mass sales, above the bestseller threshold (13,000–17,000 was the initial break-even range; Lane calculated that he would need an annual volume sale of 2m; PW 12.8.39). And they exploited a new, technologically transformed kind of book, the mass-market paperback, a phenomenon Mrs Leavis does not anticipate in *Fiction and the Reading Public*. No-one would maintain that Penguin Books have aggravated the cultural condition. Yet Penguins could not have succeeded without the vulgar '3d and 6d' store which represented for the Leavises in 1933 some of 'the worst effects of mass-production and standardisation' (F. R. Leavis and D. Thompson, *Culture and Environment*, London, 1933, p. 33).

There is a tendency among pessimistic commentators to assume disastrous climaxes and bursting points. In fact culture would seem to be more resilient and resourceful than we habitually take it to be. Indices of production and consumption have all multiplied, rival media have installed themselves, without the feared collapses. The reading public has not been reduced to the condition of denatured Epsilons; nor has it stratified as it should have done to fulfil pessimistic prophecies. These facts have lent strength to more recently fashionable theories which oppose gloom and argue that the problem of the future will not be cultural regimentation in a consumer manipulating society, but the bewildering diversities and cultural opportunities of a post-industrial, technocentric world.

Publishers now commonly endorse a pluralism of élite readerships, growing out of and dependent on a massive industrial base. Dan Lacy, Vice-President of McGraw-Hill, probably the largest single book publisher in the world, cites the astonishing increase of the American booktrade from $500m value in 1952 to $4b in the mid 1970s, with the absorption of publishing into communications conglomerates with turnovers as large as those of whole countries, and observes that the influx of new money and of new management into publishing, and the rise to a dominant position of what might be called market-oriented publishing has by no means smothered traditional forms of what might be called in distinction author-oriented publishing, but rather has given it new vigour and resources. (*Trends in American Publishing*, ed. K. L. Henderson, Illinois, 1968, p. 7)

Lacy grants that 'author-oriented' publishing can never offer the same return as those 'market-oriented' educational books whose profitability laid the ground for the American post-war boom; nor can they match the mass-market paperback or the technical publication with its precisely predictable specialist readership. Nonetheless small, editorially independent, 'literary' houses will proliferate as the conglomerates extend. Such independent houses will have little to gain from the economies of vast scale and industrial rationalisation, though they will indirectly benefit from these factors working in an expanded and fully stimulated market. Shielded by uncompeting giants they will find themselves with a clear field and a proportional slice of a business increasing at 10–15 per cent annually. (It is an aspect of Lacy's optimism about the future that he does not point out that these small, specialist outfits might be highly vulnerable if the annual increase did not materialise, or reversed itself—more of which later.)

One recognises in Lacy's view a belief that good literature is a kind of surplus value whose fractional amount swells with total book production. There are familiar and longstanding applications of this model to the world of fiction. It operates, for example, in the notion of the General Trade Publisher, a figure responsible for most of the hardback fiction in this country. The idea that the 'good' novel is somehow parasitic on less good but more remunerative novels, and dependent on their wealth-generating profusion, is often expressed in the trade wisdom that bestsellers pay for art. One may apply the principle in other ways. Publishers, for example, argue that to keep their fiction programmes ambitious it is necessary to have a large, secure market. (This view was recently urged by the British book trade at the prospect of Australia becoming an open market.) Another way of looking at it is to see the publishing of novels as a lottery in which an occasional title hits the jackpot, and pays for those that do not. (Henry Miller's *Tropics* seem to have served this function for Calder and Boyars in the 1960s). A third version might be found in the systematical, two-tier arrangement in which the unambitious work (not necessarily a novel) provides the benevolent publisher with money to 'reinvest' in literature. (Cape's publishing Ian Fleming is a case in point; this fastidious publisher usually has at least one spy or detective-novelist on its list.) This last finds corroborating evidence in America where many general publishers, responsible for quality fiction also have huge, solidly profitable educational divisions. In a smaller way Faber ('the' English publishers, as Sylvia Plath called them) carry on from their earliest partnership days as Faber and Gwyer the publishing of nursing textbooks (not, one might add, what Plath had in mind). A fourth kind of interdependency principle is the way in which small ambitious publishers (Secker and Warburg, for example) have sheltered under the protection of large broader based groups (Heinemann in Secker's case). Finally, one might also cite the way that British publishers of quality hardback fiction have increasingly bought into the mass paperback market.

In each of these representative cases 'literary' novels exist superstructurally on a mass market or 'unliterary' sources of publishing wealth. This view of fiction's economics has become generally accepted. In his sophisticated study *The Situation of the Novel* (1970) Bernard Bergonzi presents the mutuality as something quite uncontroversial. Without bestsellers, he asserts, there could be no 'literary' novel because there would be no novels, *tout court*. One might object that he takes a narrow view of possible interdependencies. Nonetheless as a representative literary-critical view of the 1970s it shows a wide divergence from *Fiction and the Reading Public* and its terror of 'commercial and economic machinery':

It is well known that the economics of novel-publishing is precarious; that first novels almost always lose money, and very few novels make much; and yet publishers are still remarkably eager to go on publishing them, because the rewards from hitting the jack pot with a best-seller are so prodigious. Yet it is conceivable that the economic basis of novel-publishing could change in such a way that bringing out novels would cease to be worth while for a publisher who wanted to stay in business: if, say, the relation between the certain loss on run-of-the-mill novels and the possible gains from a best-seller were to alter in a way unfavourable to the publisher, publishing novels at all would cease to be an attractive gamble. In that case, presumably, novels would disappear from the market, and publishers would turn their attention to more profitable kinds of book.... There is little that the prospective novelist could do, apart from circulating his work in manuscript, since the printing and distribution of a novel is a complex and expensive business (unlike the case of a book of poems which can easily be duplicated or, for that matter, recorded on tape), and few novelists could meet it out of their own pockets. Presumably for a few years the flood of unprinted novels would mount higher and higher in ever-increasing frustration, but I imagine that within a generation novels would have ceased to be written, and that some other vehicle would have been found for the 'one bright book of life' (B. Bergonzi, *The Situation of the Novel*, London, 1970, repr. 1972, pp. 16–17).

The materialist assumptions of Bergonzi's argument are easy to substantiate. Because of its bulk (50,000–250,000 words) its first-form price (consistently 10 per cent of the average weekly wage in the twentieth century) and the large sales required for the recovery of investment, the novel is necessarily ingrained into the commercial system and advanced technology; more so since, as Bergonzi points out, to be profitably pursued it usually has to be a multiple operation. One must publish novels to make money out of a novel. The form is thus peculiarly dependent on the goodwill of the idealistic-commercial publisher and such sentiments as those expressed by the editorial director of Collins (otherwise the most commercial of British publishers) in May 1976:

Every year we publish 20 or so novels which not only do not make a profit but which we suspect from the start are unlikely to do so. Why should a commercial house behave so irrationally? In part out of a belief that good fiction *must* be published, that we owe it to the novelist and to posterity to publish novels of quality. (Bk 15.5.76)

In this respect the novel is quite unlike poetry, 80 per cent of whose modern classics, it is reckoned, originate in commercially pure little magazines or self-published ventures which can be financed from personal pockets. It is a fair guess that 80 per cent of great twentieth-century novels have originated in the lists of General Trade Publishing. Fiction's destiny is to this extent inextricably bound up with the fortunes of the booktrade as a whole.

II

Bergonzi published *The Situation of the Novel* in 1970, secure that he was speculating rather wildly about possible demises of 'the one bright book of life'. By 1974 things had so gone to the bad that one might have argued that his doomsday predictions were well on the way to fulfilment. The 'everlasting boom' which English publishing had enjoyed since the war was, like much else in English life, put at risk by the world inflation and recession accompanying the oil crisis of 1973–4 and general economic austerity. Up to this point the trade had enjoyed steady, self-sustained expansion, supported by relatively stable prices and a smoothly functioning sales and distribution system. Between 1946 and 1972 the number of titles produced rose from 13,000 to over 30,000; the turnover of the trade from £27m to over £200m; the average price of a novel, meanwhile, rose only from 12s 6d to £2; and although the balance of power shifted between them, institutional purchasers and the bookshop contrived to maintain a steady demand. Now, in 1973, all that was put at risk. Perversely, once we had come to accept the booming mass-market as a necessary infrastructure, we seemed in danger of losing it.

The search for literary-historical 'moments' or 'turning points' can be an artificial and largely self-serving critical activity. But it is, I think, reasonable to see 1973 as a crisis. It took the form of general instability, largely brought about by uncontrolled price increases, together with a suddenly unpredictable market for books. This crisis will be examined in detail but some of the features which are matters of record may be anticipated here. Printing costs went up by 30 per cent a year, or more. New novels soared in price—between 30 and 50 per cent in one year alone (Bk 28.2.75). In 1972 £2 was a normal price, in 1976 £3.95. (It could be shown that the impact of this rise was, perhaps psychological rather than real. But psychology is a determining factor in bookbuying, which is guided not by need but self-gratification.)

After 1973 books came under increasing pressure from price resistance. Service and distribution costs soared—postage going up sometimes twice a year. The profits of key publishing concerns dipped, though in many cases annual turnover was markedly higher; costs were eating into revenue faster than inflation was swelling it. Hence 'fewer and safer' was a slogan more in evidence than 'fewer and better.' Public library purchase, a mainstay of marginal publishing ventures (like poetry and first novels), was cut back with the shrinking of public funds and the concurrent price spiral. In one county, new novel purchase was cut out altogether. It was, *The Guardian* commented, Fahrenheit 32: 'they're not burning our books, but freezing them out' (Grd 31.1.76). With capital spending scheduled to fall from £13m to £2m by 1980 (Grd 13.5.76) libraries seriously considered operating without fiction departments, or in makeshift shanties (there was a lot of rather apocalyptic speculation at the period). Small and middle-sized hardback publishers, on whom the production of quality novels depends, were coming under increasing pressure to forfeit a larger share of their paperback royalties, a source which had become substantial as the 'revolutionalised' paperback market expanded to 30 per cent of the total. Internationally the American Justice Department's anti-trust investigation threatened the hitherto protected British Traditional Market, on which the remarkable 45 per cent exporting record of the booktrade in large part depended. Membership of the EEC produced an ambiguous and potentially erosive situation, by which overseas-printed books might, it seemed, evade copyright exclusion. (The bi-national Penguin-Viking house had tentative plans to exploit this loophole, which they withdrew under fierce trade pressure; see ES 10.12.75, Bk 17.7.76.)

Domestic outlets were similarly under pressure. Retail bookshops, whose stock can be notoriously sluggish, aimed to reduce holdings and to speed turnover. As a result a book of anything less than bestselling popularity was that much less likely to be found on the shelf; at the same time publishers, in the interest of stimulating their cash flow and reducing stockholding costs, were shortening backlists and had become notably less co-operative on single-copy orders. 'Ordered any good books lately?' was the ironic title of one consumer's guide, pointing to the interminable waits suffered by would-be buyers, as publishers demonstrated reluctance to fill small orders. The fact that by 1975 some publishers were refusing to supply orders under £10, and others levying surcharges, led to hostility between the Booksellers' and Publishers' Associations (Bk 4.10.75). Bookshops seemed to have fallen behind the times, it was felt, especially when comparisons were made with Germany which had teleordering and efficient wholesaling or America which had high-pressure promotion methods. Indeed it seemed that the bookshop, the foundation of the trade's distributive rationale, might be doomed commercially. 'Britain's Bookshops are Vanishing Fast' ran one report, 'at present there is only one proper bookshop for every 100,000 adults, and that number looks like going down, as booksellers report a "frightening fall" in the profits of smaller businesses. "Their plight is serious and they need every possible help and assistance otherwise many will not survive"' (ES 29.4.76). Booksellers' profitability has always been low, according to *Bookseller* figures it had averaged at 4.8, 4.7, 4.3 per cent in the years 1973–5. (8 per cent was reckoned to be necessary for minimum economic well being. Bk 8.5.76.)

Hitherto the low profitability of bookshops had tended only to limit the promotion of books and the more expensive forms of modernisation, a fact which enhanced their traditional and conservative aspect. Bookshops were left behind in the supermarket and boutique revolution, often giving the forlorn impression that they were waiting for the carriage trade to return. Now, it would seem, more serious limitations were inevitable. A thinning out of the already thin ranks seemed economically necessary—especially of the most attractive kind of bookshop, the small, intimate, browsing establishment. 'In all probability,' it was reported, 'the range of stock held by even the biggest bookshops will be reduced and slower sellers restricted to a by-order only basis' (THES 2.7.76). The effect of this particular decline is potentially epochal. The small bookshop holding an extensive stock performs a vital regulatory function in the British booktrade, since it is the sole justification for the net book system, a system which involves restraint on the part of large metropolitan bookstores not to give the kind of discounts to customers which they (and only they) can afford. The Net Book Agreement works as a de facto subsidy for small retailers and for those in outlying regions and also ensures that institutional sales go through accredited retailers with set concessions. It is only through some such measure as the NBA that the optimum bookshop service of one per 30,000 of the literate population could be achieved.

The NBA is envied in the US, 40 per cent of whose sales go through bookstores, compared to an estimated 65–75 per cent in the UK (PW 8.7.74, Bk 14.5.77). The Canadian Royal Commission on publishing which reported in 1972 was similarly envious of a system which established control, and discouraged the rapacities of direct selling, mail-order and competitive discounts. It would appear, however, that the British NBA was shrivelling with the bookshops which were its raison d'être. Ironically Macmillan, the firm which had been instrumental in inaugurating the NBA in 1897, made tentative moves that would have subverted the system in 1975, by not marking the price on their slowest moving books. They backed down in the face of booksellers' protest, but the augury was ill (PW 18.8.75). The 'early selling' and the 'early reviewing' controversies of 1976–7 might also be taken to suggest a gradual loss of collective self-discipline within the British booktrade.

What was universally termed the 'squeeze' had a positively throttling effect on the 'literary' novel. After two years of this attrition the situation was sufficiently acute to warrant a *Spectator* leader on the apparently imminent fiction famine:

> Readers are in for a lean time. Fiction is especially hard-hit, and now that some local authorities have stopped their libraries from buying novels it is likely to get much worse. Our literary editor has calculated that there were twice as many published in the same period last year. It may be that writers of fiction will take their place alongside writers of poetry as minority artists. (Sp 31.1.76)

There were other symptoms of cultural crisis. Britain's only surviving large-circulation intellectual magazine, *Encounter*, went begging in the face of the Micawberish economics: Expenses £100,000, Income £40,000 (ES 26.11.75). *The New Review* (not a large-circulation magazine) got by with an estimated per-reader subsidy of £5. Some of the main literary reviews, *The Spectator*, *The New Statesman* and *The Observer* were on a circulation slide. *The Spectator* and *The Observer* seemed particularly shaky, until their respective sugar-daddies came along. 'The Arts Staggering' ran a *Guardian* feature on performing arts: 'Britain's 1,000 opera, theatre and ballet companies, orchestras and community and regional arts associations are threatened with collapse or extreme cutbacks' (Grd 31.10.75). The Royal Opera House forecast a deficit of £300,000, the Royal Shakespeare Company one of £200,000. Cash crisis in the Arts Council (which went hand extended to the government in 1975) raised fears that a network of provincial theatres, painfully installed in the post-war years, would be sacrificed to the White Elephant on the South Bank which came into operation in 1976—almost as if it had been waiting all those years for an appropriately desperate crisis. CORT (the Council of Regional Theatres) indicated that a 36 per cent increase in their Arts Council grant would be needed to prevent the provinces reverting to their former condition of 'cultural slums' (PP 6.1.76). The Royal Court, which had sponsored major innovations in post-war English theatre, was forced to close for a period at the end of 1975 for lack of ready money and a deficit of £40,000. Ronald Bryden wrote, in allusion to another terminal case of the time: 'the invalid the British theatre brings to mind this winter is General Franco. Take away the blood transfusions, heart-pacer, kidney machine and intravenous feeding tubes, and what you have left is a corpse' (PP 6.1.76).

The Government 'think tank' on the English film industry reported in late 1975 on ways that some kind of future could be 'salvaged'—this at a time when, as critics tartly noted, the best that native film-makers could offer was *The Bawdy Adventures of Tom Jones*, a shameless travesty of the 1963 production. Commenting on the report Dilys Powell took the occasion to note that, as in popular music and to some extent in popular fiction, the best talents were drawn abroad, down the so called 'fame drain':

> Creative people leave this country and go to work in Europe and America. John Schlesinger makes *The Day of the Locust* in the United States; I know it is an American subject, but there must be themes here which could engage his attention. Dirk Bogarde has not acted for years in a film made in England.... Sixteen years ago the British cinema was discovering the British working people and Karel Reisz was directing *Saturday Night and Sunday Morning*. But last year we watched *The Gambler*; and Karel Reisz made that in America. If these were isolated instances we could shrug them off. (ST 1.2.76)

Meanwhile the busiest film-maker and the 'hope' of the British film industry was Lew Grade whose ITC had 'conquered' the West End with *The Return of the Pink Panther* and was following it up with *The Pink Panther Strikes Again*. Grade modestly proclaimed his destiny: 'Don't call me a tycoon I am just a showman ... and if in any way I am contributing to what people call the Renaissance of British films, I am more than happy' (S 7.2.76). His status as a new Lorenzo was certified when Sir Harold Wilson made him a lord in his resignation honours list.

In another quarter, the BBC was announced to be cutting back 10 per cent on programme schedules, impoverished by the unexpected failure of viewers to buy colour television sets with their higher licence fee. The need was to save £10m over 1976. In August 1975 there were rumours that BBC2, a major cultural benefit of the 1960s, was about to close down altogether (ES 28.8.75). Generally the surge of energy which had made England exciting in the previous decade seemed to have dried up. And a main reason for the drying up was the financial timidity and instability brought about by double-figure inflation, budget cutbacks, the three-day-week, and uncertainties about the economic future of the country.

III

The most alarming feature of this period was the rise in retail prices. In the specific case of novels, however, it should not be assumed that rocketing prices of themselves lead automatically to disaster. Such periods have, in the past, been tonic. Two beneficial price disruptions come to mind: that consequent on the Napoleonic wars, and that of the second world war. Both were notable for explosive increases in price followed by new dispensations for the novel and, thereafter, long stable periods—historically speaking the age extending from Scott to Henry James and what, in our own time, we might call the age of Graham Greene (i.e. 1945–70). In both cases what seems to have underwritten a gradual and stable expansion was a shift to institutional, as opposed to individual purchasers: the circulating library being the institution in one case, the public library in the other. Arguably some such jolt as a threefold increase in unit cost is needed to bring about this kind of change, which in turn brings about long-lived stability.

One can see why some galvanic shock might be needed before such changes do occur. As regards its production and marketing processes, British literature is famously conservative. It is very rigidly controlled; it maintains retail price maintenance long after it has been elsewhere removed, and strenuously discourages direct selling which then inhibits the more adventurous kinds of advertising. Book advertising is less flamboyant today than it was even in the 1920s, when Gollancz launched his controversial Sunday advertisements. Certainly Britain has never followed America in this respect. A report in 1974 indicated that the booktrade spent on advertising only one sixth of what the record industry spent (Bk 1.6.74).

The British booktrade is kept in line by the Publishers' Association, the Society of Authors and the Booksellers' Association, all set up together with the Net Book Agreement in the last two decades of the nineteenth century, after a long period of damaging, Hobbesian war of all against all. On one level the professional institutions have served to maintain a gentlemanly code. On another they serve as dams against a recurrence of potentially suicidal individualism. The British trade has thus founded itself on discipline, self-control and protectionism—sometimes with a fierceness reminiscent of the Catholic Church in its most militant phase. When, for example, a lone voice was raised at the Booksellers' Association conference in 1976 suggesting the abolition of the NBA it met the rejoinder that it 'was heresy to discuss the demise of RPM' (Bk 8.5.76). Some justification for conduct which would be unacceptable in conventional trades can be found in the example of other 'open' and relatively uncontrolled book cultures. Canada, the most open market for books in the English speaking world, offers its reading public more British books than are to be found in the US and more American books than are to be found in Britain. The agency system and free import offers the Canadian public 20,000 new titles a year from each of the major English language producers and almost as many from the major French language producer; a notional 70,000 books a year is available to the Canadian. Yet Canadian literary culture is not enriched. Rather it is swamped under this annual deluge of good things. In 1970, for example, there were only 40 new fiction titles emanating from Canada. Canada's contribution to the 70,000 total is some 2,500. Smaller population would account for some of this passivity and the fact that Canada does not enjoy Britain's demographic advantage of an urbanised, dense population in a small land mass. Nonetheless the Royal Commission on Canadian publishing was more of the opinion that it was the very openness and unprotected nature of the Canadian booktrade which had conduced to the meagreness of its literature.

In Britain control has created stability, prosperity, order and professional dignity. On the other hand it has halted processes which have, for example, been evident in the gramophone record industry. The book trade has resisted standardisation of its product; it has discouraged such things as paperback reviewing or primary publishing in paperback. The inhibition on paperbacks for libraries, or on the setting up of university bookshops, undoubtedly stunted the evolution of the 'quality' or 'egghead' paperback in this country; hence it became an American speciality, with a palpable cultural loss for the UK. Similarly in 1977 the Booksellers' Association registered the strongest opposition to the imaginative scheme of selling books in public libraries on the grounds that this might encourage direct purchase from publishers 'with disastrous effects both on local bookshops and on nationally based library suppliers' (Bk 23.4.77). The professional institutions have held back the simultaneous bookclubs, long flourishing in America, and bookclub sales in bookshops, common in France and Germany (ST 1.10.76). The booktrade has made relatively little impact on the new youth market, to whom 1960s bookshops seemed antiquated and parental institutions. Here again, Britain compares badly with the US. In America young readers have made novelists like Fowles, Brautigan, Golding and Vonnegut what *Time* calls 'Lords of the Campus'. Deference to student taste in the US (and the greater flexibility of their syllabuses) meant that such authors progressed from underground or cult status to set-book authors. With up to 10 million young Americans in higher education and freshman English a compulsory course this has entailed huge sales for certain living novelists which have little equivalent in Britain, any more than we have the huge campus sale of extra-curricular books—sufficiently important in booktrade terms to warrant separate college best-seller lists.

The English booktrade is remarkable for surviving names and a physically unchanging product. Some names, like those of Longmans, go back as far as 250 years (further back than the novel itself, one might claim). There is even a kind of conservatism built into the book physically—as if it had reached the end point of its development, like the eskimo igloo. (Compare again with the audio-visual market; in twenty years we have progressed from the 78rpm shellac record through the vinyl LP to the tape cassette; from 12 inch black and white television to 24 inch colour and the video recorder.) Look at the novel of 1875, even of 1775, and it is recognisably the same kind of object as a new novel of 1975. It is produced in much the same way, by a trade organised in unions which could presumably trace their origin back to medieval guilds. (Although we are told by Woodrow Wyatt that modern printing equipment can be handled by any twenty-year old secretary after three weeks' training.) The novel is sold in bookshops, some of which have pedigrees as long as those of the older publishing houses. It may, to continue the theme, be reviewed in *The Spectator* (founded 1828) or *The Times* (founded in 1785) in terms which, Marxist critics tell us, serve to maintain the 'archaic mould of England' and further entrench 'the literary counter-revolution' (Ban 3.1975).

If one accepts that the literary-publishing complex is by nature inert, backward-looking and over-controlled it can be argued that the destruction of old forms is a precondition of any advance. One may echo D. H. Lawrence's anarchic call: 'Surgery for the Novel—or a Bomb'. Such a view might welcome crisis. Of course the crisis need not take the drastic form of threefold price increase. Something analogous was brought about in 1894 by just the opposite, a slashing reduction in the price of the new novel from 31s 6d to 6s. By the 1890s only the libraries bought three-deckers and had thus become monopoly purchasers of new fiction. The new 6s price helped shift purchasing power back to the private buyer and the fiction-carrying magazine, redressing what had become an imbalance. This era of stability—that of the 6s–7s 6d novel—lasted almost as long (50 years) as the age of the 31s 6d three volume novel (73 years). What seems finally to have brought it down was that once again the libraries came to have too great a share of the purchasing of new fiction, leaving an unexploited sector of private buyers. One consequence was the innovation of the quality paperback in 1935. In 1939, when Penguin was four years old and had sold 25m copies, John Lane (Allen's brother) reported: 'the need for a cheap series had arisen because new book sales in England were being made principally to rental libraries which supplied publishers with about 9/10th of their total sales' (PW 12.8.39).

The pattern seems clear enough. The publishing of literature, especially new fiction, goes in long plateaux, interrupted violently by short periods of transition bringing about a new balance of institutional and private purchase. The effect of these transitions is to harmonise disruptive factors, cumulative changes in the reading public, author unrest, commodity price changes or the invasion by foreign competitors with more efficient techniques.

Historians of publishing observe that such periods are necessarily painful and that the industry has no inbuilt mechanism for dealing with them. As John Tebbel deduced from his *History of Book Publishing in the United States:* 'The weakness of publishing's seamless web of continuity has been, and continues to be, its difficulty in breaking out of the patterns established early in its history' (Vol. 2, New York and London, 1975, p.x). More important, perhaps, is the fact that publishers and the book trade generally do not want to break out of its established webs and patterns, and will fight to preserve them. The successful defence of the NBA before the Restrictive Practices Court in 1962 was based on the argument that books are so important culturally as to require unique immunisation from the modern economic climate. The 'victory' preserved the trade in the methods of the late nineteenth century, just as the Traditional Market Agreement preserved the markets of that period (i.e. the Empire). It is easy to take a sinister view of this conservatism. In a challenging reassessment of the NBA in *The Guardian*, 16 March 1976, Martin Lightfoot concluded that a conspiracy was being imposed on the British people by a reactionary minority determined to maintain the *ancien régime* for their own benefit:

> It seems difficult to avoid the belief that the present situation is the result of a middle-class alliance which is not necessarily in the interests of the population at large. It is an alliance sustained by an inbuilt cultural pessimism which maintains that the potential readership of books (and especially of 'good' books) is pretty much a fixed quantity and that increased availability cannot alter this pattern.... Where commercial interests take up an alliance on a platform of such cultural pessimism, public suspicion is justified and only to be expected. At the least we are faced with the choice between open access to a smaller number of books as against restricted access to a larger number. In this raw form in which it is seldom displayed the Net Book Agreement is a social and cultural issue of some importance.

Lightfoot contends that we are witnessing a crisis; that things cannot go on in the future as they have in the past, change must come. The question which then arises is 'What kind of crisis?' Are we to take 1973–6 as a period of transition—what Tebbel calls a 'breaking out'—or what might be more aptly called a breaking down, in some more catastrophic sense? Frank Kermode has suggested on the evidence of recent changes that we are witnessing the end of a literary-cultural era:

all our notions of what a book ought to cost are founded on the now obsolete assumption that paper is cheap. It isn't, nor is the labour of the typesetter. And books, despite technical expedients and innovations, will continue to get dearer.... The shapes and forms of books are not part of the nature of things. A book of poems hasn't always been a 'slim volume', and the fact that volumes of modern poetry are usually slim is a fact bearing on the kind of poetry they contain as well as on the economics of their production. So the changes that are likely to overtake publishing in the near future will also alter, perhaps radically, the substance of writing. The present calm in 'British writing' may strike historians as appropriate to the last days, or the after life of an epoch. (DT 16.8.75)

In the chapters that follow some answer will be attempted to the question whether we are facing an apocalypse or a periodic adjustment.

Although the procedure of this book is that of a survey the material is arranged so as to present an argument, which had better be laid out at once. Up to the 1970s, it would seem, the British book trade sustained a laudable diversity in the upper reaches of our literary culture. There is, as crude evidence of this richness, the numerousness of the titles produced annually for the British market; within 10 per cent of the American figure in 1975, with only a quarter of the population and many fewer college graduates. Gross number of titles means very little, perhaps. But taken with the relatively low money turnover of the British home trade (crudely, for every million in the British sector, six million in the American, Bk 3.4.76) the calculation is that many more books sustain themselves on lower domestic sales than in the US. This confirms a vaunted feature of British literary culture: that it supports heterogeneity and caters for what are, essentially, a multitude of minority readerships. The organisation of a trade where so much of the business is concerned with small amounts of books and small amounts of money will necessarily appear ramshackle to the cold business eye. It presents, to quote Gerald Bartlett of the Booksellers' Association, 'an immensity which defies efficiency, yet is in itself in the most worthwhile terms the greatest of efficiencies' (Bk 13.12.75).

Recently this immensity has been put at risk by what is here seen as a trend, a crisis and a failure. The trend has been the increasing assimilation of the book industry to rational styles of production and marketing—'efficiency' in Bartlett's first sense. One of the consequences has been a distinct lessening of culturally philanthropic investments by 'responsible' proprietary publishers—partly because such publishers are anyway in retreat against new industrial organisation and the commercial logic that progress is on the side of long print runs and fast turnover.

The crisis is that affecting the public libraries caught between rising book prices and reduced public spending. Because the public library is uncoerced by either commercial pressure, or irresistible reader preferences, it has consistently respected the rights of diverse and minority tastes; no one, for example, takes a public library to task for there being only one date stamp in a three year old novel. One consequence of the system has been to make novels commercially viable through library purchase that in future may cease to be so. Another indirect but potent effect of the library has been educational; since it allows members to borrow many more novels than they could possibly buy (three a week, normally, representing at 1976 prices £12 worth of new fiction), they have supplied a huge reading public, constituting some 30 per cent of the adult population. Should the public libraries cease to supply this public the eventual consequences for the novel will be momentous.

The failure, as I take it, is that of interventionist bodies like the Arts Council or the cultural agencies of government to remedy current problems. Ideally the Arts Council, with its benign 'arm's length' policy, should have contributed to a plural, uncoerced literary culture. Unfortunately it has hitherto had insufficient cash or public goodwill behind it to do so. The state's reluctance to implement Public Lending Right may also be counted a failure of some significance. And I would add as another, contributory, failure that of the British critical establishment. With all the opinion-forming means at its disposal, this body has, for largely technical reasons, never assumed decisive authority.

Weighing all the evidence it seems that we are indeed witnessing a transition of some kind, equivalent perhaps to the major transitions of 1894 (the abolition of the three-decker) or of 1851 (the introduction of free trade in books, which served to divert much new fiction into magazines). The difference is that the forces for change on those occasions came largely from within the booktrade. Today the situation is complicated by outside factors which may override the trade's own energies. I have tried to indicate some of these in the first section, 'Crisis and Change'. In the third section, 'Trends, Mainly American' I suggest the way that things may go, barring some kind of economic doomsday. The second section, 'State Remedies' deals largely with the efforts of the central authorities, among whom are included the state-supported universities.

Crisis and Change

1 Fiction and the 1973-6 Library Crisis

In the first week of September 1975 the national press carried two announcements one of which might be construed as hopeful for literature, the other of which was, without doubt, very bad news indeed. The first concerned a 'Green Paper' from the Labour Party Arts Study Group, under the chairmanship of Renee Short. This projected a tenfold increase in the money allocated to arts (from £25m to £250m); that the London based Arts Council be abolished in favour of a decentralised regional system; that Arts Council activities be democratised by such innovations as a 'socialist policy for music'; that, for literature, 'direct intervention in the shape of a state publishing house with regional branches may become a necessity'. One more lame duck, the English novel, viewed the prospect of salvation by nationalisation (Bk 18.10.75).

The other announcement, three days later, was the Whitehall circular instructing local authorities on the economies required for 'zero growth' in 1976–7. 'Local spending cuts', a *Guardian* headline warned, 'will affect everyone' (Grd 5.9.75). 'Londoners face three tough years', *The Evening Standard* told homegoing commuters in a lead article that continued with the ominous paragraph title, 'FEWER BOOKS' (ES 5.9.75).

At first it may seem odd that a measure which would be principally evident in bus queues, homeless families and unwelcomely persistent garbage should imperil the English novel. But post-war fiction had hitherto depended on staple library sales. Libraries are an obvious non-essential to urban life. 'You have to have electricity or bread,' observed one publisher grimly, 'you don't have to have books' (Bk 15.3.77). In late September features began to appear containing news of four-day weeks for certain London libraries. Already, earlier in 1975, some damaging economies had been taken. Wiltshire County Council, for example, reduced its annual spending on books for the year by £25,000. Bromley borough cut new book purchase by 25 to 30 per cent (Bk 26.7.75). And fiction is an area where economising libraries instinctively make their first cuts. Ominously in Buckinghamshire no new fiction was to be bought at all in 1975, despite protests from deprived ratepayers demanding their legal right to a 'comprehensive and efficient service'; and from a worried Publishers' Association in alliance with a Library Association who branded the county as 'a dirty word in public librarianship' (Bk 11.9.76). In 1975–1976 the Buckinghamshire book fund was cut from the £290,000 the libraries wanted, to a bleak £65,000 (Bk 19.2.77). Though extreme, Buckinghamshire was not unique. A 'leading county librarian' was quoted in *The Bookseller* (26.7.75) prophesying that new novels 'would be rare or non existent in public libraries for at least a decade'. By 1976 the Library Association was contemplating 'a radical change of emphasis in which libraries might curtail their function as a major outlet for popular fiction and increase the provision of more specialised and expensive non-fiction works' (DT 29.4.76).

Rounds of cuts followed rounds of cuts. In February 1976 *The Library Association Record* reported that 'while one in three library authorities had less money to spend in real terms in 1975–1976, it is likely that only one in three will escape cuts in 1976–1977' (Bk 28.2.76). In May 1976 the librarian of the London Borough of Brent was quoted as saying 'libraries have been savaged in a way that is unprecedented in the twentieth century. We have been clobbered' (Obs 16.5.76). In June 1976 at a Councillors' Conference at Brighton the Finance Director for West Yorkshire Metropolitan County Council moved to 'scrap free library books on the rates' (ES 16.6.76); there seemed a swell of approval for this measure and later in the year Lord Donaldson (mindful perhaps of the Redcliffe-Maud Report which declared the public library to be the cornerstone of future regional cultural planning) implored local authorities not to impose on libraries 'more than their share' of cuts (T 7.9.76). In Autumn 1976 further cuts were said to be slashing library expenditure 'to the bone' (ES 15.10.76). Figures were provided to show what this meant. In the year 1975–6 the average county expenditure on library books per 1,000 population was £473; the average metropolitan expenditure £526; the average London borough expenditure £671. Taken with the average book price of around £5 and the suggested Department of Education and Science norm (250 books per 1,000 population) it would seem that the population was getting less than half an 'efficient and comprehensive service' (Bk 19.2.77). In the face of this unremitting stringency some authorities swallowed their pride and frankly asked for donations. 'Inflation-hit libraries beg for books,' ran a *Sunday Times* headline (18.4.76). The story beneath made the point, already familiar, that library austerity was 'making publishers reluctant to publish new fiction writers'.

The novel receives a death sentence so often that some theorists assume it is in the nature of the form always to be on its last legs. Nonetheless on this occasion the pressures were extraordinarily intense. That public libraries should pick on the novel for a main economy was natural enough. Public libraries began in the mid-nineteenth century providing that favourite Victorian commodity, 'useful knowledge'. They only became major dealers in fiction after the second world war, and then as a result of factors beyond their control. There has always been a pressure on libraries to relinquish a non-educational service which booksellers, especially, felt had arisen as a historical accident. War stifled filmgoing and dining-out and had the paradoxical effect of stimulating reading while inhibiting the production of new books, partly via 'war-time economy production' (i.e. programmed shortage of materials); partly because it seemed unpatriotic to write novels in the midst of such bloodiness ('only the mentally dead', George Orwell wrote in March 1941, 'are capable of sitting down and writing novels while this nightmare is going on'; *The Collected Essays, Journalism and Letters of George Orwell*, ed. I. Angus and Sonia Orwell, London, 1968, ii, 54). People wanted fiction, and less was being produced. One consequence was the spectacular boom in American novels (selling American rights was suddenly as easy as 'falling off a log,' an agent, Juliet O'Hea, recalled; T. 31.5.76). Another consequence was to force people back to the libraries—especially the public libraries whose stock of old fiction was suddenly desirable. Authors such as Trollope enjoyed a revival.

At the same wartime period public libraries had become patriotically upgraded. The annual report of the Library Association in 1941 noted that public libraries were now recognised as 'one of the readiest means of maintaining public morale under the strain of war'. Lending libraries were further imbued with patriotic rectitude by various connections with the armed services. In the early months of the war, many libraries supplied books to local military units. The Library Association collaborated in the 'Service Library and Books Fund' set up in November 1939. By the end of 1942, about 8m books had been distributed to units of HM forces at home and abroad for free circulation. 'Most of this literature, of course,' the record tells us, 'was of a recreational character' (i.e. novels; T. Kelly, *A History of Public Libraries in Great Britain*, London, 1971, p. 331). Oddly enough the American providers of books for the armed forces had taken a different path, that of the paperback novel, printed on licence for the services. The 123m paperbacks distributed by Armed Services Editions were, one suspects, a precondition for the 'paperback revolution' in the US after the war, just as wartime circulation of loan books was a precondition of public library dominance in England.

The wartime boost to the public library system was compounded by the austerity of a hollow victory. Books were post-war luxuries, and although not actually on points they were vaguely guilt-making if bought too recklessly. George Orwell, a bookman if ever there was one, calculated in 1946 that he spent £11 a year on them—less than he smoked. Naturally enough people stayed with the libraries, where one could indulge without shame. But the fiction-centred commercial libraries were in a doddering state and could no longer hold their custom, let alone enlarge their service. They were hurt by a number of war and post-war factors: the shrinkage of middle-class purchasing power; the increasing cost of menial employees like counter assistants and van drivers; the growing complexity of the book business (the public libraries had been benefiting since 1946 from the graduates of the new library schools). Commercial libraries' power to resist their public competitors was weakened by years of internal competition, especially in London, between Smith's, the Times Library, Harrods, Mudies and Boots—all of whom had maintained for far too long 'farcically inadequate subscription rates' (F. W. Swinnerton, *Authors and the Booktrade*, London, 1932, p. 62). They had never been as efficient as the public libraries in stabilising their stock, relying on rapid turnover of new books to attract customers. The most famous of the metropolitan libraries, Mudies, was physically destroyed by bombs in the War, though it had been ailing for years. Boots' and Smith's nationwide networks held on until the 1960s, but were increasingly unable to justify large floorspaces against more profitable lines of goods than used books. Smith's finally went under in 1961, Boots in 1966. At the time of winding up Boots had 121 libraries and 140,000 subscribers compared with 450 and 500,000 in the 1930s; in the last five years of the service they dropped 150 libraries despite relatively low subscription rates (30s for 'A', 15s for 'B' class privileges). This decline by no means reflected any weakness in the parent firm, merely a process which was occurring through the whole hierarchy of commercial libraries which Boots and Smith's headed. By the 1960s the myriad '2d libraries' had gone the same way as their betters, their few score hardbacks giving way to gaudy, display-racked paperbacks. All this left the public library unchallenged. With the nicest possible historical timing the 1959 Roberts Report and the subsequent 1964 Libraries and Museums Act confirmed the public libraries' importance to the state and promised an efficient and comprehensive service to every citizen, with the Department of Education and Science benignly presiding.

One's first reaction, looking back, is that the triumph of the public library was a gauge mark in the development of British democracy—a declassing of the nation's reading facilities equivalent to the National Health Service declassing of the nation's medical service. It is easy to forget how great the change was. A decade and a half ago commercial libraries dispensed reading matter with ostentatious privileges for those who could pay. The following description is given of the better metropolitan libraries (i.e. the Times and Harrods, as opposed to the more popular Boots and Smith's), as late as 1960:

> The service is a personal one. Each member deals with the same librarian all the time by telephone, in person or by post, so that even when a subscriber rings up and says he (she?) wants a 'nice new novel' the librarian will know, after a while, which kind of novel to offer. With both libraries you can call personally, order by telephone and have your books delivered, or exchange books by post (Sp 11.10.59).

With the final elimination of the commercials the 'free' library became fully respectable, purged of the associations of the penny rate, the self improving artisan and the tuberculosis bacillus. They naturally took over the commercial libraries' former role as general purveyor of fiction. The sight doused much of the democratic gratification which the booktrade may have felt. There appeared the much maligned lady in the chauffeur-driven car, scooping up armfuls of the newest novels, bought on the rates. The sight was alike obnoxious to authors who felt they lost royalties, to booksellers who felt they lost sales and to publishers who felt that it created a false psychology of 'free' books against which any reasonable pricing level seemed exorbitantly high. Above all it was free *novels* that irritated. 'One cannot obtain free beer, cigarettes, chocolates, theatre or cinema seats on the rates,' complained one typically irate bookseller, 'so why fiction?' (Bk 7.2.75). One could and did, and public library expenditure continued to rise. Between 1967 and 1973, a period of modest inflation, it maintained an average annual increase of 13.54 per cent (Bk 13.9.75). Over £16m was spent on books for English and Welsh public libraries in 1972–3. The estimated expenditure on books had risen to £23m by 1975–6 (Bk 6.10.75. Later estimates put these figures higher; £20m in 1972–3, £28m in 1975–6; see Bk 1.1.77). Public libraries in the mid 1970s held some 110m volumes, and operated a network with close on 11,000 outlets (T. 7.9.76). Britain's library service was, according to Lord Donaldson, Minister for the Arts, 'the finest in the world' (DT 7.9.76; all these figures are somewhat vague given the problems of definition. For a slightly different set of statistics see *The Author* Summer 1977).

In 1951, looking back over 150 years of the production of novels, the booktrade historian Michael Sadleir concluded that the library was the hub of English literary culture. Its dominance came from the interconnection of market imperatives which, Sadleir foresaw, would serve in perpetuity to preserve a very high price for new fiction and borrowing from libraries as the main access to it:

successful novelists will not work under market-value in the cause of cheap fiction. The English public borrow novels from the libraries; they will not in the first instance buy them. As for the libraries, they buy just as few copies of any novel as they dare; and the number of copies, not the price, is what interests them. (M. Sadleir, *XIX Century Fiction*, Cambridge, 1951, ii, 175)

The 1960s would seem to have seen the culmination of the process—the lending system triumphant, and the public library doing the lending. The public library would dominate, it seemed, forever. It was as unlikely to lose this dominance as, say, the national orchestras, art galleries, museums or state-run hospitals theirs. 'The ordinary reader', wrote Maurice Temple Smith (a publisher) in summer 1973, 'is no more likely to return to buying his books than his 17th-century ancestor was to perusing handwritten copies in monastic libraries' (Aut Summer 1973). As if to confirm this, the bookselling network built around the 6s novel and the new price system of the 1890s perceptibly withered. The main chain, W. H. Smith, diversified into gifts and stationery merchandising. Just how far things have gone back in the last twenty years may be reckoned from the following advertisement, taken at random from *The Spectator*, 3 July 1953:

> A GOOD REVIEW?
> GET THE BOOK FROM SMITH'S TODAY!
> EVERY BOOK REVIEWED OR ADVERTISED IN TODAY'S SPECTATOR CAN BE OBTAINED FROM ANY OF SMITH'S BOOKSHOPS—THE BOOKSHOPS WITH THE FINEST SUPPLY SERVICE IN THE WORLD.

Let anyone who doubts the decline navigate the path through the magazines and jigsaw puzzles to try the same experiment at his local Smith's today. Smith's still sell books, of course, and their profits go up every year (£15.6m in 1976, before tax on a turnover of £324m Bk 16.4.77). But their bookstock is strictly segmented into bestsellers that go like daily papers, paperbacks that go like magazines, gift-books that go like calendars and safe reference books that never grow old on the shelf. Nor with a turnover practically equivalent to the whole of the British booktrade could Smith's think for a minute of becoming exclusively or even largely involved in quality books again.

II

By the 1960s, survey after survey showed that the English were, as Anthony Blond put it, 'an electorate of 25,000,000 stingy book-buyers' (A. Blond, *The Publishing Game*, London, 1971, p. 56). In 1967 we were shown to spend only one pound on books for every three in Holland, four in Norway and New Zealand, and seven in the USA (Blond, p. 49). A table in 1968 showed the UK sandwiched between Turkey and the USA, spending half as much disposable income on books as the Netherlands (Bk 19.4.75). This, of course, did not mean that as a nation we disliked books. Britain led another kind of world league table, with one-third of the population registered library users. Addressing the Lords on the subject of public lending right in 1975, Lord Willis asserted that in America 14 books were bought for every 13 borrowed; in Holland the ratio was 12:18; in West Germany 7:5 and in the UK 4:38 (Bk 12.7.75). The figures were the subject of some dispute (Bk 18.10.75, Bk 1.11.75); nonetheless the main point stood. The British, it would seem, are booklovers—so long as they do not have to buy the books. This represents a feature of the age, rather than a national 'stingy' characteristic. According to another estimate (also disputed) in 1920 one book was borrowed in Britain for every ten bought; in 1965 the figures were reversed, ten borrowed for every one bought (NR Nov. 75).

Since nearly three-quarters of the 600m library loans every year are fiction the novelist and his publisher clearly have a vital interest in the institutional purchaser. It is not merely commercial self-interest. Imaginative publishing ventures were undertaken in the confidence that the library sale would make them minimally profitable. One example may be given, that of Hutchinson's commendable 'New Authors Ltd'.

New Authors was started in 1957, as a subsidiary of Hutchinson, 'to publish first books with a profit sharing scheme, and no options on second books', and came under the direction of Michael Dempsey, 'a young whizz-kid editor of great talent' (Bk 13.9.75. It is from Dempsey's account in *The Writer in the Marketplace*, ed. R. Astbury, London, 1969, that the following details are taken). Although it was intended originally for all varieties of creative writers New Authors became, de facto, a novel-publishing enterprise (for reasons connected with institutional purchase patterns, presumably) putting out five-or-so books a year. The aim was to take an author's first work and trust that the second would be submitted to the parent Hutchinson. New Authors was to be, in other words, a fiction nursery (among its discoveries were Beryl Bainbridge, J. G. Farrell, Julian Mitchell, Maureen Duffy). New Authors was non-profit making, all surplus was to be distributed among authors (none accrued, apparently). Dempsey, writing about the scheme some ten years after its inception gives two particular cases, which may presumably be taken as representative of the series' sales market. One novel, published in early 1967, sold 2,243 of a printing of 3,000; of those sold 2,050 went to public libraries. The other novel, published later in the same year, sold 1,500, 1,300 of which were taken by public libraries. In citing these figures Dempsey was intending to make a critical point about the miserable support which the buying public gives the young novelist. 'Somewhere along the line,' he concludes, 'a lot of things have gone wrong' (*The Writer in the Marketplace*, p. 59). With hindsight, however, one is more likely to be impressed by how securely underpinned the venture was by the public library.

Dempsey's figures give a graphic example of how the 'promising new novelist' with no brand-name to sell his work in the bookshops is dependent on enlightened institutional purchase both for sales and circulation. No one goes into Foyle's and thinks: 'I must buy an interesting work of fiction by someone I don't know.' On the other hand people do go into public libraries and experiment with writers they have never heard of—why shouldn't they? all they stand to lose is the use of one of their six tickets for a fortnight.

The New Authors figures may be suspected as a misleading guide to the whole field of new fiction. They are, however, confirmed by Tom Maschler of Cape, in an interview of 1969: 'Now, the average sale of a first novel in this country at the moment is probably something like 1400 copies, maybe only 1200, of which perhaps as many as 90 per cent are sold to the libraries. That's the *average*' (P. Firchow, *The Writer's Place*, Minnesota, 1974, p. 244). And Cape, like Hutchinson, would aver that it is on first novels that the continuing literary health of a culture depends.

Throughout the twentieth century 1,000 has been generally taken as a minimum break-even point for fiction. With generous library purchase, the novel had an insurance policy on its durable, first editions, a large number of which would be taken promptly off hand, without any excessive advertising display or salesmanship. At first sight it appears to be somewhat analogous to the mid-nineteenth century when Mudie was the main purchaser of expensive three-volume novels. But there are important differences. Mudie was a commercial dealer in a freer market than obtains today. Mudie could extract up to 60 per cent discounts from publishers, with whom he dealt direct; the more copies he took, in effect, the less he paid per copy. Public libraries have a hard-won 10 per cent discount from specially licensed middlemen. There is no improvement in terms however many they should choose to buy. Mudie was much more responsive to fashion and prejudice, taking up to 3,000 of a novel if it had hit the public fancy and only a handful if it did not or he thought it would not (and none at all if it were in any way morally objectionable). Once a novel had the bloom off, and had been replaced in the public favour, Mudie would sell off surplus copies in his sales department, a practice alien to public libraries who customarily pulp their old stock.

From this summary it can be seen that Mudie operated like a huge bookshop in the nineteenth-century bookworld. He was as fickle and unreliable as the public itself. Although he could usually be relied on to take a minimum amount, there was no sure way of knowing which novels he would take a lot of.

Modern public libraries are, by comparison with Mudie, reliable and controlled. They are extremely reluctant to buy excessively of any one novel, however popular. But, in the late 1960s at least, they could be expected to buy a commercially reassuring number of any novel emanating from a respectable publisher. Writing in 1977 T. G. Rosenthal, managing director of Secker and Warburg, estimated that in the post-war boom the 'safe library sale' of a 'good literary first or second novel' with good reviews had been 1,500. (In 1977 he estimated that it had sunk to 'something like 300 to 400' T 26.2.77.) 1,500 was not a vast number when compared to Mudie's occasional purchases. But it was steadier and could be taken to guarantee a modest edition. If things went well it would act as the springboard to subsequent, larger editions. Take away the 'safe library sale', or even render it less safe, and one removes a lot of the intellectual adventurousness of the booktrade. *The Guardian* in January 1976 painted a gloomy picture of a British book world with the library springboard gone:

Libraries account for about 20 per cent of the total British sale of books. They're important sales because they free publishers from the fickle taste of the public and sheer commercialism of trade. They have meant that creative, experimental, academic, worthy, even dull books can be published. Peter Owen summed up many publishers' view of the situation as disastrous. 'We cannot now publish fiction unless it's by a well-known writer. An average first novel will be lucky now to sell 200 copies. And yet you can't print much fewer than 2,000. We've an author who used to sell in the thousands; now he's selling 500 or 600. We may have to drop him. . . .' A publisher used to be able to reckon that a 2,000 print order on a little-known novel, or non-fiction book, would sell at a price so that 1,500 was his break even point. He would be able to expect 1,200 library sales and so had only to get 300 bookshop sales to cover his costs. An acceptable situation. Now though, with libraries buying perhaps only 50 copies of that same book, the publisher is in trouble. (Grd 31.1.76)

Most commentators were agreed that the eventual consequence would be a period of literary stagnation, a prejudice against innovation and unknown authors with unknown prospects. Such was the view of T. G. Rosenthal at Secker and Warburg, a man with direct responsibility for commissioning new fiction for one of the country's top quality publishers:

who . . . will be able to blame a librarian who reasons that if he has got, say, £3 with which to buy one novel, that he ought to buy the new Alastair Maclean or Catherine Cookson because it will be read by from 60 to 100 people before it falls apart, rather than spending the same amount of money on a marvellous first novel which Secker published last year called *Emily Stone* by Anne Redmon which will probably be borrowed only six or seven times—an unfortunate decision for the poor librarian but by no means an improbable one. (Bk 7.6.75)

The library point of view was understandable enough. They had no desire to persecute the publishers or drive emerging authors back into the garret. In such matters they had proved themselves better partners than the previous circulating libraries. Public libraries have never imposed their will on publishers by refusing to purchase any novel costing more than a certain price (it was this ultimatum by the commercial libraries which kept novels to an 8s 6d ceiling in the 1930s). Nonetheless public libraries were held in a 'financial strait-jacket' by the rigidity of the rates system which keeps them to a set budget. Their institutions are expensive to run. Customarily they expend only a fraction of their income on books. In 1975, for example, Islington libraries' spending exceeded £1m for the first time. Of this six-figure total only £125,000 went on new books (ES 10.12.75). But the seven-eighths which went on administration was irreducible—it might even have to rise since salaries are usually incremental. Unlike the book funds they could not be cut down or cut off. In 1975 there was, for the foreseeable future, a standstill or worse by order of government. Estimated library expenditure in 1978–79 was to be £149m, £6m *less* than in 1975–76 (Bk 28.2.76).

Accompanying this was the erosion of money value by inflation running in double figures (and as high as 40 per cent in some months in 1975). There was the unprecedented rise in book prices. Finally there was the fact that most libraries could comfortably operate with the 100m books in stock, without replenishment for a year or so at least. Not surprisingly the axe fell where it hurt the libraries least and the authors most. 'You could say there are three Bs in librarianship', declared the Surrey County Librarian in May 1976, 'Books, brains and buildings. You can't save money on existing buildings, it's difficult to save it on staff, but cutting the book purchase is an easy way of showing a saving' (Obs 16.5.76). Insidiously the libraries tended to boycott novels costing more than £4 (hence the popularity of the £3.95 price in 1975–76 and the fact that cloth-bound fiction had only half the average price increase of books generally, Bk 15.1.77). But literary novels, selling under 2,000 in 1977 should cost something around £6. Only by long print runs could prices of under £4 be justified.

Libraries, then, could live off their stock for a while. But the producer could not hibernate until the good times came back. One possible solution was government handouts, which were efficacious in saving ship yards and multinational car manufacturers over the same period. Other countries in similar circumstances had moved to preserve the library base. Sweden has, proportionate to the population, the same level of library loans as the UK. Its Commission on literature which reported in 1975 discerned a decay in literary standards and anticipated a remedy by putting forward a proposal for a state subsidy which would, in effect, purchase 1,250 copies of any 'quality' novel (with an eligibility limit of 400 titles a year) for libraries and bookshops. In this recommendation Sweden was following the initiative of Norway, which had operated the scheme for ten years. Essentially this scheme entails the state taking direct responsibility for the library sale, recognising it as the main preservative of literary well-being in the advanced culture which, in company with other north European countries, Scandinavia enjoys (Bk 29.3.75).

III

It is not merely devil's advocacy to continue this section on the 1973–6 library crisis with the question 'so what?' Despite the short term hardship and disruption a kind of literary 'cull' might be thought to be no bad thing in the long run. If we accept that institutional patronage has fostered the novel, we should also examine the possibility that libraries may have confined the artist. Patronage is, not to play with words, often paternalistic. Is it really desirable that a novelist should have to frame his work to the preferences of a colossal, single patron, noted for his strong ideas about the intellectual and moral welfare of the nation? Librarians are doubtless conscientious. A survey in 1973, for example, demonstrated that 'any one copy of the TLS is read by 83 per cent of librarians with responsibility for book buying.' But it is not conscientiousness or responsibility which is at issue; rather it is the character of the library as library— inert, respectable, class-ridden, representing the culture of the rate payer. Other misgivings have been voiced, often among the library service itself, as to the 'community class barriers' which the libraries set up. Libraries are particularly irritating to the radical young and their spokesmen in the alternative press. A more humdrum criticism is that libraries have never quite shaken off their utilitarian nineteenth-century role and are much happier catering to pigeon fanciers or model aeroplane enthusiasts than they are in providing new (as opposed to recently published) fiction.

On a more theoretical level, one may speculate whether it is desirable that a novelist should have to serve a system which forces him to overproduce. For although they may take enough to provide some small profit, libraries do not of themselves take enough to provide the author, working on a 10 per cent royalty and no PLR, with a decent living; unless, that is, he brings out a new novel every year or so. The kind of treadmill which faces such a writer wanting to live by his pen and unable to hit a large buying readership is described by Colin Wilson in the account of his start in the profession:

> A novelist who churned out a novel a year might reckon to make anything between £100 and £1,500 a year. The latter sum is adequate [Wilson writes in 1968] but as most writers are extravagant by nature— they hanker after good food and comfortable travel—it is certainly not enough to allow complete freedom of mind . . . a writer who produced a book every three years (as many writers do) would obviously make less money than any navvy or dustbin man. (*Voyage to a Beginning*, London, 1968, p.158)

It is noticeable that many novelists writing for the British public do, in fact, produce at extraordinary speed. In spite of 'blocks' Doris Lessing has managed to bring out 21 volumes of fiction in as many years; Iris Murdoch, still a young novelist by traditional standards, is on her eighteenth novel in 20 years. Melvyn Bragg managed 9 novels in 9 years (despite doing much else); Simon Raven 14 novels in 15 years. A number of British novelists have been forced to the expedient of writing under different names finding, as they do, that they need more than one novel a year to live and that the public will not take more than one novel a year from a single identifiable author. This group includes not only genre-novelists like Jack Higgins but solid writers like Donald Payne and even major literary artists like Anthony Burgess (19 novels between 1958 and 1968, under his own name and that of Joseph Kell).

Another possible consequence of the library system is the shortness of the average English novel, when compared with its American or European equivalent. Writing to *The Bookseller* in 1973 Peter Owen commented on what had become an established fact of English publishing since the war: 'publishers have become unenthusiastic about novels of more than approximately 60,000 words' (23.6.73). Owen put it down to escalating costs; but a contributory factor is the library user's requirement to have a novel, six of which can be read in a fortnight by a somnolent borrower who customarily spends half an hour or so at the exercise in bed before going to sleep. (It should be said, incidentally, that public libraries are much more generous as to their allowance of books, and much stricter as to length of borrowing time, than their commercial predecessors). The public library may be supposed to exert a formative influence on the novelist who wants to succeed, especially at the beginning of his career. The two week, four/six book rule encourages a shortness and broad readability. Writing in *The New York Times Book Review* in December 1975 Anthony Burgess commented on the difference between library supported English novelists and the university supported American novelists as one of bulk and complexity—permitted in one case, denied in the other:

> In England we have long lost the knack of fictional longitude. Economics has nearly everything to do with it. [In America] everybody seems to be on campus with a professional sinecure, honor-bound to spend ten years or so on a bulky masterpiece. In Europe things are different. Universities

and novelists have nothing to do with each other. Our position is essentially that of Dr. Samuel Johnson forced to write the novella *Rasselas* in a week to pay for his mother's funeral. (NYTBR 14.12.75)

(It may be noted in passing that only about 8 per cent of American books are bought by libraries, about half or a third of the amount bought here; Bk 4.9.76. Public library book purchase in America over 1976–7 was estimated at approximately £84m. UK expenditure for the same period was estimated to run at some £30m for a population only a quarter as large as that of America; Bk 23.4.77).

Serving one client limits a literary form and enslaves its practitioners. This was George Moore's objection to the Mudie library tyranny of the late nineteenth century:

At the head of ... English literature sits a tradesman who considers himself qualified to decide the most delicate artistic question that may be raised, and who crushes out of sight any artistic aspiration he may deem pernicious. And yet with this vulture gnawing at their hearts writers gravely discuss the means of producing good work; let them break their bonds first. (Quoted by G. Griest, *Mudie's Circulating Library*, Bloomington, Indiana, 1970, p. 149)

The recent English novel, in length, quality and readability bears a heavy impress from the public library system—though whether it is as pernicious as Mudie's 'tradesman' bondage of the Promethean artist is another question. Certainly libraries themselves would reject the accusation and mount a convincing defence. By their nature and original statute they are in the business of raising standards. They do not, as did the commercial libraries, pander to crazes by purchasing illimitable copies of short-life bestsellers. Public libraries select their books on other grounds than mere popularity. In fact they subtly arrange their layout to deprecate the merely popular book. The 'western' shelf has a distinct aura of cultural shame about it; readers at my library do not linger or care to be seen alongside it.

Libraries catalogue acquisitions to the highest bibliographical standards and place new novels alongside classics. The 'C' shelf will hold Conrad and Chekhov, as well as Christie and Cartland (though the latter two are more likely to be out on loan). Since they do not, like the commercials, have sales departments dealing in their own second-hand stock local authority-run libraries keep novels on shelves for a long time. A sense of the tradition of literature, and of its canons, is given by the public libraries in a way that it never was by Boots or Smith's. The stabilising function of the public library is, one might claim, even more valuable in the disorienting world of rapidly successive bestsellers and short-life paperbacks which we inhabit.

In *Adam Bede* George Eliot describes tradition as a kind of 'gum'. As such its cohesiveness has an ambivalent quality; it holds together but it also impedes and clogs the necessary processes of change. The public libraries' orderly procedures and cultural caretaking, while admirably preserving tradition, can by excess convert to stodginess, or even downright philistinism. Public libraries are, as they were in the 1850s, supported by the rates and accountable to the ratepayers' representatives on library committees. There has been a provable bias against the avant garde and the 'shocking' in library book selection—whether it is aesthetic or moral shock which is concerned. In the twentieth century public libraries have almost universally indulged in a number of furtive practices to inhibit books (usually fiction) which they regarded as dubious. In his study *Censorship and the Public Libraries* (London, 1975), A. H. Thompson gives an entertaining survey of myriad fatuous suppressions and interferences. Yeovil, for example, went in for a system of 'white spots' in the 1960s 'to help people—they are mostly members of women's organisations and elderly folk—to pick out harmless and innocuous love-stories' (p. 120). Many libraries had (and some still have, one gathers) 'poison shelves'. Others made up 'hot lists' with the aid, sometimes, of excitedly 'worried' readers. 'X' certificates, warning stamps ('there are some passages in this book which may be disturbing'), reserve lists, clandestine cataloguing, have all been practised by benevolently protective authorities. Throughout the 1960s Edinburgh had a 'fiction annexe' whose sole purpose was, it would seem, to make it practically impossible for ratepayers to get novels of a 'strong meat character'.

There is, in England, a line of official disapproval of dangerous novels, from the Bishop of Wakefield's burning *Jude the Obscure* to the (now) Bishop of Liverpool testifying against *Last Exit to Brooklyn*. Persecution, however, is not necessarily dramatic. In the public library post-selection censorship is probably rarer than a pre-selection timidity. My own public library does not have, or does not record itself as having: *The Naked Lunch*, *Cain's Book*, *Last Exit to Brooklyn*, any 'obscene' Genet, either of Miller's *Tropics*. Charter bookshops are obliged, by the terms of their 1960s charter, to provide any book asked for, and do so; and if the English were principally buyers, rather than borrowers of books with cultural guardians doing the actual purchasing, one doubts whether *Last Exit to Brooklyn* would have had to undergo three trials before publication (it promptly sold 13,000 in hardback, which indicates that reader resistance was not the cause). The situation has probably improved since 1954, when a survey showed that a large number of libraries were reluctant to stock such works as *Ulysses* and *The Naked and the Dead*. (As a schoolboy in the late 1950s I remember that the Colchester public library copy of *Ulysses* was stored obscurely in the 'reference library' and that certain pages had been razored out, certainly by the librarians.)

In understanding the institutional mind the case of *The Naked and the Dead* is particularly instructive. As has been said, librarians dutifully read the quality press to help make their judgements. On 1 May 1949, the *Sunday Times* had a special front page editorial on the imminent publication of Mailer's novel in England. The editorial declared:

> Mr Mailer is a writer of exceptional gifts and much of the book has real value, but large parts of it are so grossly obscene that it is quite unfit for general circulation. No decent man could leave it lying about the house, or know without shame that his womenfolk were reading it.... In our opinion *The Naked and the Dead* should be withdrawn from publication immediately.

The public librarian, over half of whose patrons are 'womenfolk' and children, must be expected to be peculiarly susceptible to this kind of instruction. Bookbuyers, on the other hand, are gloriously indifferent to such pontificating. There can be few better advertisements for a book than to be thundered at on the front page of the *Sunday Times*. In consequence 50,000 copies of *The Naked and the Dead* sold like hot cakes while librarians dithered with their consciences (PW 4.6.49).

In their adult-book choices one suspects that the libraries keep in mind an average user who conforms to the pattern of ratepayer and voter, with a lot of leisure time: women in a word. Margaret Drabble has said that, judging from her correspondence, her average reader seems to be the 'intelligent housewife who never buys a book' (Firchow, *The Writer's Place*, p. 115). It is not by any means a shameful admission, as Drabble is astute enough to know. Ian Watt in *The Rise of the Novel* demonstrates that the intelligent, leisured lady of the early eighteenth century was the indispensable condition for the invention of the genre—Samuel Richardson wrote novels for the 'intelligent housewife who never bought a book'. Doubtless it is this estimable reader (their 'womenfolk') whom the public library both caters for and thinks to protect. In so doing the library is culturally interventionist; it chooses the books you may choose. Whether the power is exercised wisely or unwisely, it is nonetheless an infringement. One can argue from recent movements in the book trade that it is not merely a reserve power. The paperback revolution of the late 1950s and 1960s gained much of its energy from fiction which the public library could be expected to disapprove of: *Woman of Rome*, *The Ginger Man*, *Lolita*, *Lady Chatterley's Lover*, *The Naked and the Dead*, *Catch 22*, *Candy*. Anyone who wanted to keep up with the moving frontiers of permissive fiction was forced out of libraries; paperbacks often had the glamour, as it were, of an informal *Index Librorum Prohibitorum*.

England in the twentieth century has been marked by an atmosphere of passive, but pervasive censorship which the public libraries, if they did not create it, have not defied. Much important fiction has been conceived in a mood of caution. Some might not use so polite a word. In a note to the English, bowdlerised version of his story, *The Time of her Time*, in the early 1960s, Norman Mailer alleged that English writers had shirked their fight, were cowards, in effect. Has the time not come, he asked

> for the British writer to face the disagreeable fact that compared to us in America, he has been slack, has fought his battles with too little, and surrendered too often to those peculiar betrayals which are worked in the name of good taste, caution and the public trust? (*Advertisements for Myself*, London, 1961, repr. 1963, p. 356)

One can extend the charge to English publishers. Until Calder and Boyars, in the 1960s, Britain had no twentieth-century publisher equivalent to Horace Liveright who, in America in the 1930s, made it his business to publish controversial works, and pick fights with the Society for the Suppression of Vice. It was Sylvia Beach, an American, who first published *Ulysses* in Paris and Bennet Cerf of Random House, who first risked publication under a commercial imprint. The Penguin *Lady Chatterley* followed previous trial and publication in America. *Lolita* came similarly late to the English market. *Last Exit to Brooklyn* has already been mentioned, but the tradition of the naturalist novel to which it belongs recalls larger issues. Naturalism, as with Zola in France and Dreiser in America, has provoked epic battles between art and authority. The same battles have, it must be granted, been fought over in England—but always late and always on a minor scale. From Vizetelly's prosecution through that of *The Rainbow* to Sir Cyril Black's suit against Calder and Boyars, Britain has shown itself as decades behind France, years behind America and not far ahead of bigoted Australia and South Africa.

As we have seen, Mailer blamed pusillanimous authors. George Orwell, angered by what he saw as a 'trahison des editeurs' faced with *Animal Farm*, condemned the English publishing establishment as gutless and far too worried about their professional reputation. There may be elements of truth in both allegations. But one might also argue for another important, inhibiting pressure. As the mid- and late-nineteenth century shows, libraries, when they dominate a literary culture, act as powerful reinforcers of conservatism, prudence and 'responsibility'. To some extent libraries give the readers an instrumental power over the authors. 'The British reader of fiction', Giles Gordon (an experimental novelist) observes, 'is conservative down to its boots' (Grd 21.10.76). The public library joins with him in enforcing his conservatism on the producers of fiction.

IV

There is, when one thinks about it, a certain felicity in Jane Austen's having dominated the bestseller list in 1975 with *Sanditon* (it sold 22,000 in the first ten weeks and eventually 30,000 in hardback, figures which would have astonished the original author Bk 29.1.77). For the kind of fiction Austen practised lives on. The English novel, as exemplified by Drabble, Snow, Angus Wilson, Elizabeth Taylor *et al*, is still very much about Sense and Sensibility, Pride, Prejudice and Persuasion. Consciously and often proudly so, one might add. On the publication of her eighteenth novel, *Henry and Cato*, Iris Murdoch indicated her sense of literary pedigree to *Guardian* interviewer Stephen Glover:

she writes 'social novels' in the tradition of Dickens, George Eliot or Tolstoi . . . 'I don't think the English novel has veered back,' she tells me, 'because apart from a few eccentrics, and some very clever ones, too, such as Joyce, it hadn't gone very far away. The English novel tradition is very strong, a stronger tradition than that of the French novel, and it has just gone on.' (Grd 23.9.76)

Bergonzi, in *The Situation of the Novel*, fixes on a similar remark by Margaret Drabble, in a 1967 broadcast:

I don't want to write an experimental novel to be read by people in fifty years, who will say, ah, well, yes, she foresaw what was coming. I'm just not interested. I'd rather be at the end of a dying tradition, which I admire, than at the beginning of a tradition which I deplore. (p. 78)

Less guardedly the same novelist, in conversation with an American interviewer, observed: 'Oh dear, I do have this awful leaning toward the conventional novel' (Firchow, *The Writer's Place*, p. 112). Kingsley Amis, was less apologetic, if equally complacent, with the same interviewer:

I think that one of the reasons why, according to me, the English novel has got it over the American novel at the moment is because of things like English snobbery, and English conservatism and English class consciousness and all that kind of thing. Because I think that all this so-called wave of modernism has hit the English novel less hard than any other kind of novel. It seems to me that, little as I know of it, thank God, the French novel is in smithereens now, because of that wave. (*The Writer's Place*, p. 35)

One notes that the French do not have to the same extent as the British a public library system dominating their literature, and acting as a breakwater for any new waves. Only 4–5 per cent of the French population is estimated to use a public library as opposed to 20–30 per cent in this country (Bk 26.6.76). One may not generalise too easily, but it is tempting to assume, as I have done, a link between libraries and traditionalism, between booksellers and avant gardism. (The point is perhaps easier taken if one thinks of what a bookshop in the neighbourhood of a university, and what a public library in the same neighbourhood would stock.) French book culture is dominated by the bookbuyer, and as the commission looking into the question reported: 'French bookbuyers are young, educated, well-to-do city dwellers.' (To which one hears the echo—English book borrowers are middle-aged, moderately educated provincials). A survey in 1976 confirmed that the majority of British public library users are in the 45–65 age group. It seems evident that it is the *élite* nature of French reading-buying patterns which has enabled movements in 'pure' literature like the *nouveau roman* to flourish; certainly this is the view of publishers like Jerome Lindon, whose Editions de Minuit have put out many titles by experimental novelists. It would also seem logical to assume that it is stress on purchase rather than borrowing which accounts for another famous feature of French literary life; the vast sales-reward of their prizes. Almost every year commentators wonder at the fact that the Booker (value £5,000) adds only some 5,000 to 10,000 to the winner's sales. The Goncourt (Value 50 fr) whips up sales of 5,000 *a day*, and total additional sales of a quarter of a million (see ST 9.1.77). There is no other fiction prize in Britain which does anything for an author's sales. In France the Prix Femina is credited with adding up to 150,000, the Renaudot with up to 100,000 extra sales (PW 9.4.73).

Finally one might add that not everyone shares Amis's relief at being spared the likes of Camus, Sartre, Robbe-Grillet, Butor, Sollers, Beckett, Le Clézio, Sarraute, Tournier.

In this chapter I have considered libraries from two aspects. First in connection with the recent crisis which seems seriously to have hampered their role as patron of the novel. Secondly, and in a longer perspective, I have considered exactly what that patronising role was, and whether we might not be better off without it. It is difficult to strike a balance between immediate alarm and sage complacency at the cutting down to size of an institution which had to some extent over-reached itself. One thing is clear, however. Michael Sadleir (and more recently Redcliffe-Maud) was over-confident when he predicted that the library must always remain at the centre of our literary culture, dictating the physical form of fiction and, indirectly, its content. Recent events, if nothing else, have shown that now we may have to adjust to a situation where libraries matter less. To be true, this shift is unlikely to be as sudden as was feared in 1975. 1977–

8 estimates for book expenditure indicated a 7.13 per cent increase over the previous year's levels. As *The Bookseller* noted: 'a certain gloomy satisfaction is in order. The figures were expected to be much worse' (Bk 23.4.77). Given the rate of inflation for book prices (20–30 per cent, Bk 15.1.77), erosion rather than collapse seemed the danger, though in the long run the result would be the same.

2 Fiction in a Siege Economy

The cosy world which we were told would go on forever, where full employment would be guaranteed by a stroke of the Chancellor's pen, cutting taxes and deficit spending, is gone.
Prime Minister, September 1976

Unfortunately the immediate problems of the mid-1970s did not begin and end with the libraries. In other ways the novel was painfully squeezed by the inflation which the government set about 'attacking' in 1975, and almost as severely by the drastic weapons chosen for the attack. Publishing was unlucky in that printing is a skill, practised by a highly unionised workforce, and requires an imported raw commodity. Its products are not sold at the point of manufacture and require transport, often several times before they reach the customer. Books are highly diverse and require intelligent (or expensively automated) handling at all stages of their movement, and careful stock-control when they are immobile in the warehouse. There is, today, no full-scale wholesaling system as there was in the nineteenth century, and as there is in modern Germany. To quote a publisher on that favourite subject of books' 'difference':

I heard of a man in the cement business with a turnover exceeding that of Oxford University Press. He makes three grades of cement and has 19 customers. OUP have 18,000 titles and probably 2,000 customers in the UK alone. Here is where books *are* different. (Bk 21.4.73)

(It was estimated in Autumn 1975 that the British booktrade has 300,000 titles in print, and some 1,700 active publishers.)

Publishing has a slow return on investment. Years may elapse before manuscript follows the advance payment, months before print follows manuscript, and books may have to be kept years more on a backlist awaiting eventual sale. The paper they are printed on has to be paid for within days. And the final commodity is not essential to life, nor even to comfort, so purchase is extremely discretionary. As has often been noted, price resistance begins at a surprisingly low level.

Between mid-1974 and mid-1975 printing costs shot up 30 per cent, and the cost of paper by 36 per cent. In view of such reports as Collins's in March (Bk 29.3.75) that they had experienced increased costs of 60 per cent in paper and binding materials, the overall increase was, in fact, not as bad as feared. Warehousing and stock-holding costs had meanwhile gone up 50 per cent over the year. Overall increases in book prices were between 25 and 35 per cent (Bk 8.1.77), but the price of many books was lapping the general rate of inflation, itself galloping. Saul Bellow's new novel, *Humboldt's Gift*, one of the major literary events of 1975, was advertised at 'circa £4' in the May trade papers; when it emerged in October it actually cost £4.90—representing a 50 per cent annual increase.

The British increases took place against a progressive drop in the price of books, and particularly novels. Up to 1975 the real cost of a novel was less than it had been in 1901, taking the 1977 pound as worth 6½p in 1901 currency and the price of new fiction 6s and £3.95 respectively. The new disproportion in book prices was, however, more readily measured against contemporary indices. In 1973 the latest novel was, averagely, cheaper than the latest LP record (though by no means as much cheaper as it had been ten and fifteen years earlier). In mid-1975 the situation was reversed. At £3.95 the new novel was more expensive than the new LP. Nor was the inflation in novel prices clearly evident in the £3.50–£3.95 price range. A survey by Jeremy Brooks in *The Sunday Times* revealed that these prices could mask costs per 1,000 words from 3.7p to an 'outrageous' 11.6p (ST 3.4.77).

The shop price of a book is as much the result of distribution and transport, as of production costs. In this critical period books were hit heavily by multiple increases in postal charges (part of the government's move to reduce public spending by cutting subsidies to social services, particularly the Post Office which made *The Guinness Book of Records* with its deficit). Bookshops customarily order small amounts of books, and use the letter and parcel post for the necessary communications of their trade. Between 1971 and 1975 there was an estimated 400 per cent increase in publishers' and booksellers' postal rates (Bk 29.11.75), an unprecedented imposition on the trade. In the face of these rises some publishers were driven to look at ways of circumventing the parcel and letter post, so taking the trade back to pre-Rowland Hill days.

One fact remained in spite of all ingenuity. The British publisher was, for the first time, at a serious disadvantage to his foreign competitor. In the House of Lords on 19 March 1975, Lord Beaumont delivered a barrage of telling, but unavailing statistics to show this.

Even allowing for substantial discount of the public tariff, the price of posting a 7oz magazine in Britain is twice what it is in Sweden, 15 times what it is in France, 17 times what it is in Italy and 100 times what it is in Spain. Looking at books, the comparison is almost as bleak. An ordinary publisher posting a 2lb book here would have to pay almost twice what he would in Germany, Belgium and Denmark: almost four times what he would in Sweden; more than ten times what he would in Spain and more than 25 times what he would in Italy. (Bk 5.4.75)

(Whether the Italian ever got his 2lb book was another matter. The press in 1975 carried reports of Italian mail being sold for scrap by unscrupulous postmen.) In the same debate Lord Allan (Chairman of Longman and Penguin) estimated that the American publisher was favoured with a 50 per cent advantage in postal charges.

Commodity increases could be blamed on 'world shortages' (a drearily familiar evasion of the time) and production increases on 'cost of living adjustments'. But the postal increases were a deliberate and, publishers thought, vindictive imposition. 'Industrial genocide' was a phrase used to describe a situation where it might now cost as much to send a book by mail as to make it.

Most dangerous, in the English speaking market, was the growing advantage to north American producers. America had inflation around 13 per cent in late 1974, falling to single figures in 1975 (Bk 21.6.75). Their postal rates were pegged to lower increases than the British, were stepped less steeply up the price range, and Congress was friendly to the publishing lobby.

The comments collected by a British observer at the 1975 Montreal Book Fair are probably as loose as conversation usually is, but nonetheless reflect a real emergency for the British publisher:

The effect of the different rates of inflation between Britain and America is to make British books less acceptable there, so eroding a major British export market. At Scribner's concern was expressed about British price levels . . . 'British prices are becoming impossible' said Milton Gladstone of Arco . . . George Blagowidow of Hippocrene . . . said: 'British books are being priced out of the market here. Your inflation of 30 per cent is way beyond ours of about 4 per cent in book prices. Several publishers who import British books have said to me that they would now rather buy rights or nothing at all.' (Bk 21.6.75)

The same points were made by the chairman of Routledge and Kegan Paul, reporting on his firm's annual performance in 1974–5:

Book manufacturing prices in the UK have risen to higher than American prices, which has produced anomalous patterns of trading: to make matters worse overseas postal charges have been increased to levels much higher than the equivalent American charges. This aspect of Government policy is destroying our competitive situation in overseas markets. (Bk 13.9.75)

As Franklin implies, much of the prosperity of English publishing lies in exporting success, itself a result of English being a world-wide language and long-standing American lack of interest in exporting. As the 1977 President of the Publishers' Association, Graham C. Greene, put it—exporting is the American publisher's jam, but the English publisher's bread and butter (T 31.3.77). In the post-war period between 40 and 50 per cent of British production was exported. As far back as before the war it was 30 per cent and it never fell below 20 per cent, even at the peak of wartime hostilities and the stringencies of War Economy Standard. Key firms, like Penguins, have more than half of their sales overseas; in 1976 58 per cent of Collins's sales went to overseas markets.

Since less than 10 per cent of American production was exported in the 1970s, the future danger was that with differential cost rises they would become the more efficient producer and win markets from the British. Fear for the security of overseas markets was heightened by the anti-trust investigation, filed in New York in November 1974, which, by naming British publishers as 'co-conspirators', threatened the old 'empire' agreement of 1947 (the Traditional Market Agreement). The TMA had been set up, ironically, in apprehension of American expansiveness after the second world war. In essence it was a pact among British publishers not to make any agreement with an American publisher which did not entail the 'whole package' of rights to the seventy-or-so countries which formed the immediate post-war British empire. In effect the TMA had given British publishers a clear field in such rich markets as Australia and Africa (a situation regularly described by indignant Australians as cultural colonialism).

It was suspected that the privileges of the TMA, and the benefit to English producers was 'brought to the notice' of the Justice Department by the American paperback houses. (Another theory blamed the 'malice' of 'individual Australians'; Grd 31.5.77.) American paperback firms were the most aggressive of the trade exporters, and with British price rises their long-run books were for the first time price competitive (PW 5.7.76). The TMA was dissolved in Summer 1976 with the American publishers' signature to the consent decree. According to *Publishers' Weekly*'s dry comment, the American trade 'were not dismayed at the prospect of its demise' and welcomed 'a whole new era of competition in the publishing and selling of English language books throughout the world' (PW 5.7.76). British publishers did not welcome it. It emerged that the PA 'consented' only when Joel Davidow, chief of the anti-trust division's foreign commerce section went to London and 'convinced the British that he could make life so difficult for them that compromise would be the better part of wisdom' (PW 5.7.76). An offer, to use the cliché of the period, they could not refuse. The effects would not be immediate, but as a British authors' agent warned in 1977, 'there are no easy markets any more' (Bk 26.2.77).

Domestically publishers were pushed around, as well. Precise figures are hard to come by, but it seems agreed that a lot of publishers specialising in new, hardback novels, make their substantial profit only remotely, from overseas and subsidiary rights sales (Aut Autumn 75). The paperback rights, of which publishers had traditionally taken 50 per cent, were coming under increasing pressure. In January 1976 it was announced that the 'monolith' had finally cracked, and the Society of Authors had succeeded in extracting from the Publishers' Association a new norm, 70–30 per cent in the author's favour.

This was undoubtedly a short-term victory for writers. Whether it would prove a long-term benefit was another question. An American commentator, observing the same trends a little earlier over there, saw it as ultimately self-defeating:

> A surprising number of hardcover publishers now survive on their half share of sales to paperback companies. Those bestselling authors who try to cut down the publisher's share do so at the risk of wiping out hardcover publishing. The hardcover side of the industry is as shaky financially as newspapers are. (Aut Winter 73)

American pessimists on this issue could point to the alarming fact that certain best-selling writers (Jacqueline Susann was the first) already claimed 100 per cent of their paperback rights. 70 per cent might merely have wedged the gap open for final expropriation.

In Britain it could, however, be argued that the success of authors in squeezing a larger paperback shareout was not necessarily a bad thing, since together with the general expansion of that area it accelerated a movement by hardback publishers to buy into the paperback industry. This meant that hardback firms would share paperback profits—rather than simply picking up subsidiary rights money. But this consolidation might be thought to have dangers in its turn, since it would insidiously tend to cramp the choice of hardback titles in favour of those that have eventual appeal to the 'mixed drugstore public' that the American paperback currently aims at.

II

Of course all books were hurt by price rises and sharper business conditions. But the literary novel, like poetry, is marginal and particularly at risk when costs get out of hand, or when the economic conditions are unstable. Publishers were not, apparently, being bankrupted (a fact which was eventually viewed with some surprise). But they were finding an unwelcome imbalance between turnover and profit, and they trimmed their business accordingly. The tendency was to encourage concentration on the single, rapid-selling, bestseller, by a brand name author, with good rights, serialisation and paperback sales prospects. A likely casualty, again, was the first novel by the promising young author. Such novels are long-term investments—even where they are not positively bad investments. They may have to wait years until subsequent success reawakens interest, or until the full earning capacity of the book is revealed. T. G. Rosenthal of Secker and Warburg, one of the most fastidious of the 'quality' novel producers, reckoned that 'at least half' of their books were counted on to make losses in their year of publication (Bk 31.5.75). This is entirely against the imperative of rapid cash flow when money is losing value at 20 per cent and the return on investment in publishing an average 10 per cent. In a symposium on financial planning and cost control in March 1975, the printing, publishing and bookselling industries were advised to ask themselves: 'can you modify or reduce the levels of stocks carried? Remove excessive stock and slow moving lines... any means that can be found of shortening the purchasing, manufacturing cycle should be utilised' (Bk 22.3.75).

Publishing finance flows from several sources: immediate sales, subsidiary rights, the backlist, borrowing. It seemed likely in the mid 1970s that publishers were inclined to go for quick money and print for a shorter time—at least where certain categories of books, including novels, were concerned. This could be seen in the sudden remainder boom. In *Publishers' Weekly*, Malcolm Oram reported:

> Publishers' need to raise cash quickly and the rising costs of warehouse storage have together produced brisk business for the remainder trade. Phil Edwards of BSC Remainders, one of Britain's two largest dealers, told PW: 'In the late 1960s the stuff I was being offered was always at least five years old. Now it's often under two years and sometimes under a year. It's not just the small publishers either. It's the big ones who are really trying to unload.' (PW 18.8.75)

Murray's Remainder Service pointed out in their prominent advertisements in September 1975: 'Remaindering is no longer the poor relation of the publishing business... it helps the whole publishing industry keep pace with inflation' (Bk 20.9.75). Backlist economics were further damaged by the introduction of anti-inflationary price codes, and under Shirley Williams 'voluntary restraint' as to the repricing of books in stock (Bk 7.2.76). John Boon, of Mills and Boon, addressing fellow publishers in November 1975, at a conference entitled 'Books in a Siege Economy,' reported: 'There is no need... to explain the economic necessity in times of inflation for pricing up one's backlist. The Price Code changed all this. It was forbidden to price up books in stock... so the financial basis of the list was destroyed' (Bk 29.11.75). Mills and Boon's adjustment was to concentrate on short-life paperbacks, fast exports and generally items with a quick turnover.

It seemed the backlist which allows the discriminating customer to pick a single book (as opposed to the backlist which allows the retailer to restock with fifty paperbacks) might be a casualty of the age. This particularly hurt serious fiction. The backlist consolidates the 'oeuvre', the coming together of all the parts of an author's achievement into a grand design. This was eminently demonstrated in 1975 with the completion of Anthony Powell's twelve-volume 'A Dance to the Music of Time'. The critics who reviewed the last segment, *Hearing Secret Harmonies*, all set it in the context of its predecessors. In *The Observer* Kingsley Amis wrote, 'my feeling when I laid the book down was like the sadness that descends when the last chord of a great symphony fades into silence.' And Michael Frayn had an article in the same celebratory issue, 'exploring the extraordinarily complete world that Anthony Powell has created' (Obs 7.9.75). The 'symphonic' and 'fictional microcosmography' aspects of Powell's work arise from a grand sense of the simultaneous existence of the whole cycle. In mid-1976 when the 'Alms for Oblivion' series finished there was a similar retrospective and cumulative tone to the reviews and features on Raven. Both 'A Dance' and 'Alms' were themselves intimately concerned with time ('Time hath my lord A wallet at his back . . .'), particularly with time passing and being refound in fiction. For this reason it was necessary that all parts of the series should reverberate to every single novel as it emerged.

In aesthetic terms the backlist helps create the persistence effect without which linear products (like sequence novels) have no 'structure'. The backlist permanence of English fiction has coincided with a large number of novelists writing 'chronicle novels'—Waugh's 'Crouchback' trilogy, Hughes's 'The Human Predicament', Olivia Manning's 'Balkan' trilogy, Snow's 'Strangers and Brothers', Henry Williamson's 'Chronicle of Ancient Sunlight', Lessing's 'Children of Violence', other trilogies, quartets and multi-work series by A. S. Byatt, J. I. M. Stewart, Lawrence Durrell. All have an ambitious scale partly guaranteed by the durability and memorability of the hardback novel which circulates in libraries and which stays on a publisher's list for years. And this, in spite of the fact that the novel generally has a shorter effective selling period than almost any other kind of book.

As it is we now foresee a universal paperback situation where, to paraphrase Warhol, every novel is world famous for three weeks. It is not just that paperbacks compete for scarce space in bookshop shelves and window, and consequently displace each other. Ephemerality is built into their very nature. It is this ephemerality which Alvin Toffler gleefully hails as the future of the book in his *Future Shock*:

We have witnessed the virtual disappearance of the solid old durable leather binding, replaced at first by cloth and later by paper covers.... Thus in the US a paperback appears simultaneously on more than 100,000 newsstands, only to be swept away by another tidal wave of publications delivered a mere thirty days later. The book thus approaches the transience of the monthly magazine. Indeed many books are no more than 'one shot' magazines. (Alvin Toffler, *Future Shock*, New York, 1970, repr. 1971, pp. 161–2)

This question of the backlist would seem to be another area in which we see Britain's future in America's present. Toffler overstates when he says that the American hardcover has virtually disappeared (the book clubs prevent that happening—though they too deal in tidal waves of short-life books). But the tendency has been towards shorter duration. One may quote the novelist Ronald Sukenick on this subject, writing in *The Village Voice* on 'The Ecology of Literature':

[American] publishers... may still publish you, but at the slightest indication that your book won't have a quick-buck success they may not even bother sending it to the stores. They will probably pulp it as fast as they can without even telling you—the thing isn't even worth the storage space. Books disappear as effectively these days as works by deviationists in Russia. I know a book dealer who has accumulated a collection of the significant novels of the 60s that is literally worth a fortune because these books have become so rare. Novels in the 1970s become rare in a matter of months. (VV 5.4.73)

In Britain it is already the case that the bigseller or 'fiction front-runner' takes up most of a publisher's promotional effort. Commercial publishers, as they are rightly called, cannot be expected to shift resources to bolster up the 'uncommercial novel' which used to get by on low costs, generously extensive reviews and consequent library sales. Nor is it simply the library sales and the costs which are increasingly uncertain: if certain quality newspapers merge or go under, as is frequently mooted, then the 'free' coverage which quality books get in reviews will be severely reduced (similarly if papers and journals go slightly down-market, as happened with *The Listener* on the last change of editorship; the book pages were curtailed). The long, disinterested review by some famous and expert reviewer, in a newspaper with standards, is the best of advertisements—and it costs only a review copy.

III

John Calder's figures are probably a little hyperbolic, but they convey a strong and traditional sentiment about the right way to market novels:

> Our list consists mainly of fiction ... [He writes of Calder and Boyars.] Our list is broadly speaking, an intellectual list, and we very seldom remainder a book. When we publish a book we expect to go on selling it for the next century. That is really our criterion. Is somebody going to want to read this book in ten years time? ... If we don't see the book lasting ten years, our tendency is to say no. (Firchow, *The Writer's Place* pp. 66–7)

Taking Calder's ten-year rule, consider the case of William Golding and his *Lord of the Flies*. Golding was already the author of four still-born novels and over 40 when he tried a number of publishers with this work in the early 1950s. Everything had been slow to come in his career. Like Graham Greene and Richard Hughes he had published the *de rigueur* Shelleyan volume of Oxford undergraduate verse in 1934 ('Thorns of Life'—compare Greene's 'Babbling April' and Hughes's 'Ecstatic Ode on Vision'). Unlike these authors whose first novels made print four or seven years later, Golding had to wait until 1954 for the publication of *Lord of the Flies*.

Golding was in 1953 an unknown and that bane of publishers' readers, a schoolteacher who wrote on the side. Some publishers, like Cape, showed a mild interest in the manuscripts he sent them and the novelist, with all the pliability of the unpublished, offered to make the changes which would render the works acceptable. Unsuccessfully. Returning *Strangers from Within* (i.e. *Lord of the Flies*) Cape concluded: 'it does not seem to us that you have been wholly successful in working out an admittedly promising idea. We should suggest, however, that you might care to offer it to Messrs. André Deutsch.' In other words it might be publishable, but Cape preferred some other firm to take the risk. So did Deutsch (M. S. Howard, *Jonathan Cape Publisher*, London, 1971, pp. 246–7). It must have been a hard period for the author, who was sustained by an addiction to writing which he was later to compare to that of the alcoholic's for drink (Sp 7.7.61).

Finding no luck with the obvious publishers of novels, Golding tried *Lord of the Flies* on Faber. This was something of a long shot. Faber's were, however, by no means unknown as publishers of novels, and they have always shown unusual verve with science fiction—which genre might be said to include *Lord of the Flies*. Anyway, Faber accepted and the work was published, as first written, in Autumn 1954. Looking back in 1962 Peter du Sautoy remembered the decision as a somewhat risky one for the publisher:

> I think we took a bit of a risk with William Golding and his novel *Lord of the Flies*. . . . I think it was a risk, looking back on it now. Incidentally, it was a book which had been turned down by a large number of publishers, so that they must have thought so too. (*Books are Different*, ed. R. E. Barker and G. R. Davies, London, 1966, p. 145)

The reviews the novel received were largely laudatory, but not so as to lift it above other novels of the time, then judged equally good, if not slightly better. Praise was grudgingly mixed with censure and some comments were, one imagines, furtively eaten by their authors in later years ('only a rather unpleasant and too easily affecting story' NS 25.9.54; 'a tendency to be too explicit' Grd 28.9.54; 'overall dullness' Sp 1.10.54). There is a curiously flattening effect in finding *Lord of the Flies*, as one does, reviewed sixth out of six, even if it is regarded as the best or second best of the week's bunch.

Nonetheless the book held up and Faber reprinted. E. M. Forster made it his choice of the year. Although a Penguin edition did not appear until 1960, the novel seems slowly to have attracted a wider readership; by word of mouth advertisement, one imagines, and its suitability as a progressive school text. A roughly similar pattern was evident, yet much magnified, in America. There, however, *Lord of the Flies* was well received critically when it came out in 1955 ('a triumphant literary effort' NYTBR 23.10.55). Sales were nonetheless torpid. The novel sold only 2,383 before going out of print (Time 22.6.62). Golding's second novel, which appeared in Britain in 1955, was not published until 1962 in the US. But, significantly, exegetic articles began to come out in both England and America almost at once in learned journals, with two on *Lord of the Flies* in the *Kenyon Review* alone in 1957. This represented a much faster than average reaction time. One assumes that the rich scent of religious themes, mythic symbolism and classical motifs had quickened academic nostrils. From being an academic discovery Golding gradually became a favourite with American students, by the natural processes of intellectual percolation downwards. His cult standing was given a huge impetus by his college lectures in 1962. By this time he was, as *Time* put it, a 'Lord of the Campus', and had overthrown Salinger (in his turn Golding was to be overthrown by Fowles and Tolkien):

Lord of the Flies is required reading at a hundred US colleges, is on the list of suggested summer reading for freshmen entering colleges from Occidental to Williams. At Harvard it is recommended for a social-relations course on 'interpersonal behaviour.' An MIT minister uses it for a discussion group on original sin. At Yale and Princeton—where Salinger, like the three button suit, has lost some of his mystique as he becomes adopted by the outlanders—the in-group popularity of Golding's book is creeping up. At Smith, where *Lord of the Flies* runs a close second in sales to Salinger's *Franny and Zooey*, 1,000 girls turned out for a lecture by Golding. The reception was the same at the thirty campuses Golding visited during his year as a rarely resident writer-in-residence at Virginia's Hollins College. (Time 22.6.62)

The process continued mounting until the mid-1960s, when the ten-years-old *Lord of the Flies* topped the bestseller lists for a couple of years. By 1966 it had sold almost two million copies. In 1964 Frank Kermode wondered at the triumphal entrance of this, by now antique novel, in areas normally reserved for newcomers:

William Golding's *Lord of the Flies* has sold over a million copies in the American paperback edition alone. It has, by all accounts, succeeded *The Catcher in the Rye* as the livre de chevet of educated American youth. I doubt if anybody is really qualified to say why this should be so: books make their way inexplicably. This one was published in 1954, and certainly it was noticed; E. M. Forster commended it and 'everybody' talked about it, but with a sense that it was caviar rather than chowder—a book to tempt an intellectual into believing he had discovered a classic at its birth, but hardly a best seller. In the years that followed Golding did much to confirm this belief, but very little towards making himself a popular novelist. (Frank Kermode *Continuities*, New York, 1968, p. 186)

One main deduction is, surely, that *time* had helped make him a popular novelist, allowing the mysterious convections of popular taste which Kermode describes. The book was around for a large public eventually to catch on to it; it was not withdrawn prematurely or buried under an avalanche of other books.

A number of features emerge from *Lord of the Flies*' ten-year-long journey to the top of the bestseller list, and from Golding's career generally. The first is that good novels may need a long time to make themselves properly felt. They resist being hurried or pushed—no amount of advertising would have sold a million copies of *Lord of the Flies* in 1954–5. Had Faber let the novel drop out of sight in 1955 or 56, as caviar to the general, it would probably never have ascended to the heights that it did. Secondly it emerges that a classic which is also a first novel, needs very often a publisher to take his courage in his hands, as Faber's did and Cape did not. Many writers would not have had Golding's pertinacity. (Though, one may note, the pertinacity of beginning novelists seems to be one of the wonders of literature. David Storey's first published novel *This Sporting Life* was his seventh written and was itself turned down by more than a dozen publishers; Obs 10.10.76. Some writers even see the initial obstacle as a necessary ordeal; Paul Scott had his first novel rejected by seventeen publishers and comments philosophically, 'writers must have failures early on. It sorts out those who go on. You need a lot of stamina' T 20.10.75. Rejection slips, it would seem, are the fledgeling author's night on the hillside.)

Thirdly, as Kermode notes, Golding's career continued in a very distinctive way. His subsequent, increasingly widely spaced novels (half a dozen in twenty years) were increasingly complex, artful and difficult. (None, incidentally, had anything like the sales success of *Lord of the Flies*.) Partly this was the result of his becoming a full-time novelist, and this switch to an 'artistic' career must have been underwritten by the steady year-in, year-out sale of his first novel. By 1976 it had graduated from academic discovery, through youth cult book to being required reading for American schools and colleges and, in the text book form, had reached a sale of just on six million. In Britain *Lord of the Flies* was on the 1976 paperback bestsellers list with a sale of 150,000 (ST 27.2.77).

As it is, books have already been written about Golding's books. He has a consolidated oeuvre and critics solemnly discuss his 'evolution.' But for the success of *Lord of the Flies*, and the funds it generated directly and indirectly (in reviewing and lecturing) Golding might have written nothing more, or might have 'adapted' his fiction, as he was initially prepared to do for his first readers in Bedford Square. And the success of *Lord of the Flies* is clearly the consequence of an established habit of 'long-term' publishing.

In the present state of affairs, one can see a number of points where a Golding of the mid-1970s might be cut off, chivvied, or turned aside. A publisher under pressure might be less willing to gamble on an unknown and elsewhere rejected writer. He might be unwilling to keep the work in print until it made its 'inexplicable way,' hastening it on to oblivion after the first smallish sales were totted up. Finally, even after success, he might not be so patient with Golding's later, increasingly taxing and less saleable fiction. Golding might be coerced into 'doing it again' rather than following his own tricky path to artistic self-fulfilment. One may conclude by quoting Charles Monteith of Faber, in December 1975. The forbidding comments seem directly aimed at any latter day Golding:

> We shall be publishing fewer titles next year than we published in 1974, 1973 or 1972. Young writers will find it difficult to get published. It is nothing to do with our attitude; it's to do with the economy generally. All decent publishers are prepared to risk a loss on first novels, or on poetry, because they believe in writers. It's part of literary concern. The books that will tend to suffer are first the young, unknown author's book. (NR Nov. 75)

The main deduction one would draw, however, does not concern the exclusion of new talent—though this is a real possibility. Rather what seems of historical significance is the change in the characteristic tempo of English literary life. Middle-aged 'first novelists'; matured novels; slow accession to popularity—these appear to have been indicators of an unforced pace, a commercially low pressured atmosphere. This seems to have changed. Here again the American example might be invoked as a portent. In the US authors in the 1975–6 period were given a painful reminder of the new acceleration in literary tempo by the spate of advances which were recalled, and contracts revoked when books failed to arrive on the dot (see the article 'Publishing's Dirty Little Secret' in *More*, Dec. 76). The old generosity as to 'slow' authors was suddenly and strikingly altered.

IV

Publishers who want to stay in business have to answer to economic circumstances. Two trends were discernible in 1975, which suggested that publishers were thinking more about the bottom line than they used to. First, there was a threatened thinning out of titles, especially those of a prestige nature. Secondly the trade was, as a spokesman of Associated Book Publishers put it, 'concentrating on the most profitable parts and seeking to cut out the more marginal publishing' (Bk 23.8.75). Hutchinson's chairman put it more bluntly in his comments on how to improve his firm's 1974 profit (£397,000) to turnover (£7,750,000) ratio: 'this improvement can only be achieved by vigorous exploitation of a smaller number of new titles' (Bk 14.6.75).

The publishing habit of letting bad books pay for good is well known. So too is the trade adage that of five books, three make a loss, one covers costs and the fifth makes a profit; or that publishers should be prepared to lose on the first three books of a good author. For the higher-minded publisher the books he loses on are a kind of proud wound. This presumably accounts for Rosenthal's making public, without any shame, that half of Secker and Warburg's list loses money in its first year (and, Rosenthal suspects, for the first five years after publication, Bk 31.5.75)—a resigning matter in most businesses. But cultural philanthropy of Secker's kind is only feasible when good books by good authors can be produced fairly cheaply; when they sell minimally well and are thus justified as covering overhead. Finally this kind of high-mindedness can only be ventured on when economic stability allows costs to be recovered in a currency equivalent to what was paid out a few years earlier. There is also the consideration that Secker and Warburg may not always be independent in the matter of what they publish. Since 1951 the house has been part of the Heinemann group who look after Secker and Warburg's finance, travelling, distributing, accountancy and exporting. To quote Warburg on the original agreement: 'they took over in fact what makes a publishing house a *business*. . . . What was left for Secker and Warburg to do? Everything that was individualist or personal' (F. Warburg, *All Authors are Equal*, London, 1973, p. 142). Heinemann have made record profits for fifteen years (£15.5m turnover in 1976 profits over £3m; Bk 30.4.77). Secker and Warburg rest on a pyramid of coarser grained books which are not allowed to make losses in their first year (Pan publications, for example, in which Heinemann have a third interest). And what would happen to Secker were they to become too unbusinesslike is another question. Pessimists might point to the unhappy and brief liaison of the conglomerated Random House and avant garde Grove

Press, formed in July 1972, breaking up in November the same year. The original reason for the union was financial—Grove too needed someone to take care of the *business*. The reason for the break was, in large part, irreconcileable differences over the value of backlist items. (Random House, had, for example, destroyed Mishima's *Madame de Sade*, which Grove could not accept; PW 27.11.72). In America, at least, it would seem that the 'business' and 'personal' elements could not be so easily separated when books stopped moving from the warehouse.

In 1975 there circulated horror stories of 'quality' books, nine tenths of whose print run remained unsold, eating up money. In an exceptionally gloomy article in *The Guardian*, 4 July, Peter Owen reported on his firm's drastically reduced sales of fiction:

> A novel which sells 2,000 copies on publication in hardback is virtually a bestseller today: the average sale for a novel of literary merit by an unknown author is 200 to 300 copies; an established author sells between 500 and 800 copies; the paperback houses, who need a sale of 25,000 copies to make a book an economic proposition, are publishing increasingly less quality fiction. I am cutting down print orders on all fiction. Recently we had to pulp unbound stocks of more than 40 novels of merit, well reviewed on publication, for which there was no market, not even as drastically reduced remainders.

Crushed between rising prices, increased handling and holding charges, falling sales, increased profit imperatives, the marginal novel might not, in future, even reach eligibility for pulping. Some commentators found Owen's gloom excessive, and perhaps aimed at drumming up parliamentary interest in the plight of publishers (Public Lending Right was down for debate in parliament on 4 July and his article was quoted). But most agreed that what was to be expected was a period of stagnation; a prejudice against innovation; against unknown authors with unknown prospects.

V

These economic facts communicate themselves to authors as a general inclemency, and generate a certain mood among them, or at least among the more artistically ambitious of them. For some time there had been a collective sense of living on a dwindling income, of following an unrespected calling and a general bewilderment which was, it could be persuasively argued, connected with the political and economic diminution of Britain as a world power. Addressing Americans on this subject in 1974, C. P. Snow observed:

I would guess that any country that has felt its power decline rather sharply will feel at least an inward turn. . . . Between the wars, writers still had the confidence of the past rather strong in them, and that would be true of, say, Wells, Bennett and to some extent Lawrence. . . . That is gone completely. We haven't come to terms with our destiny in the way the Swedes have, for instance. (SR 6.4.74)

Recent economic hardships, for fiction writers especially, could easily convert bewilderment into despair. In the early 1970s Kay Dick took a tape recorder and conversed with a group of her novelist friends: Pamela Hansford Johnson, Olivia Manning, Brigid Brophy, Maureen Duffy, Francis King, Isobel English and Muriel Spark. The conversations are largely metaphysical in nature, pondering especially the question of death. But running through them, as a kind of melancholy obsession, is the financial hardship of the modern novelist. Time and again the speakers return to the spiritually lowering and enervating effect which shrinking sales and decreasing respect for the English novel have produced in them. Francis King, for example:

I'm very gloomy. I sort of feel very pessimistic about things in general, particularly about things in England. No, I don't foresee a very agreeable future for any of us. I think it's very discouraging for a novelist that fewer and fewer novels get read, they sell in smaller and smaller quantities. (K. Dick, *Friends and Friendship*, London, 1974, p. 130)

Pamela Hansford Johnson agreed, comparing the situation unfavourably with what it had been when she started writing in the mid 1930s:

I think I'd loathe to be a young writer today. It's far harder to get going. The costing is so much higher, and all that. The sales of novels are slumping very badly. . . . Very miserable. It reflects the time, I suppose. (*Friends and Friendship*, p. 23)

It is, on such evidence, a dispirited age of authorship. One has the sense of genteel poverty, of sensibility fighting an ever harder battle in an economically hostile world, and undramatically cracking up. This mood is certainly not a new thing, born in the 1970s. But it seems to have been given a firm twist in this critical period.

It is tempting to prophesy doom and learn to make do with the novels already on the shelf. But easy analysis is complicated by the observable fact that in one sense the mid 1970s were not hard times for the novel. The bestseller never sold better. Even at a massive (for early 1975) £3.60 Arthur Hailey's *The Moneychangers* broke records. Pan were supposed to have given £75,000 for the paperback rights (ES 6.3.75), after the book sold over 200,000 in hardback in America, assisted, as the trade papers said, by 'saturation national advertising'. The film rights were bought by Paramount, it was a Literary Guild full selection, *Reader's Digest* paid the highest price in twenty years for the 'Condensed Book' rights, and it earned a record sum for television rights. The news that Hailey had signed a contract, an American reviewer observed, had lumberjacks sharpening their axes for the papermills and booksellers oiling their tills. Michael Joseph brought the triumphant author to England on a promotion visit in May. Pre-publication sales were 50,000 in hardback. (Pan's pre-publication advertisements in December 1976 screamed out '1,000,000 copies in print . . . 500,000 copies already sold in Pan Export Editions' Bk 27.11.76. By January the novel had won its Golden Pan with 1m sales; Bk 8.1.77). Figures even of this magnitude were less impressive than the multi-stage selling operation involved; as planned the book would pass progressively through American hardback, serialisation, bookclub hardback, British hardback, American paperback, translations, finally film and TV adaptations—generating millions in many currencies en route. In its first form in Britain the book stayed in the *Sunday Times* bestseller list for twenty-two weeks. In America the *Publishers' Weekly* advertisement had run: 'THE MONEYCHANGERS: If you're a bookseller think of it as money in the bank.' They did, in spite of savage notices. So too, apparently, did grateful British booksellers see the novel as money in their banks.

Clearly, then, some novels were still being bought and were still a profitable investment for some publishers. Nor was it simply trash which succeeded. One of the most interesting literary phenomena of 1975–6 was the highly ambitious work *Ragtime*, which was marketed in much the same way as *The Moneychangers* and had, in some ways, another spectacular success (see chapter 4).

One saw a situation in which some publishers, like Peter Owen, claimed to be pulping what they felt were good, but no longer saleable, novels and other publishers actually reported that sales were up in bestselling lines of fiction (Bk 23.8.75). In the third quarter of 1975, there was a 28 per cent improvement in booksales reported, which kept the trade ahead of inflation (Bk 8.1.77). 2,389 new fiction titles were published in 1975; the figure was down some 4 per cent in 1976—but still remained high enough to confound earlier prophecies as to a drastic thinning out (S.Tel 23.6.76). There were also huge coups in fiction publishing to report in the last quarter of 1976, like the Hamlyn-Heinemann-Secker 'Operation Pickle', in which bumper packages of Orwell, Kafka and Maugham were made up, to sell at a paltry £3.95. These omnibus volumes sold 550,000 in a month, and as Secker and Warburg reported, were designed in large part to finance a continuingly ambitious programme of new fiction. They represented a strikingly successful entry by Hamlyn into 'literary' areas of publishing. And yet, at the same time, the trade was almost unanimous in proclaiming that times were hard for the young, ambitious novelist—and likely soon to become impossible.

What one sees in this evidence is an emerging 'pattern of extremes', particularly when it is taken together with the library crisis. One can explain what the term means by quoting a very sanguine view on the prospects for fiction by a publisher connected with the country's largest single producer:

> Despite economic pressures on the family purse more people are buying novels than ever before. Mr Philip Ziegler an editorial director of Collins recently reported that Collins novels in one form or another are selling a record number of copies.... 'The successful novelist has never had it so good,' said Mr Ziegler, 'nor has the fiction publisher. Nor—hush, hush—has the bookseller.' But there are some difficulties. The greatest problem hardback publishers now face is dwindling library sales. Reduced funds for book purchases, coupled with soaring costs, mean that where 20 copies were bought two years ago, the order may now be for twelve, ten or even six. Inevitably this falls hardest on the less established novelist, since, traditionally, something like 70 per cent of the print of a first novel ended up in libraries. (STel 23.5.76)

If the report is trustworthy, it may be assumed that whereas the economic structure of the industry was secure enough, the kind of patronage which it offered, and quality of its product in its top range, had altered. The general tendency, if continued over a long period, would be to move the trade's central commitment away from the multitude of relatively small-selling titles of a diverse nature which had hitherto been its characteristic. Such was the stand which the Publishers' Association took in their 1962 defence of the Net Book Agreement; that every book, however minor its appeal, should have its democratic chance of publication:

> Books should not remain unpublished simply on the grounds that they have limited demand, because among books with such limited appeal are found the most significant and valuable products of our civilization. It is essential that there should be the greatest variety of books published and available to the reading public, because in such variety there is cultural health. (Aut. Spring 67)

Although the trade might not show any great lessening of turnover, this essential variety might well be thought even more at risk than it had been in 1962. Against the above quotation one can place the observation of the official historian of Bantam Books, the largest and most efficient paperback firm in the world: 'The smart publishers have rid themselves of the compulsion to publish every title for every buyer, thus freeing the paperback strategists to concentrate on particular markets' (C. Petersen, *The Bantam Story*, New York, 1975, p. 127). The British book trade's new interest in such things as 'generic advertising', television promotion and High Street marketing (see Booksellers' Association Conference, 1977, Bk 30.4.77), suggested that it, too, might be getting 'smart'.

Despite all the worry of 1973–5, the English publishing system survived. Admittedly things had looked bad, at times. Of all publishers canvassed at the Frankfurt Book Fair the British alone said that 1975 was *not* their best year (PW 3.4.75). But it looked as if English gloom would not last forever. In April 1976 there were encouraging trade figures, the inflation rate came down ten points and generally things seemed to be looking better. Profits in publishing held up, and improved in some cases. Of course there was the terrible run on the pound in June, which plunged it through the psychological barrier down below $1.70. But sudden devaluation on this scale, in the short term at least, could only help an industry which exported 40 per cent of its product. What 40 per cent devaluation did for the international price of the British book was to offset the effect of 30 per cent inflation (though it should be noted that the collapse of sterling was not an unmixed benefit to the British book trade and their overseas outlets—see the interesting article 'Oxford Veterans meet in Cologne', Bk 14.2.77). With some surprise it was noted in late 1976 that the expected decimation of titles had not occurred, there had been no bankruptcies, no massive lay-offs in the trade. Things, in fact, seemed not all that changed. Indeed, in late 1976, optimism seemed in order again; '£351m turnover shows books can beat inflation as companies look to an even better year' ran a *Times* headline (T 1.11.76). (In fact the estimated turnover in 1976 was £405m, and perhaps nearer £500m if undeclared exports were taken into account; Bk 30.4.77. Projections for 1977 included a record 36,000 titles.) According to Paul Hamlyn, whose firm had had an exceptionally good year, publishing was 'recession proof'—'The book business', he claimed, 'is not affected by boom or slump' (STel 2.1.77). There were, however, those who claimed like Rayner Unwin (Chairman of Allen and Unwin) that because publishing has 'an exceedingly long pipeline' the effect of the crisis would not be felt until 1977–8, when the rest of the economy was pulling out the trough (publishing being behind the times in everything, including misery), but pessimists were a minority (Bk 18.10.75).

But if nothing else, some of the vulnerable structure on which the British booktrade rested had been shown up very clearly: library sales, exports to protected markets, reliance on subsidiary rights, the net book system, uneasy equilibrium between new hardback and reprint paperback. The picture presented was of a system rigid, yet fragile. If the crisis was alleviated, even if it was a false crisis, this did not mean that salvation and security were at hand, at least not for the literary novel.

3 The American Future of British Fiction

The sixties were not yet seven months old when I heard, quite by chance, from a close American publishing friend that a plan existed and was well advanced to sell the Heinemann Group of Publishers of whom of course we were a not unimportant part, to an American house. The news seemed to me at first incredible, but if it were true I had no doubt that it would be a bad, perhaps even a disastrous, day for the whole British publishing trade. It was not that the Americans were inefficient—far from it—nor that they were harsh taskmasters—we have plenty of them over here—it was much simpler. The trouble with the Americans was . . . that they were Americans.
F. Warburg, *All Authors are Equal* (London, 1973), p. 287

The economic crisis masked a number of longer-standing, and arguably more serious threats to the traditional production of English fiction. There had been, over the previous decade, an observed trend away from the middle-sized independent firm with its figurehead publisher, towards the very large, board run group or conglomerate in some cases, formed by mergers, link-ups and expansionist 'industrial publishing'. The absorption of Penguins into the gigantic Longman Pearson Group on the death of Sir Allen Lane in 1970 was the most publicised of these developments, and seemed to mark a new era of what was sometimes called 'slide-rule publishing'; a style of operation which was accountant-dominated, impersonal and, above all, American. Nor was it just a question of style. The late 1960s were a period of growing apprehension of 'The American take-over of Britain' as J. McMillan and B. Harris entitled their 1968 book. It was seen as a new, and practically irresistible imperialism ('we are not without cunning. We shall not make Britain's mistake. Too wise to try and govern the world, we shall merely own it,' ran *The American Take-over*'s epigraph). Publishing, it was felt, would fall like all the other British dominoes. Rationalisation was a prelude to expropriation.

Here, if anywhere, it seemed that the direst predictions of *Fiction and the Reading Public*, its 'monstrous and impersonal machinery', were on the way to fulfilment. A major transubstantiation of British culture was threatened, and with it the nightmare of intercontinental standardisation. Speaking on the Third Programme in June 1968, Maurice Temple Smith (a publisher) declared:

> What would be wrong—in my view disastrously wrong—would be if... the distinction between British and American publishing began to break down; and at present, although the British stake in America remains small, the American stake in British publishing is increasing noticeably. It would be absurd to retreat from this into a sort of Gaullist redoubt, barricaded against some supposed American malevolence. That would be to miss the whole point, which is that the commercial tide in publishing is set strongly towards larger and larger markets, and the only point at which that process would have to stop would be when the entire English-speaking world has coalesced into one vast market. It would be futile to console ourselves with the thought that this wouldn't make much practical difference. The same forces that make for larger markets also make for uniformity within the market, and there would be a real danger of the present fruitful differences being ironed out in favour of a profitable uniformity, homogeneous and insipid. (List 6.6.68)

In the nineteenth century, according to the famous insult, there was no American literature—only English literature published in America. Soon it seemed there might be no English literature, only American literature published in England.

Warburg's 'disaster,' like Temple Smith's, was one of takeover, dollar imperialism—actual penetration by American firms going multinational. This was a logical deduction from postwar developments in the American publishing industry which may, for perspective's sake, be reviewed briefly in the next section.

II

America was less shackled by wartime shortage than Britain, and the insatiable demand for reading matter which accompanies war triggered off a phase of high growth. Before this the American booktrade had been severely hit by the depression of the 1930s, and between 1930 and 1946 presents a much more violent and extreme aspect than British publishing and bookselling. The effect of the bust-boom sequence was to shake the US trade out of the 'genteel' or 'gilded' age. One result in the postwar period was the unbridled and intensive exploitation of bestsellers, and short-life paperbacks. At the same time demographic and social changes actually served to transform the whole character of American publishing, turning it into a different kind of business from what it had been. There was a 65 per cent increase in the birthrate between 1945 and 1947, sending a huge bulge through the school system. At another level the GI Bill of Rights heralded an era of universal higher education. Congressional Acts of 1958 and 1965 diverted hundreds of millions of dollars into educational publishing.

Whole categories of booksale were developed in America that are, at best, embryonic in Britain. Campus bookshops, for example, turned over 17 per cent of the American trade's nearly three billion dollars in 1973. (General retailers took only a little more, with 22 per cent; PW 30.7.73.) In 1975 there were 2,559 registered college book-outlets in the US (*The Bowker Annual of Library and Book-trade Information*, New York and London, 1976, p. 190). In Britain the Publishers' Association has actively resisted campus bookshops because it feels that 'general' bookshops should enjoy student trade. To quote one of their spokesmen in 1962, at the height of the new university boom: 'we do like to see in university towns bookshops run by booksellers who carry a wide stock, not only textbooks, and books of that kind' (*Books are Different*, ed. R. E. Barker and G. R. Davies, London, 1966, p. 192). This hostility to specialisation and new selling techniques retains the broad generalism of the old fashioned bookshop, but at a certain cost. For the importance of the college-university market is that unlike the school market (where Britain's publishing is apparently very healthy) it overlaps, at least in arts and social-science subjects, with the unspecific, educated readership among the population. Britain had little equivalent to the 'quality paperback' (called 'egghead paperback' over here) in the 1960s, and this was at least partly due to the discouragement of campus bookshops.

There was, however, a more significant reason. Post-Robbins Britain aimed for a university population under a million and with austerity even this seemed beyond reach. With a population four times as great, America had by the 1970s achieved college education for 10m. Expansion is the general feature of American postwar publishing; but in education-related divisions the expansion was manifold. (For exact figures see K. L. Henderson (ed.), *Trends in American Publishing*, Illinois, 1968, p. 33.) And the period commonly referred to as the 'paperback revolution' should, perhaps, be more properly if less vividly known as the 'schoolbook revolution'. Mid-1970s figures show the American booktrade resting on four huge domestic pillars, each with a 1975 value of half a billion dollars: (1) elementary and high school books ($643.1m); (2) trade ($549.2m); (3) college text books ($530.6m); (4) Professional ($501.2m). Compare the following figures released by the Department of Education and Science for 1974–5, of amounts spent on books: education authorities, £43m; public libraries £22m; university and national libraries, £4.8m. This amounted to a total of £69.8m out of a home market turnover of £162m, and a total home and export market of £281m. These figures suggest that the UK is much more dependent than the US on non-institutional 'trade' and export publishing (Bk 25.12.76).

The education boom coincided with changes in the structure of the American booktrade. There was the 'abdication' of a generation of powerfully individual publishers, fearful of inheritance taxes and conscious of a lack of family interest in dynasty making. Some new appointments were flagrantly untraditional. After the death of Alfred Harcourt, William Jovanovich was appointed to the presidency of what is now Harcourt Brace Jovanovich, in 1954. The thirty-six year old Jovanovich had previously headed the school book division. His elevation was, if one is to believe published accounts, resented in a house which prided itself on being the leading 'literary' publisher in America (see Peter Davison, *Half Remembered*, New York, 1973, pp. 158–60). In the shake up Robert Giroux, the most esteemed of literary editors, left the firm after fifteen years as editor-in-chief, taking many of 'his' famous authors like Lowell and Eliot with him. Nonetheless subsequent events would seem to have proved Jovanovich's appointment historically correct. (Certainly he must have felt so himself. One of his bitterest accusations against 'snobbish' English general trade publishing is that it has ignored the all-importance of educational books, and will pay for it.)

Expansion manifested itself in two large, transforming convulsions. The first was a series of mergers and takeovers by which general publishers allied themselves with educational publishers. (Harper acquired Row; Harcourt, Brace acquired World; Holt acquired both Rinehart and Winston.) In the 1960s the second stage was set going by Wall Street interest in a business that was now economically significant and much safer by virtue of educational publishing. This eventually led to the incorporation of major publishers in conglomerates whose size made the publishers no longer seem major. RCA, for example, acquired Random House in 1966 and sold it to Times-Mirror in 1977, MCA acquired Putnam's in 1975, CBS Holt in 1967. The costs involved were huge: the RCA-Random deal involved some $35m, the CBS-Holt deal $225m (PW 4.8.75). Bantam, the largest paperback company in the world, was acquired by NGC in 1968; NGC became part of the larger combine AFCC in 1971; Bantam was put up for sale in 1974, for $120m. It was eventually acquired for $70m by IFI International, an affiliate of Instituto Finanziario Industriale.

Most people instinctively dislike the idea of conglomerates meddling with books, films or even—in the most bizarre case of CBS and the New York Yankees—baseball. What, it may be asked, is a firm like Gulf and Western doing in publishing? (They own Simon and Shuster and Pocket Books.) The answer would seem to be—'why not?—they are into everything else'. This is how the *New York Times* describes G&W: 'the conglomerate whose various parts range from A (for auto replacement parts) to Z (for zinc) with a pause at M (for movies, as in Paramount Pictures)' (NYT 1.8.76). A wry portrayal of the firm, and of the philosophy of conglomeration generally, is given in Mel Brooks's hilarious *Silent Movie*, where the conglomerate 'Engulf and Devour' (company prayer: 'Oh Mighty Dollar/To Thee we Pray/For without Thee/ We are in the Crapper') manouevres to take over 'Big Pictures Studio' (motto: 'Ars est Pecunia'). One of Brooks's multitudinous comic points is that large commercial machines gobble up smaller commercial machines.

Not surprisingly, perhaps, those gobbled up put a rather more serious and braver face on it. Bennet Cerf of Random House, the man who in his youth had heroically taken the risk of publishing *Ulysses*, declared on his firm's union with RCA in January 1966: 'our conviction that publishing and electronics are natural partners for the incredible expansion immediately ahead for every phase of education in our country' (C. Madison, *Book Publishing in America*, New York, 1966, p. 510). As Cerf implies, publishing could no longer raise within itself the capital and financial expertise for modern expansion programmes. There was an element of the marriage of convenience on the other side, too. The conglomerates preferred to diversify rather than accumulate profit and risk heavy taxation. Moreover companies such as CBS and RCA were prohibited from acquiring a bigger slice of radio and TV by monopoly laws. There is also some warrant for Cerf's view that if books wished to develop as a medium, the conglomerates were necessary partners. It was they who had created the new media. CBS put millions into the development of television, before they ever got a cent back. They were also pioneers in the development of the long-playing record. It is quite feasible that some future mutations of the book will need the wealth and technical skill of the conglomerates. Nonetheless, no-one looking at what CBS and RCA (via NBC) had done to recent American television could be altogether hopeful. (For a somewhat jaundiced chronicle of a communications giant see R. Metz, *CBS: Reflections in a Bloodshot Eye*, New York, 1975.)

The new coalescence of publishing, education, Wall Street and electronics and the gigantic business organisations that went with it, had, as has been said, a transforming effect. With a turnover of nearly $4b and a non-publishing top-management, the trade's distinct traditions tended to be ironed out. To quote Dan Lacy of McGraw Hill: 'Eccentricities peculiar to publishing have tended to disappear as publishing firms have conformed more and more nearly to management practices of American corporations generally' (Henderson, *Trends in American Publishing*, p. 4). Books, to invert the axiom, are no longer different—different that is from auto parts or zinc.

Ironically, then, super growth in the US produced some of the same results as zero growth in the UK—at least where quality literature was concerned. Conferences called by the National Endowment for the Arts, the National Society for Literature and the Arts, and various publishers in 1975–6 set about discussing such topics as 'Can Poetry and Serious Fiction Survive?', 'The Future of Hardcover Fiction: is there one?' and, ultra trendily, 'The First Novel as an Endangered Species' (PW 10.11.75, NYTBR 28.3.76, SR 9.8.75). It was not, as in Britain, library cuts but the profit imperative of 'responsible' American publishers ('don't gamble with the stockholders' cash') which was producing the environmental hazards for novels.

Other national publishing industries with a shared language

viewing postwar events in the US could not but fear for their traditions. On the one hand growth was necessary for economic survival—all industry was 'concentrating'. But the American evidence suggested that above a certain threshold, growth must be financed from outside publishing with a necessary loss of autonomy and personal style. A solution which the Canadian Royal Commission examined in 1972 was for the state to provide capital. But 'baling out' in Britain was restricted to firms considered vital, and manifestly broke. British publishing qualified on neither count. Capital could, however, all too easily come from the USA.

Additionally there was something frightening about the ease with which century-old American publishers had first merged, then disappeared into conglomerate mazes. Observers in the 1960s were justified in thinking that the new corporate American industry was on the march, and would not be satisfied with intra-national expansion. No-one doubted that whole national industries could be wiped out by strong neighbours. England herself had, with the takeover of Oliver and Boyd, Nelson and Constable in the 1960s, virtually extinguished the Scottish industry. The magazine *Scottish International*, gloomily marked the event as the end of an era which had begun 150 years before, when under Scott and Constable, Scottish publishing had led the world:

> A few independent publishers remain, but Scotland can no longer claim to have a publishing industry of her own which gives some priority to the books of local writers and books of native themes and topics. Scottish books must now be good enough to withstand the competitive scrimmage of English dominated mass marketing, both at home and abroad but particularly in the South of England. Thus in a world of more books, more readers, more writers, the writers and readers of Scottish books are in a worse position than they ever were. (Scot I Jan. 68)

Disgruntled Scots might take bleak satisfaction at the prospect of American publishing now doing to English what English had done to Scottish.

III

Americans did buy into British publishing in the expansionist 1960s. But, in the event, nowhere near as much as had been feared they would. As it finally emerged, the list of acquisitions is quite short.

All in all *Publishers' Weekly* estimated in 1974 that the turnover of US-owned publishing in Britain amounted to 12 per cent of the total (PW 25.11.74). And this had to be offset against the so-called 'springback' in the 1970s: many shares were bought back from American investors. More spectacularly British firms set up branches, or took over American publishers in *their* homeland.

At 12 per cent, publishing reflected almost exactly the same degree of American ownership as the British economy generally. But, since penetration had been particularly high in 'communications' industries, British publishing had obviously repelled a challenge rather well. Patriots might also swell their breasts at evidence that British publishing was not always an easy morsel for foreign firms to swallow. Harcourt Brace Jovanovich, for example, took over Rupert Hart Davis in 1961 and had a very incompatible time of it, according to published accounts. Hart Davis was retained as managing director and in 1963 refused to bring out HBJ's current bestseller, *The Group*, because he considered it a mediocre novel (it was left to Weidenfeld to make money from McCarthy's novel). Jovanovich, apparently disgusted by the caprices of British publishers 'let him have the firm back' (Madison, *Book Publishing in America*, p. 497). There were dark murmurings in the British press, hinting at typical American ruthlessness; 'the inside story, not a pretty one, cannot be told yet,' wrote *The Spectator* (4.10.63). On his side, Jovanovich had some hard things to say about the hoity-toity amateurism of British publishers in his *Now Barabas* (New York, 1964): 'The comfy, cottage aspect of British publishing that the English themselves seem to find so necessary has always been, I think, largely pretentious, and it is an anachronism in these times' (p. 40).

As national property the publishing industry emerged from the 1960s intactly British compared to, say, the motor industry. The English novel, English poetry and English drama were, too, less overcome by American influence than either film or television. It appeared proven that the British literary-publishing complex was sufficiently massive and confident of its traditions not to need—at the moment anyway—the kind of protective legislation which Canada had introduced. In this proximate territory a number of frankly anti-USA laws have been enacted to fortify Canadian control of Canadian literary culture. One such is the ruling that Canadian advertisers cannot deduct as business expense advertisements in a publication with less than 80 per cent Canadian editorial content. (This ruling halted production of *Time*'s Canadian edition; NYTBR 1.8.76.) Another ruling insists that any takeover needs certification by the Foreign Investments Review Board, as being 'in the best interests of Canada'. Hence Simon and Shuster's Canadian subsidiary ran into trouble when its US parent was taken over by Gulf and Western, and Simon and Shuster (Canada) eventually sold out to an Ontario firm (NYTBR 1.8.76). These measures, aggressive though they were, have still not served to raise Canada from its status, admitted in the Royal Commission Report, of a 'regional' and 'domestic' division of the US market.

Despite evidence of stout British sovereignty, a general impression of creeping Americanism remained. Indeed Americans themselves noted it, with that offensively condescending nostalgia which top nations reserve for the heritage of countries they are taking over. Reviewing Anglo-American relations in the NYTBR in 1974, Joseph Epstein observed:

> So much of English life—its publishing, its social science, its liberationist movements—seems an open imitation of its American counterparts, as such usually no better but in fact rather shabbier than the original.... American novelists arouse more interest than natives ... and in literature it's beginning to look like dark for the British Empire. (NYTBR 23.6.74)

Having resisted chequebook invasion, British publishing would, if we believe Epstein, seem voluntarily to have 'imitated' its rival, and Americanised itself.

Epstein offers impressions. Nonetheless hard evidence can be adduced to support the 'self Americanisation' thesis. The modernisation of Macmillans, since 1963, is an example. In effect this changed Macmillans from a family firm not much different from what the brothers had founded in 1843, to a board-run, multi-divisional operation on recognisably American lines. (As part of the modernisation the St Martins Street premises, with all their sentimental associations for the firm, were sold for capital and a new complex established at unromantic Basingstoke—about as far away from the 'Row' as it was possible to get.) An even more dramatic series of examples was evident in Penguins. First there was the merger with Longman Pearson, immediately on Sir Allen Lane's death. Then came the crisis of 1975, and the thinning out of both list and personnel. This was followed by an obscurely visible power struggle between, it was suggested, the 'men of money' and the 'men of books' (ES 9.7.76, ES 11.11.76, ST 13.6.76). There was also the takeover of Viking, a famous American firm with an annual turnover of $15m. Under the headline: 'PENGUIN JOINS US GIANTS IN £4m TAKEOVER' *The Guardian* business section reported the move thus:

The Penguin book group is expanding its interests in the US by taking over a leading American publishing company, Viking Press, in a deal worth up to $9m.... Penguin which is combined with Longmans in the Longman Pearson group is a company in the banking, publishing and industrial empire of the S. Pearson and Son group.... Mr Jim Rose, chairman of Penguin becomes chairman of the Viking Penguin Board, and Mr Thomas H. Guinzburg, president of Viking, will become President and chief executive of Viking Penguin.... Mr Rose said yesterday that the new deal meant Penguin could now buy world rights to books in hard cover and paperback, 'This will be the pattern of things to come.' (Grd 11.11.75. The sums involved were the subject of some journalistic disagreement.)

In a similarly prophetic mood, Penguin's American Vice-President was quoted in *The New Statesman*, 9 May 1975, as saying after the Anti-Trust investigation blew up:

I don't think British publishing will go to the wall.... But to survive it will probably have to become more like the American publishing. It may have to offer fewer titles in print and sell more of them. (NS 9.5.75)

(In November the Anti-Trust suit was given as a main reason for the Viking operation; Bk 15.11.75.) The 1976 figures for Penguin showed, perhaps coincidentally, a marked improvement of turnover to profit ratio (1975: £17.25m/£2.32m; 1976: £18.7m/£3.21m; Bk 30.4.77).

Penguin, for so long the symbol of the best in English publishing, would seem set to become the first of the 'English-US Giants', a 'united publishing house', serving, as their advertisements put it, 'the English-speaking world'. If this *was* the pattern of things to come it was, perhaps, a rather grim outlook for the majority of English publishers. As Anthony Cheetham of Futura put it, 'most of us are too broke to try that route' (Bk 13.12.75). Only the biggest and most buoyant British publishers could buy themselves out of trouble by acquiring an American subsidiary. For many it might well eventually go the other way.

Arguably such a development as the Penguin-Viking link-up was inevitable. William Jovanovich's view in 1964 was, as we have seen, that the 'comfy and cottage' aspect of British publishing was a perverse anachronism. It must, to use the phrase of another forward thinker, be dragged kicking and squealing into the twentieth century, and this meant accommodation with America and American methods; rising to the 'American Challenge' as Servan Schreiber titled his influential book. Jovanovich's view (like Harold Wilson's and Servan Schreiber's) may seem to have been founded on incontrovertible economic realism. But the British publishing industry demonstrated in 1962 that it was quite capable of defying not just current merchandising practice but current merchandising law, on the grounds that 'books are not ordinary merchandise'. There are strong arguments for wanting to preserve the 'cosiness' of a book-trade, and to work with smaller than efficiently gigantic units.

IV

Whatever the ruling or fashionable philosophy of the profession many publishers of British novels have obviously realised that for wide sales the market is best seen as a large, Anglophone, Atlantic community. A casual survey of bestsellers in the late 1960s and early 1970s indicates a vogue for works with international themes—espionage, hotels, war, airports, international finance. Some writers, like Arthur Hailey, represent a literary conjuncture which is hard to identify nationally (born in England, resident in Canada, main market and setting for his fiction the USA). Bestselling authors like Deighton, Forsyth, Clavell and Higgins live out of Britain, for tax reasons presumably, flitting like the action of their narratives from one exotic setting to another, as the accountants direct. Forsyth, for one, is very bitter on the subject. But it is arguable that exile is in some way a fitting desert for a writer who does not 'belong' to England anymore. 'It is not something that I designed to happen,' he writes, 'it just happened that foreigners also liked my books to the point that 80 per cent of what I have earned in the last three years has been in foreign currency' (T 8.9.76). *The Day of the*

Jackal topped the bestseller lists in fourteen countries and, so its cover tells us, has sold 5m plus. Similar success met *The Dogs of War*, a story of multi-national companies, foreign mercenaries and African bush wars, success boosted by the Angola war in 1975–6. This novel followed *Jaws* as the second-bestselling paperback novel of 1976 in Britain (ST 27.2.77).

Subjects like Forsyth's reflect their market just as much as Jane Austen's three or four country families, or Raffles' London clubland. The wideawake English publisher now thinks of the English-speaking world when the bestseller is projected. The glossily international Bond books, which regularly sold a million in American paperback, obviously set a pattern (only one of the Bond books, incidentally, had a British setting for its main action).

Fleming, like Forsyth, was a product of the English public school. His career involved him in the government service, and he began his novel writing career late in a busy life. The Bond books were published by Jonathan Cape, at the recommendation of Fleming's personal friend and contemporary, William Plomer. In this way Fleming can be seen to have some membership in the established coteries of English literary life. But what of the younger bestselling authors, who have no such rootedness, and whom the tax laws drive into exile? Why should they retain their Britishness, simply because that is the land of their origin? They might even be impelled by motives of fiscal revenge to disown themselves. One can quote the angry Anthony Burgess, in 1976: 'I shan't go back there [i.e. the UK] The British Government has frozen £40,000 of my assets until they decide how much I owe.... It is an evil brutal system' (ES 28.4.76). And if not fiscal revenge, then the revenge of the wounded sensibility. John Fowles, for example, complains of the way in which American readers and critics value him, and British don't: 'he is... delighted by the attention he receives here [the US], and contrasts it bitterly with his standing in his native land.... "They hate to see my success here: they like to talk about American vulgarity as a way of berating me"' (PW 25.11.74). Why should such authors not establish themselves where their main sales are and where they are appreciated? This is more than ever the case after the abolition of the Traditional Market Agreement. An eventual loss of British authors as national property is apprehended by T. G. Rosenthal:

There is a risk that because of the great richness of the US market some British authors—whatever their old loyalties—will be published by an American house first. Even the most successful book in Britain sells at best 10 per cent of the quantity it would make in the US market. (PW 1.3.76)

The example of Jack Higgins (né Patterson) may be cited to support Rosenthal. Higgins was a prolific, not terribly successful author of male action novels, when his work *The Eagle Has Landed* was recognised by the American publisher Holt as a potential best-seller. The novel has a straightforward international theme; a wartime German assassination attempt on Churchill. *The Eagle Has Landed* was released first in America, where it topped the bestseller list for weeks, earning the writer some hundreds of thousands of dollars before making any appearance in the British market. Bantam paid $200,000 for the paperback rights, and were rumoured to have given twice that for the rights of the next novel (*Storm Warning*) which was quick in coming. At the time of his inevitable departure from England to a Channel Island tax haven, Higgins had an estimated £350,000—most of which was American earned (as reported on BBC 'Tonight' 12.4.76). Within two years *The Eagle Has Landed* had sold 15m in 31 languages. Fortuitously Higgins's daughter, sixteen year old Sarah Patterson, had simultaneously made a reported £30,000 with her first romantic novel, *The Distant Summer*. This was published by Hutchinson and Arrow paperbacks, serialised in *Woman's Own*, sold to the Master Storyteller Club, American rights were taken by Simon and Shuster and Pocket Books paperbacks, it was made an alternative Doubleday Book club selection, and taken as a Reader's Digest Condensed Book. The Pattersons, father and daughter, could hardly but see their writing futures as linked with the American market.

At a higher level than the Pattersons or Forsyths, the same pressures are detectable. The careers of Anthony Burgess and Muriel Spark, for example, have been changed by the fact that they are now international writers, who live abroad (in Italy) and sell most of their books abroad (in America) and would cease to be able to do the one unless they did the other. Muriel Spark has graduated from English and Scottish settings to American, middle Eastern and high European, parallel with her advance in professional life. The same tendency is evident in Burgess's work (though less clearly since much of his early fiction grew out of his expatriate service as a teacher in Malaya). The publisher's synopsis of Burgess's 1977 novel bears repeating.

With *Beard's Roman Women* he has produced a highly original and entertaining novel about a middle-aged script writer living in Rome whose life fluctuates between a lovely photographer, four liberated girl rapists and a series of surreal telephone conversations with his supposedly dead wife. As an unusual counterpoint to the story the book has been illustrated with photographs of Rome taken by David Robinson. (Bk 29.1.77)

It may seem a crude observation, but where a novelist lives, or where he no longer lives, will have an effect on a product which is essentially inspirational in origins. If Muriel Spark writes about the Italian and American rich in her latest novel, rather than penurious Peckham, it is partly because she is now rich and has no need to pass her time in SE London. If Burgess lives in Italy he will tend to write about Italy.

So too will what a novelist perceives to be his or her major market have an effect. Margaret Drabble was reported by *Publishers' Weekly* as having almost 18,000 of her hardback *Realms of Gold* in print within a few months of its appearing in the American market (PW 3.11.75). One does not know how many were printed in Britain but it is hardly likely to have been many more. How long will such a novelist continue to see the 'intelligent [English] housewife who never buys a book' and is responsible for a paltry 1,200 library sales as her *first* reader? Another somewhat accidental example may be had from Piers Paul Read's 1976 novel, *Polonaise* (a work with a recognisably international theme and action). A few weeks before publication it was discovered that the work unintentionally libelled an English peer, who was disinclined to be satisfied with the publisher's apologies. 11,500 British copies of *Polonaise* were pulped at a cost, it was said, of £7,000 (ES 27.9.76), and the 19,000 copies printed for the American market were simultaneously put at risk (they were eventually issued with a sticker apology; PW 7.11.76). The novel had also been printed up for the American-based journal *Cosmopolitan*, before the unlucky mistake was discovered. The episode was newsworthy and generated some compensatory publicity for Secker and Warburg. But no one seemed surprised that a British author, and a highly regarded one, should be selling a third less of his novels in the 'first' market. Again, one cannot but think that some consciousness of the relative disposition of his national readerships must gradually condition Read's fiction. (Although it should be noted that Read has resisted the pressure which he feels, as a successful novelist, to emigrate, out of respect for 'the subtle but certain bond which should exist between a writer and his own people'; T 23.9.75.)

The doyen of English international novelists is Graham Greene. His 1973 novel, *The Honorary Consul* was twenty-seven weeks in the American bestseller list, which means it probably entered the highest, 250,000-plus bracket. Can a writer ignore the fact that he has five to ten American purchasers for every British? Of course Green (Berkhamsted, Balliol, Foreign Office, *The Times*) has an inbred Englishness which he could never blend out, however long he lived abroad and even if his novels sold not a copy in the UK. But it is interesting to consider the case of the writer whose appellation as 'the new Graham Greene' was one of the critical clichés of 1976, and who has taken the logic of Greenian fiction a step further.

Paul Theroux, born in Massachusets, in 1941, travels widely but is now apparently resident in England. His reputation was made in the mid 1970s, with a travel book, *The Great Railway Bazaar*, and a novel about international terrorism, *The Family Arsenal*, a work given painful topicality by the 1975–6 Provisional IRA bombing campaign in London. This is recognisably Greenian (*The Honorary Consul* was also about international urban terrorism). But what Theroux brought to the Greene formula was new and appropriate publishing tactics. The following comes from an interview which the novelist gave to *Publishers' Weekly* in 1976:

> he finds the way in which he is published on both sides of the Atlantic, sometimes here [the US] first, sometimes there, as helpful in getting him authoritative review attention. 'I'm sure it helps that *Arsenal* was approved of by most English critics, and obviously the comparisons to Greene don't do any harm. And then when *Bazaar* which came out here [the US] first, got to England, it got attention from all the big guns—Angus Wilson, V. S. Pritchett, Paul Scott.' (PW 26.7.76)

A novelist whom Theroux admires, and has written a monograph on, is V. S. Naipaul. A West Indian, with strong feelings for his sub-continental Indian origins, Naipaul too is based in Britain, where he emigrated in 1950. Naipaul writes travel books of distinction (and sometimes, as with *An Area of Darkness*, to controversial effect), and in his fiction deals with international themes. His 1975 novel, *Guerillas*, deals with another variety of urban terrorism, that associated with Black Power, and the later career of Michael X. Like Theroux, again, Naipaul has a major American reputation; he is one of the few English authors under forty-five to have been written up at length in *The New York Review of Books*. The battle between Deutsch and Secker for him in early 1977 was sufficiently newsworthy to make the gossip columns.

One can compile an impressive list of such internationally minded novelists, prominent in 'English' letters at the moment: Dan Jacobson, South African and Jewish, whose novels to date are set abroad and sell well in America, though he lives and works in Britain; Ruth Prawer Jhabvala ('what *is* that Polish woman with the Indian name called?' Dame Rebecca West asked absentmindedly on 'Tonight', as she listed the important 'English' novelists now writing); Mordecai Richler, Canadian, was for a crucial period of his writing career domiciled in England; Thomas Keneally, an Australian, has been based in Britain in the 1970s; Sarah Gainham was born in London, but has been resident in Europe since 1947, as much of her fiction reflects; Anne Redmon is American and lives in London; David Plante was born in the US in 1940, educated partly in Europe, and has been resident in England since 1966; Gabriel Josipovici is a British subject, but of origins sufficiently foreign to debar him from receiving the Somerset Maugham award, after he had won it (one of the more bizarre literary episodes of 1975; see Obs 6.7.75); Frederic Raphael was born in America, educated at Charterhouse and Cambridge, and is largely resident in America and France; Brian Moore, born in Northern Ireland, became a Canadian in 1948, has been based in America since the late 1950s—is claimed as the literary property of all those areas, but most plausibly by Great Britain. Moore's statement in a Radio 3 broadcast in 1976: 'I have become a literary nomad' could be echoed by many of the more influential British novelists of the day. So too could Raphael's self analysis:

> I am conscious of being foreign in England and I find myself at home to some extent in many other places, yet I cannot sever myself entirely from the country where I live [he means the UK at the time of writing] or from the language in which I write. (*Contemporary Novelists*, London and New York, 1976, p. 1145)

A case could be made that this corps of writers represents the vanguard of current English fiction—writing not for England but the English-speaking world. There is, of course, resistance to the idea. Although he has won practically every British prize and honour worth having, V. S. Naipaul is still relegated by some literary historians to the provincial category of 'West Indian Novelist'. One influential reviewer stigmatised Theroux's superbly accurate *Family Arsenal* as 'the work of an alien'. When Prawer Jhabvala and Keneally were shortlisted for the 1975 Booker prize there were Podsnappish calls for rules to restrict the award to 'English' writers, and headlines about 'Hauling down the fictional flag' (Grd 30.10.75). The same cavils would have been brought against Teodor Korzeniowski (Conrad) and Henry James.

On the evidence of the last fifteen years the British publishing industry is capable of withstanding direct takeover. It retains an unviolated national identity unlike, say, Scotland, Canada or Belgium. At the same time, perceptible changes in the direction of 'Americanisation' or 'internationalisation' have taken place, both in the structure of the booktrade and, more importantly, in the flavour of many of the novels it produces. This will, in all probability, advance still further when the effects of the lost Traditional Market Agreement emerge, and protected markets become part of a large Anglophone territory.

In the future a lot will depend on a permanent national integrity in British publishing. If it can develop international consciousness, while continuing to own itself, then the prognosis is good—and would be even better if some tax system could be devised to keep the more successful authors resident. Nonetheless even with this happy outcome, some problems can be foreseen for international fiction. National prejudice remains a barrier. There is some question whether quality fiction can adapt to the marketing techniques needed to sell it internationally without damaging artistic concessions. Integration which does not involve subjugation of the weaker culture to the stronger, or subtle forms of prostitution, is tricky. These matters are considered closely in the case of a single novel, *Ragtime*, in the next chapter.

4 *Ragtime*, A Novel for Our Times

RAGTIME is set in America at the beginning of this century. Its characters: three remarkable families whose lives become entwined with people whose names are Henry Ford, Emma Goldman, Harry Houdini, J. P. Morgan, Evelyn Nesbit, Sigmund Freud, Emiliano Zapata. It is a novel so original, so full of imagination and subtle pleasure, that to describe it further would only dilute the pure joy of reading. Turn to the first page. Begin. You will never have read anything like RAGTIME before. Nothing quite like it has ever been written before.
From the cover of the American paperback edition

Everybody's reading RAGTIME
Macmillans' advertisement

One of the better selling and more publicised novels in England in 1976 was the most publicised and best selling novel in America in 1975, *Ragtime*. There is, unfortunately, nothing unusual in this sequence. We are used to the English book of the year being the American book of last year. A string of blockbusters from Philip Roth, Norman Mailer, Thomas Pynchon, Saul Bellow and Kurt Vonnegut has induced in many Britons an exasperated sense that really important novels happen more often on the other side of the Atlantic. But *Ragtime* warrants attention on other scores than its having been just another successful intruder on the English literary scene. From the first everyone saw *Ragtime* as epochal. As one of its American publishers portentously put it: 'We view the book as a literary work, a watershed publishing event with sales longevity' (PW 26.4.76). What he meant by this oddly metaphorical description was that *Ragtime* was doubly significant; initially by virtue of its being a great novel which would in time become an American classic. Secondly, *Ragtime* was significant because the way in which it was to be sold ('total merchandising' as it was called, by analogy with total war) would transform the manner in which, henceforth, the American booktrade handled its most important books.

It is as a portent, or 'watershed publishing event', that I want to consider *Ragtime* here. Is it in fact the novel of our times, for both Britain and America? More particularly does it in fact indicate a fruitful hybridisation of quality fiction and bestsellerdom? Or is it merely a creature of American sales 'hype'? What does it tell us about the present state of the inter-Atlantic reading public, and the booktrades which serve it?

I

When *Ragtime* appeared in July 1975, the American reviewers joined in an ecstatic stampede for the novel. As is often condescendingly observed by Englishmen, they have a stop marked 'Great American Novel' which is pulled out at least once every twelve months. It was extended to the full for *Ragtime*: 'it will be the most accoladed novel of this year' (*The New Republic*), 'As exhilarating as a deep breath of pure oxygen' (*Newsweek*), 'A unique and beautiful work of art' (*Saturday Review*). The book's jacket came to be encrusted with similar preposterous superlatives from highly reputable sources. There were many others to choose from: 'a fabulous tale' (*Time*), 'an exceptionally original and pleasurable novel' (*The Atlantic*), 'An extraordinarily deft, lyrical, rich novel . . . as original as it is satisfying' (*The New Yorker*).

Ragtime had the wildest reception of any novel since *The Naked and the Dead*. On the face of things the immense success of the book was baffling. None of Doctorow's three previous novels had done outstandingly well. The first, a cowboy novel, *Welcome to Hard Times*, was out of print in 1975. (It was best known in England as an unsuccessful Western film.) The second, *Big as Life*, disappeared without trace soon after publication; 'deservedly' according to Doctorow himself (ES 9.1.76). The third, *The Book of Daniel*, a thinly veiled novelisation of the Rosenberg trial and execution, was very favourably reviewed, but enjoyed no great sales and fell flat in Britain. Four years later, in 1975, it and Doctorow were largely forgotten.

No one would forget *Ragtime*, if only for the record breaking statistics so publicised about it. Just under 250,000 sold in hardcover in the first year in America (PW 9.2.76); paperback rights were bought in August 1975 for an incredible $1.85m, the highest amount ever (sceptics claimed that Bantam was out to ruin the competition; they said no, they were merely outbidding other houses at the auction who had gone to $1.7m; PW 22.3.76). Before publication the novel's film rights were bought by Dino de Laurentiis for an epic treatment, to be directed by Robert Altman, the hottest director in Hollywood, and one who had specialised in wry treatments of American themes. The price Paramount gave was unspecified, but reputed to be over the million. The book was also taken as a Book of the Month Club choice before publication. Once published it stayed in the bestseller lists for forty weeks.

Ragtime was credited with having, almost single handedly, created a resuscitating boom in American bookselling. *The New York Times Book Review* reported in September 1975:

According to the American Booksellers Association . . . business in July [1975] was up from 5–10 per cent over July last year—even 30 per cent in a few stores . . . the booksellers . . . attribute the phenomenon to two hot titles of the season, namely *Jaws* and *Ragtime*. *Jaws*, of course, achieved a second paperback life due to the popularity of the movie (and its accompanying publicity hype) while *Ragtime* is simply a widely praised hardcover novel that has caught the public fancy. Last summer [1974] the booksellers say, there were no such books. The importance of these hot books is their 'coat tail effect'—that is they lure people into the shops; once there they often buy other books. (NYTBR 14.9.75)

The hysteria about *Jaws* is understandable enough. But *Ragtime* was, by comparison, an ambitious novel by a self-conscious literary artist who had supported himself on Guggenheim and Creative Arts Program Service fellowships while writing it. How had it managed to become 'hot'? Unlike, say, *The Naked and the Dead*, *Ragtime* had neither sex, violence nor bad language in large quantity. Unlike Vonnegut and Pynchon, Doctorow enjoyed no youth cult support. As a forty-three year old teacher of Creative Writing and retiring by nature, he was not a newsworthy personality. Nor had he any previous wave of popularity to ride. And *Ragtime* had its success in the bookshops at a time when, as the trade reported, ordering policy was 'very conservative' (PW 1.3.76); this itself was a reflection of the rather tightfisted way the American public generally was viewing the hardcover novel at its new price of nearly $10.

The first point to make is that Doctorow wanted the work to be widely read. On the other hand it wasn't a case, as it had been with Mario Puzo a couple of years earlier, of the novelist cynically deciding 'to grow up and sell out'. Doctorow still had ideals, even if he was fed up with his small readership and what he called 'exclusionary' status. Writing shortly before *Ragtime* was published, *Publishers' Weekly* carried the following report:

Ragtime is much the most accessible book of the four Doctorow has written, and he is glad of it. 'I've always wanted my work to be accessible. Literature, after all, is for people, not some secret society. It probably seems so accessible this time because I was very deliberately concentrating on the narrative element. I wanted a really relentless narrative, full of ongoing energy. I wanted to recover that really marvellous tool for a novelist, the sense of motion. Two or three hundred years ago it was much more common—Defoe had it, Cervantes, more recently Edgar Allan Poe. You have to make sacrifices for it, of course.' (PW 30.6.75)

The novelist put it rather more politically six months later, in *The Evening Standard*: 'Reading is an elitist activity, and that's a shame. All it means is that society is stratified by class and the need is to try and bridge the classes and eventually democratise them' (ES 9.1.76). Doctorow, it would seem, wanted no less than to re-assemble the great nineteenth-century reading public; to break down the stratification which had separated the mass market from the best literature. His background was one which gave him unusual dexterity and technical skills to carry out this task:

Doctorow was in publishing himself for many years before he left five years ago to devote himself to writing (with occasional teaching, currently at Sarah Lawrence). He began as a reader for Columbia Pictures, where for three years 'I read just about everything that was published'.... Thence to New American Library, where he worked his way in five years to senior editor. Finally, in the mid-1960s, he went to Dial Press as editor-in-chief. In his early publishing days, 'I just saw it as a means to survival while I continued writing,' and he would put in 20-hour days between the office and his typewriter. 'Then when I got to Dial I found it very interesting and creative, and I began to neglect my own work because editing and publishing was such fun.' (PW 30.6.75)

The authorial will to succeed and an impressive background as a professional technician do not of themselves explain why *Ragtime* should have succeeded so extravagantly. They do not, for example, explain why Random House, and the subsequent paperback publishers Bantam, should have put such sales effort behind the book. From the start Random House went all out for *Ragtime*. The advertising budget was lavish. Typical of the largesse was the publisher ('almost unprecedentedly' as *Publishers' Weekly* remarked) sending out a specially produced gift edition 'to friends of the author and publisher' (PW 30.6.75). It was, Random House said, a token of their 'enthusiasm' for the novel.

American advertising budgets run, as the advertisements themselves proudly tell us, into the hundreds of thousands of dollars. A full page in *The New York Times Book Review* costs, apparently, some $6,000. At these prices, publishers do not let their enthusiasm overwhelm their commercial judgement. One may also suspect that publishing houses will put on a convincing display of in-house 'enthusiasm' if they think it will sell them more copies, and that any specially printed gift edition may be more in the nature of a *douceur* than a spontaneous effusion of proprietary excitement. Nonetheless there is no need to think therefore that the promotion campaign behind *Ragtime* was entirely cynical. I had an opportunity to ask the executive in charge of advertising Random House's edition of the novel whether he thought it was a machine-made or a natural success. His answer ran roughly thus:

> What happened first was a number of guys at Random House read the typescript and thought it was a winner. So they generated excitement—fever you might call it—phoning people telling them about it. It got selected as a Book of the Month Club choice. [America, much more than Britain, has the practice of new novels being sold at concessionary prices by book clubs.] Then came the film rights. When they got a huge offer, the critics began to prick their ears up. A real break for us was the *New York Times* breaking their review before publication date. [*Ragtime* was reviewed both in *The New York Times* and *The New York Times Book Review*.] Then came the paperback auction; they put it to six or seven big paperback houses, asking for offers and saying what their floor level was—say $500,000. When they got nearly $2m the thing was unstoppable. Doctorow's on radio, TV, in feature articles. The book's on the bestseller list for the rest of the year.

When asked if it could have been done, however good *Ragtime* was or wasn't, he said 'No—otherwise they'd do it all the time.' He cited the example of another book which had recently been given the advertising works, Muhammad Ali's *The Greatest*. It had flopped, he alleged, despite the author's modest prophecy that 'this will be the greatest book ever in the market' (PW 3.11.75). He thought *Ragtime* had succeeded because it deserved to succeed, and because it had incalculable lucky breaks, like Joshua Rifkin's Scott Joplin revival and the connected popularity of *The Sting*, and the whole nostalgia boom of the 1970s.

It may be that *Ragtime* was lucky. But one should not overlook what looks like intelligent anticipation on the publisher's part. Undoubtedly Random House foresaw that 1975–6 was a propitious time for 'The Astonishing Bestseller About America'. There were a lot of booksales in the bicentennial. Not everyone appreciated this in advance. Pyramid were pleasantly taken aback by the mammoth sales of their tawdry 'American Bicentennial Series' of novels by John Jakes. Instead of the 100,000 which they thought would be 'doing well' this five-part series was printing 2½m per title towards the end (PW 5.4.76). *Ragtime* flourished on the same wave of national narcissism. Americans, in 1976, wanted to read about America in its historical context.

Ragtime was not just an anniversary, however. It was, among other things, a novel deeply hostile to the capitalism which made twentieth-century American superpower. The climax in which the black Coalhouse Walker Jr is besieged in J. Pierpont Morgan's house (now Library) is angrily symbolic. One cannot doubt that the author is on the side of the anarchist faction who are present in the action. More immediately, the death of Walker invokes the death of George Jackson:

> In the bright floodlit street the black man was said by the police to have made a dash for freedom. More probably he knew that all he must do in order to end his life was to turn his head abruptly or lower his hands or smile. Inside the Library, Father heard the co-ordinated volley of a firing squad. He screamed. He ran to the window. The body jerked about the street in a sequence of attitudes as if it were trying to mop up its own blood. The policemen were firing at will. The horses snorted and shied. (*Ragtime*, New York, 1975 repr. 1976, pp. 349–50)

In the post-Watergate era America was tolerant, even desirous of self criticism. And it should be said that Doctorow was sufficiently tactful in pressing his political theme for none of the first reviewers to think it worth dwelling on as a feature of the novel; although undoubtedly the tart, anti-American aftertaste helped sales in this peculiarly masochistic period of the nation's history.

Finally one should record a pervasive gimmickry in *Ragtime*. One gimmick is the extraordinarily clipped style; developed apparently in the interest of creating the desired 'narrative energy'. Less original was the use of actual historical figures and dense historical factuality, woven into the fiction. This was known to be faddishly popular with the American novel-reading public. In 1974 one of the blockbusters was Nicholas Meyer's *The Seven-Per-Cent Solution*. Set in the same period as *Ragtime* this involved fictional Sherlock Holmes with historical Sigmund Freud (who also makes a substantial appearance in *Ragtime*). Meyer's book is flimsier by far than Doctorow's, but the superficial attractiveness of the two books owes much to the device of wilfully confusing actual and fictional personages.

II

It is not flattering to suggest that part of *Ragtime*'s immense success is owed to historical opportunism or derivative modishness. But in autumn of 1975 anything could be forgiven the novel. It had, apparently, achieved a double which had previously eluded every novelist since Dickens. Authoritative and trustworthy reviews guaranteed its literary value; the novel was, if critics' words meant anything, a 'classic'. At the same time it was selling in a way unknown to any but the most popular fiction—14,000 a week in September (PW 22.9.75).

It was this dual aspect of *Ragtime* which induced Bantam to give $1.85m for the paperback rights, then the largest sum ever paid, by the firm that proclaimed themselves 'the largest paperback company in the world and the most profitable' (Bk 20.9.75). To maintain their profitability with *Ragtime*, as crude calculation will show, they would have to sell over 5m at the usual price before they got a sight of their purchase price, plus advertising and interest costs. Generally speaking only Mickey Spillane, Jacqueline Susann, Peter Benchley or Peter Blatty could be relied on for this scale of sales. (*Ragtime*'s record in fact stood until 1977 when Avon gave $1.98m for Colleen McCullough's romance *The Thorn Birds*, a much less ambitious investment than Doctorow's 'literary' novel.) Clearly however, Bantam reckoned on getting their money back. They expected to recoup in two instalments. *Ragtime* would be issued in July 1976, coinciding with two peak buying periods: the bicentennial month, and the summer vacation when everyone always bought their paperbacks for the beach. Every year Bantam have what they call a 'Beach Book . . . a big easy-read novel you can take wherever you're going' (C. Petersen, *The Bantam Story*, New York, p. 84). *Ragtime* would be the season's beach book, and Bantam printed 2½m in readiness. At the same time, for their $1.85m outlay Bantam had the novel for ten years, twice the usual lease. They calculated that *Ragtime* would sell year in, year out, as it became absorbed into the canon of college and school taught 'Great American Books'. To this end a 'Teacher's Guide' to *Ragtime* was prepared. This handy volume was distributed free at the MLA conference in 1976–7. It contained, for the benefit of the schoolteacher, useful sections on how to circumvent censorious Parent Teacher Association groups, who felt the novel too frank. Bantam declared themselves sanguine about their investment in Doctorow, and Marc Jaffe hinted at some surprises, a few months before their edition came out:

> The most important ingredient from the start was the total enthusiasm of everyone in the company about that book. At no time while we were thinking about it was there any estimate, from sales or editorial, that we would sell fewer than 2m copies. There were several elements in this book that rarely come together as they did here. It was an assured bestseller, there had been a fabulous prepublication effort by Random House, and it was a BOMC choice and had made a very big movie sale, all before the bidding began.... And it's our prediction that we will break through into millions of sales on *Ragtime* at a price of $2.25 for a novel of conventional length. And that probably won't be the only edition. And we were able to get a longer license on the book than we usually do—ten years instead of five. That's because when we were looking at the figures involved we were convinced this could become a long term book, on the order of *The Catcher in the Rye*, *A Separate Peace*, Steinbeck's *The Pearl* —all important books we've kept in print for many years and which have sold in the millions. We don't just see it as a quick blockbuster, we're not just in business for that. We have some very exciting marketing plans for the book, but they're still in the development stage, and I'll just say they involve something that's never been done before. (PW 22.3.76)

As Jaffe hints, Bantam were intending to put more money out to recover the millions already spent. They had also expended considerable imagination. There was to be the usual apparatus—posters, streamers, mobiles, fliers, chapter handouts, all with the famous *Ragtime* logo. There was to be much more besides. Bantam provided *Ragtime* paperbags and a special display 'piano' holding 35 of the dual cover paperback, arranged to look like keys. Some of the stores placed a cassette recorder in the piano for the *de rigueur* Scott Joplin.

'In the heavily trafficked areas of the city', *The New York Times* reported, 'the book will be delivered in oldtime cars and trucks' (NYT 23.7.76). Thirteen '*Ragtime* Mall Festivals' were arranged, all over north America. Saturation advertising was bought. 'Newspaper advertisements are scheduled in the top 50 markets, 60-second radio spots have been created, bus cards will appear in the top 20 markets for one month and banners advertising the book will be flown over the beaches during the Fourth of July weekend,' PW reported (26.4.76). The most spectacular event was described in *The New York Times*, 18 July:

> Next Tuesday, when the White Sox play host to the Yankees, it'll be '*Ragtime Night*' at Chicago's Comiskey Park. The ushers will be wearing skimmers and gartered shirts, bands will be playing turn-of-the-century tunes, there will be an antique car rally and fireworks.

Bantam, like Random House, provided two editions; one selling for $2.25 (2½m in the first print run), the other an enlarged, boxed edition with 15 illustrations by Carol Yeh at $5.95 (30,000 first printing; NYTBR 23.7.76).

III

Even as they were launching this extraordinary sales-campaign-cum-circus there must have been some gloomy foreboding at Bantam headquarters. For as the winter of 1975 drew on, sobriety began to break in on all the 'accolading'. After the initial, celebratory review ('simply splendid. A bag of Riches') *Village Voice* (4.8.75) ran a reassessment by Greil Marcus, asserting the novel to be a confection, 'dead on the page' (interestingly he likened it to another hit of the season, *Nashville*, directed by *Ragtime's* future director, Altman). In January 1976 *Atlantic Monthly* ran a piece, 'The Most Overrated Book of the Year Award'. This booby prize was won by *Ragtime*. In *The New York Times* Books of the Year, it was rather more tactfully stated that *Ragtime* (which the paper had hailed hysterically six months before) had met 'strong opposition' from judges (NYTBR 28.12.75). There were other dissenting voices now heard. Raymond Sokolov, writing in *The Washington Post*, was moved to caution readers against early extravagant claims (his own included). In a sober reassessment in *Commentary*, October 1975, Hilton Kramer drew attention to the novel's unregarded tendencies, denouncing the 'almost complete unanimity with which its earliest reviewers agreed to ignore its patently political purpose':

> Our culture is now so completely permeated with the myth of American malevolence that an ambitious political romance like *Ragtime* which distorts the actual materials of history with a fierce ideological arrogance, is no longer in any danger of being recognised as having a blunt political point. The reviewers who are responsible for making this book a phenomenal success are, in this sense, at one with the audience to which it is addressed: an educated class that has grown morally obtuse about the world in which it lives and prospers.

The bandwagon had done something of a U-turn. *Ragtime* was no triumph of fiction, but a sympton of America's cultural sickness and moral obtuseness.

This was how the book stood in January 1976; not exploded, but rather vulnerable looking. On 19 January first publication of the book was scheduled by Macmillan in England. (They and Pan had bought rights, of course, when the novel's stock was sky-high.) Macmillan's faith echoed that of Random House and Bantam: 'We believe,' a Macmillan's representative declared, 'that *Ragtime* is that almost mythologically rare bird, a bestselling novel of the highest literary quality' (Bk 1.11.75). On the face of it, the advantages of publishing late were considerable. The novel's American fame would prepare the way for it. The fact that they felt they could bank on enormous sales meant that Macmillan's priced the novel (which must have been an expensive purchase for them) at £3.50—a lowish sum by the standards of 1976, and equivalently lower than Random House's $8.95. Otherwise the English and American editions were absolutely identical—stressing that in Macmillan's eyes, at least, there were no national barriers any more to bestselling fiction.

Promotion for the book was huge, by English standards. 'Publicitywise' in *Macmillan News* ran the following item on the novel:

> Macmillan London will be publishing *Ragtime* in January, and it promises to be one of the most important works of fiction for the firm for many years. Jeremy HADFIELD has produced a superbly illustrated and designed promotional folder which, if there were awards for promotion pieces would be an Oscar winner.

The trade advertising was confidently modest in manner—the *Ragtime* logo, with the caption: 'the most widely discussed and critically acclaimed novel of our time'. Pre-publication vibration was created by the widely circulated information that Macmillan had printed 85,000 copies. Doctorow was brought over for the launching party to which, apparently, every conceivable reviewer was invited. Copies of the novel were scattered broadcast. ('I must be the only person in London without one,' grumbled *The Bookseller*'s dyspeptic Quentin Oates.) Doctorow was interviewed and made the main feature on *The Evening Standard* middle-pages, space normally reserved for pop stars and film idols.

In the light of this publicity it was a matter of keen interest as to how the reviews would turn out. For one thing, the revisionist opinion in America was percolating into England, at least at those higher levels which the reviewers inhabit. For another, there was a provincial *hauteur* among English reviewers about the grandiose claims of the Great American Novel, and the lightheadedness of American reviewers where it was concerned. 'EH' in *The Bookseller* had been sounding cautionary noises about 'over-indulgent America' since September (Bk 3.1.76). Auberon Waugh indicated a substantial jaundice that lay ahead of any GAN in a paragraph in his *Spectator* column, two days before *Ragtime* came out:

> It arrives... with Glowing Testimonials from the *New York Times Book Review*, *The New Republic*, *The Boston Sunday Globe*, *The New York Times*, *Village Voice* and 'Liberal' (or perhaps one should now call them 'radical') reviewers on *Time*, *Saturday Review*, *Newsweek*, and *Literary Journal*.... It has already sold 265,000 copies in hard back and we are told that Macmillan has printed 85,000 copies over here. I think and hope that Macmillan will be looking very silly at the end of the day. (Sp 17.1.76)

Doctorow had made a bad impression in his recorded interview. Especially his populist aim of reaching the 'proletariat' rankled with the British public, who felt that they didn't need some jumped-up pinko American Professor of Creative Writing to throw culture their way. A letter to *The Evening Standard* ran:

> How snobbish of Mr Doctorow to say that he wants his book to be read by 'people who do not normally read books... people who work in factories and garages.' It may surprise Mr Doctorow to know that people who work in factories and garages do in fact read books. If they have any sense, however, there is one book they will *not* read. (ES 16.1.76)

'Publicitywise', then, *Ragtime* had two strikes against it before it even appeared in the British bookshop.

One supposes the literary editors must have been in something of a quandary. *Ragtime* was not all it had been cracked up to be, apparently. Yet evidence was on record that it was the most important novel in years—perhaps the most important novel of the century. It was so big it could not be ignored; could not even be given the merely usual treatment. It was, as Marcus Cunliffe put it, not just a bestseller, but a 'best bestseller, before it has even sold a copy in England' (Grd 22.1.76).

The quandary was resolved in what must be seen as the oddest spectacle in the reviews since the reception of Colin Wilson's *The Outsider*. *Ragtime* was given pride of place in all the journals: either huge solo reviews, or generous lead spots in double and (in only a few cases) group reviews. It had more column inches than any other novel of the year with the exception of *Gulag 2* and (again in some cases only) *Humboldt's Gift*. But unlike these other two, *Ragtime* was universally deplored. Some reviewers, like *The Spectator*'s Peter Ackroyd, seem to have seen it as the ultimate indictment of the flimsiness of American civilisation: 'it could only succeed in a culture which has no roots, and no soil' (Sp 24.1.76). In the *Standard* Auberon Waugh pronounced it, as he had promised the week before, 'a pretty good load of rubbish' (ES 20.1.76). Emma Tennant, in *The Listener*, wondered if it were the product of a computer (List 22.1.76). Frank Kermode, in *The New Review*, suggested that the book warranted another Q. D. Leavis coming to judgement with another *Fiction and the Reading Public* (NR Jan. 76).*The Times* thought it 'pretty pretentious and vulgar', adopting like many others a rather dowager-like tone of disapproval: 'the author has an irritating trick of using long words without having taken the trouble to ascertain their precise meanings' (T 22.1.76). *The Times Literary Supplement*'s Russell Davies, in a full-page hatchet job, picked on the unfortunate reference to garage hands: 'I see no great future for *Ragtime* here, and certainly no destiny for Mr Doctorow as the British petrol-pump attendant's Balzac' (TLS 23.1.76). In *The Daily Telegraph* Martyn Goff contented himself with observing that 'American novelists of any note seem to yearn to write the Great American Novel' (DT 22.1.76). Francis King, in *The Sunday Telegraph*, took much the same line: 'the rapture with which it has been greeted amazes me as much as if some Scott Joplin frolic had been equated with a Debussy Prelude' (STel 18.1.76). The most savage of savage reviews came some time later from Paul Levy in *Books and Bookmen*, who denounced *Ragtime* as a 'bicentennial ripoff', in itself 'merely a bad book' but 'outrageous' in the way it had been foisted on the public (BB July 76).

It was, as *The New York Times* observed, 'a sort of Boston Tea Party in reverse' (NYTBR 7.3.76). The best that any blurb-seeking Macmillan editor could rake up, assuming that they ever cleared their 85,000 and had the gall to reprint, were a warm review in *The Guardian* from Cunliffe (a professor of American studies, and therefore perhaps biased), a warmish one in *The New Statesman* from Philip French (a reviewer with a weakness for Hollywood style gloss) and some kind words in *The Financial Times* from C. P. Snow who never had unkind words for anything he reviewed. (Pan, in fact, cut out the British quality press altogether and took their tags from the *Mail* and *Express*.)

The reader might have been forgiven for asking why so ordinary a novel should be given such a large stage on which to flaunt its ordinariness. It might be true that, as Ackroyd said, New York critics were 'easily fooled' and that 'it is left to us quiet and cosy English critics to notice that the book is sentimental and meretricious'. It was also pretty clear that English critics were not to be had for the price of a few publicity drinks. But why should your wide-awake and incorruptible reviewer and his editor give the novel such huge coverage? Anthony Thwaite in *The Observer* resolved the embarrassment by striking the pose of the fearless investigator into one of the curiosities of modern literature: 'In the normal way, I wouldn't give so much space to such a trivial, preening confection; yet one has to try to account for the rapture with which it has been received in the United States' (Obs 18.1.76). In fact this kind of account was notably what the reviews failed to do. Thwaite's defence is, to say the least, hollow. When, six months later, John Gross was asked why, as editor of *The Times Literary Supplement* and a noted pro-American, he had allowed Russell Davies to go on at such monstrous length, he replied: 'the reviewer asked for more space than usual, and I gave it to him' (PW 9.8.76). Again this does not tell us why, and one can be fairly confident that the *TLS* will not give a whole page to every reviewer who might care to shoot his mouth off a bit about the latest bad American novel. And had the English critical press forgotten the adage that bad publicity is preferable to no publicity?

Ragtime was given the full treatment not because the novel was so exceptionally good that it called for attention; that much was clear. Nor would it be true to see the English critics as without will, unable to resist joining a Gadarene rush. But they do seem to have sensed, correctly I think, that *Ragtime* was a highly significant novel; significant because it represented in some sense a takeover attempt on their culture. It was a novel marketed in the ultra-American fashion; as such it conflicted with and threatened the whole economy of the British industrial-critical complex. It is as an alarmist response that the reviews, *en masse*, should be taken.

Some of the differences between the American and British systems will have been deducible from the account of Bantam's total-merchandising campaign. America is, as Malcolm Cowley noted in the 1950s, 'a country without literary cafes or salons'. But it does have supermarkets, media and hardsell advertising. In present-day America, the bestseller lists are used to generate fast sales, in much the same way that the top fifty generates record sales; the number one blazon is fiercely competed for. American book suppliers have a sale-or-return system for hardbacks (and profligately so for paperbacks) which encourages the retailer to overstock for display purposes —at worst he need only pay freight on returns. Booksellers give discounts to favoured groups of purchasers. American paperback firms allow retailers up to 75 per cent of the costs incurred by co-operative promotional advertising (PW 5.7.76). All this makes for a sharper selling market than Britain is used to. America in consequence has always led in such display fields as book jackets and paperback covers (which over there were pictorial from the first), point-of-sale enticements, book club come-ons, preview gimmicks, newspaper advertising of books (relatively restrained in Britain), promotional odysseys, saturation of local press and radio channels (only now beginning to happen in Britain).

American 'hype' as it is called had by the mid 1970s reached the pitch of a distinct publishing art. Jacqueline Susann, for example, will merit a place in literary history, not for her execrable fiction but for the way she and her television producer husband, Irving Mansfield, sold it. 'The Invasion of Normandy', a Susann press agent recalls, 'was child's play compared to the way Jackie and Irving orchestrated a media blitz' (NYTBR 11.7.76).

Jacqueline Susann, promotion machinery and even Ed Doctorow could have been shrugged off by the English book trade and reviewing circles with an 'autres pays autres moeurs'—were it not for the fact that Britain was moving inexorably towards the American way of doing things. There is as yet no reliable bestseller list (and consequent bestseller obsession), but *The Sunday Times* and *The Evening Standard* are undoubtedly on the way. Mass market paperbacks in Britain had gradually assimilated to the American pattern. Increasingly British authors were undertaking promotional odysseys through America. (Characteristically they saw it as a descent into Hell—see Gordon Williams's *Walk: Don't Walk*). The Net Book Agreement had been flouted by supermarkets which gave stamps with book purchases. Commercial radio in the mid 1970s opened the way for advertisement and magazine items about the latest book. The 'early reviewing' (i.e. by television and radio) controversy of 1977 indicated that the media were making significant inroads into the newspaper and magazine reviewers' territory. 'Promotion', it might seem, was taking over the function which once belonged to 'critical judgement'.

The English critical establishment might be expected to take this skid towards American habits very hard. For the main tendency of the American marketing system is to forestall judgement, and to settle matters before the reviewer even appears on the scene. There is something characteristically premature about the way in which the Americans put their books out. Books are often paid for before they are written; editors interfere with them before they are complete; the Kirkus Book Service (a system which has no equivalent in Britain) offers a 'tipsheet' assessment of books months before their publication—for professionals 'previews' are thus much more important than reviews; often before books are in print they are sold to bookclubs and paperback firms. The sums made in this way are released to impress the public. Before *Jaws* had a single copy in print it was famous that the novel had earned Peter Benchley $7,500 on the strength of a four page outline; that Bantam had before publication paid $575,000 for the paperback rights; that Book of the Month Club had taken it as half a dual selection; that Universal had guaranteed $250,000 for the movie rights; that before publication

Deutsch gave £10,000 for the British rights (Bk 38.6.75), that Pan had bought paperback rights 'for a substantial five-figure sum' (Bk 14.7.75). While *The Godfather* was still unprinted and unfinished it was sold (without the author's knowledge, consent or approval) to Fawcett for $410,000—then a record (M. Puzo, *The Godfather Papers*, London, 1972, pp. 36–7). In 1973 Norman Mailer had a million dollar advance for a book, before a single word was on paper. The fact that Avon and Bantam had 'slugged it out like gladiators' with bids of $1.85m and $1.9m for the paperback rights of *The Thorn Birds* (PW 13.4.77) was world-wide news before the novel sold a copy.

Figures of this size, and at this stage, create an impetus which flattens any critical resistance. American reviewers themselves are well enough aware of the fact. The literary editor of *The New York Times*, John Leonard, complained in 1974:

> Whatever it was the writer . . . was trying to communicate is obscured by the market value, the paperback deal, the escalator clause, the multimedia package. Instead of a one-to-one relationship between you and the artefact, we approach the artefact dizzy with publicity, a dollar sign planted like an axe in our skulls. (NYTBR 3.11.74)

Where a novel has whipped up significant pre-publication excitement, publication dates may be flagrantly flouted, both by the publisher and reviewer. It is not unknown for a novel to head the bestseller list before it is officially available. American publishers are adept at getting preview notices for novels from the famous, to release with the new work. All this helps make fiction-reviewing 'uneventful'—of secondary importance if of any importance at all.

Already, as has been said, these processes are on the march in Britain. Take the advertisement for Paul Theroux's *The Family Arsenal*, produced in the same season as *Ragtime*. The advertisement appeared on 24 January, some two months before publication. Yet everything good seems already to have happened to *The Family Arsenal*. The advertisement is largely in the past tense. It has its film rights sold; its Penguin paperback rights sold; it is sold in extract to *The Times* and is a prestige book club choice. The new Greene is discovered (a judgement dutifully repeated in reviews on both sides of the Atlantic, incidentally). All the reviews of *The Family Arsenal* can do, we are persuaded, is clinch the affair by a

ritual congratulatory ceremony; to provide blurb matter for many subsequent editions. The book has been 'judged' a success before any critical judgement has in fact taken place.

These points are made even more forcefully by the American trade advertisement (from *Publishers' Weekly*), with its telling proclamation:'THE FAMILY ARSENAL is already a winner.' The advertisement also serves to show how close British and American practice has moved, though there is still a palpably harder pressure behind the *Publishers' Weekly* item.

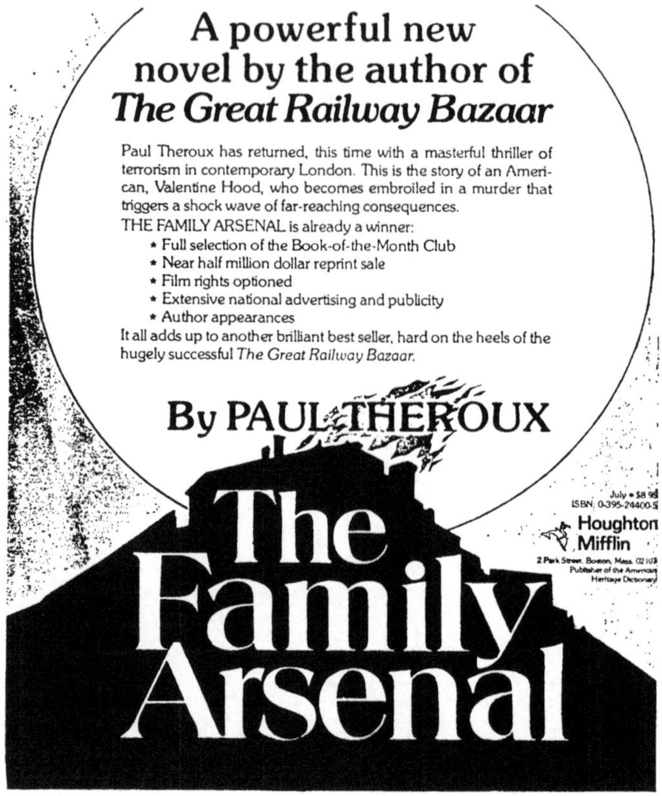

IV

It was in reaction to this Americanising tendency that I believe the English critics felt obliged to make an issue of *Ragtime*. For this was the prejudged book *par excellence*. And if *Ragtime* succeeded, against all criticism, it would argue the critics negligible. The affair shaped up as a struggle between the merchandisers and the reviewers as to who were the real opinion formers.

It was therefore a matter of great interest to see how *Ragtime* would actually sell in the face of adverse judgement. The 'Tea Party in reverse' can hardly have been the reception the publishers wanted; nonetheless Macmillan made the best of a bad job. For weeks after *Ragtime* was published almost the only sizeable advertisement to be found in the journals proclaimed 'love it or hate it—everyone's reading it. . . .' Were they and would they? After a slow start in the lists (3 in the *Sunday Times* in its first week) *Ragtime* was reported as the most sought after book in London a fortnight later (ES 10.2.76). Everyone was, for a while at least, reading *Ragtime*. 'Tills

are rattling in ragtime' declared *The Evening Standard* on 17 February—'the first big seller of 1976.' *Ragtime* stayed in the *Standard* list until 16 March. In the more precise *Sunday Times* list it held a place until 2 May (its eleventh appearance). It was number 1 on 15 February, and maintained the second and third places in subsequent weeks against opposition from Agatha Christie and Alistair MacLean.

At the end of 1976 *The Evening Standard* credited *Ragtime* with a sale of 23,000 in its annual bestsellers list. (This figure was presumably exclusive of the Literary Guild printing, which may well have brought sales up to near Macmillan's 85,000). Looking at the whole list as given by the *Standard* it is evident that *Ragtime* was, in literary terms, the 'best' bestseller of the year—with the exception of Solzhenitsyn who had been abnormally helped by his historic Panorama broadcast:

The Golden Gate. MacLean	105,000
Lenin in Zurich. Solzhenitsyn	85,000
Storm Warning. Higgins	85,000
Sleeping Murder. Christie	79,000
Touch Not the Cat. Stewart	60,000
The Deep. Benchley	50,000
Trinity. Uris	40,000
The Navigator. West	39,750
Cry Wolf. Smith	37,000
Twinkle Twinkle Little Spy. Deighton	37,000 (est)
Four Swans (Poldark). Graham	29,750

RAGTIME	23,000
In the Frame. Francis	22,000
The Boys from Brazil. Levin	20,000
Dolores. Susann	18,000
Surface with Daring. Reeman	18,000
Passage to Mutiny. King	17,000
The Alteration. Amis	17,000 (est)
Saville. Storey	17,000 (est)
The Widower's Son. Sillitoe	15,000
Henry and Cato. Murdoch	12,000

(ES 29.12.76)

It seems the critical assault did not halt *Ragtime*'s bandwagon, though it may have brought it up short of the forty weeks it had run in America. Doctorow's book was holding off the critically-acclaimed Booker-Prize winning *Saville* and the Murdoch and Amis items published later in the year. And Pan were reported as having done well with advance sales of their paperback version in January 1977, with 50,000 sold before publication in Britain to the export market and 250,000 scheduled for home sales (Bk 8.1.77). In spite of Macmillan's experience Pan chose to promote *Ragtime* as 'The most acclaimed Bestseller ever published' (Bk 15.1.77). Clearly they were hoping from it the kind of vast success which a decade earlier Corgi had had with *Catch 22*—an American book which only really took off with its paperback version. But although *Ragtime* made W. H. Smith's 'Top Ten Paperbacks' it seems not to have held its place there very long.

V

It would be convenient for the case I am making if *Ragtime* had, in fact, done all that its second American publisher hoped. It did not. Its later career in America was something of a flop after all the ballyhoo. The English critical backlash has been outlined and this, as has been noted, followed on a sizeable recantation of critical opinion in America. It seems the American public were turning, too. The sales of *Ragtime* in paperback were miscalculated in advance. Though good they were not fabulous. The *New York Times Book Review* summed it up thus, in September 1976:

This year's big regret is E. L. Doctorow's novel *Ragtime*. Bantam has sent out 2.6m copies of this prizewinning hardcover bestseller since early

July, surrounding them with highly imaginative floor displays and elaborate pageants with a pre-World-War 1 flavour. It now looks as if it'll be getting an uncommonly high percentage of those copies back from the dealers. What went wrong? 'The book's one of those New York literary clique things' (Midwestern distributor). 'The kind of title you can sell only in upper middle-class neighbourhoods' (Florida). 'Ideal for the college trade, but school was out' (New England). 'The price ($2.25) is too high, the cover unexciting, there's not been enough advertising to arouse the public's interest' (large national chain). The loudest complaints came from retail food chains that made coveted high-trafficked floor space available for display bins, but sold relatively few copies. Many paperbounders feel *Ragtime* was such a great disappointment chiefly because it had raised too great expectations. The book did do quite well in the largest cities, rated among the summer's top five on most bestseller lists. Bantam's faith remains unshaken: it believes the novel will be a strong backlist title for years to come, that eventually it'll recover the record-setting $1.85m paid for reprint rights. (NYTBR 5.9.76)

At about the same time it was given out that Altman had been sacked from the filming of *Ragtime*—supposedly because of the box office failure of his other 'American' epic on Buffalo Bill Cody.

Ragtime, then, was at best an equivocal success. It failed, at least in terms of the instant epoch-making results which had been expected from it. It may well be that the paperback was too long in coming, and that in turn the tie-in movie was too slow. Impetus was lost that could not be regained. Random House might have been advised to sacrifice a few weeks on the hardcover bestseller list, in the interest of quicker follow up. Nor should one dismiss the possibility that in the final analysis *Ragtime* was not as wonderful as first impressions had suggested.

Nonetheless, one suspects that *Ragtime* is only the first of many such Anglo-American bestseller high quality novels to be urged with ever greater sales force and sophistication on the English-speaking reading public. If there were mistakes made in the second and third stages of *Ragtime*'s promotion sequence one can be sure that they will be corrected next time round.

5 The Reviewing Establishment

Critics in England do not accept bribes, but they discover one day that in a sense their whole life is an accepted bribe, a fabric of compromises.
Cyril Connolly, *Enemies of Promise*

One of the most arresting features of the *Ragtime* case is the display of the allied ranks of the English reviewers massed against the allied ranks of the American reviewers in flat disagreement. How efficacious is the English critical establishment when it comes to the maintenance of objective standards? To what extent does it control or temper literary discourse in the country? Does it achieve what we, or even what mercenary elements in the booktrade want it to do—discriminate the good from the bad, stimulate the sale and circulation of worthy books?

The answer to these questions would seem to be 'hardly at all'. The fact that the British fiction reviewing establishment should be something less than perfect is the more surprising when one considers its advantages. An extraordinary feature of the London literary world is its concentration of serious, review-carrying journals. A worthwhile novel can hope for notice in some, or all, of a score of mass and large-sale, London-based papers and journals, with a total readership of around 10m presumable bookbuyers and borrowers. If one adds the London-based broadcast media the figures swell to double the figure:

Dailies with a review section weekly: *The Times*, *The Guardian*, *The Evening Standard*, *The Daily Telegraph*, *The Financial Times*, *The Daily Mail*, *The Daily Express*.

Sundays with a review section: *The Sunday Telegraph*, *The Sunday Times*, *The Observer*, *The Sunday Express*.

Weekly journals: *The New Statesman*, *The Listener*, *The Spectator*, *The Times Literary Supplement*.

Monthly and Bi-monthlies: *Books and Bookmen*, *The New Review*, *Encounter*, *The London Magazine*.

Media book programmes: Read All About it, The Book Programme, Kaleidoscope, Critics' Forum, *et al*.

One may compare this with other metropolitan situations. The following complaint, for example, is made by K. McCormick, writing in *American PEN:*

In New York City there are three daily papers—*The New York Times, The New York News* and the *Post.* The *Times* is the only one which makes any pretence at reviewing books and carrying book advertising. It is, therefore, in a monopolistic situation. (PEN Summer 1972. *Times* here means, as it would not in Britain, Daily and Sunday issue.)

There is, of course *The New York Review of Books,* set up in a 114-days printers' strike of 1962–3, which left millions of dollars of book advertising looking for a home. Although it presents itself as the 'premiere literary-intellectual journal of the English-speaking world' (P. Nobile, *Intellectual Skywriting,* New York, 1974, p. 4), with twice the circulation of *The Times Literary Supplement* the *NYRB* does not, unlike its despised competitor, *The New York Times Book Review,* offer a comprehensive fiction coverage. As a fortnightly (and sometimes a monthly) publication it rarely carries more than a dozen titles under notice, reviews late and invariably goes for the heavier topics of the day (much the same could be said of the magazine, *Commentary*). Nor do the international weeklies, like *Time* and *Newsweek,* have the intimacy with a single cultural centre evident, say, in *The New Statesman* or *Spectator.* The same point would emerge from a comparison of the BBC's book programmes and the breakfast show interviews with novelists in which the American networks specialise.

The impact of the English fiction review is heightened in two ways, first by the fact that the London press is, by and large, the national press and the London broadcast media the national media (a situation which does not obtain in America). This gives a small, highly interknit coterie persuasive powers over most of the population. Secondly, fiction reviews in England are concerted to appear on, or as near publication day as possible. (In America, by contrast, the gun is often flagrantly jumped.)

The synchronisation which one observes in reviews of the British novel does not happen in any other branch of literary production, and it should give the newly published novel the *éclat* of the newly opened play, musical, concert or film. And yet, the cases are definitely not the same. The drama and film review has much more effect on ticket sales, and one imagines is more trusted than the fiction review. Bad reviews can kill plays, films and musicals; fiction reviews often seem irrelevant. As Lord Goodman puts it 'the serious Press, for practical purposes, enables the performing arts to survive' (STel 1.9.76). The serious novel could probably survive quite happily without the serious Press. In what follows a number of explanations are considered for the apparent impotence of the current fiction reviewing establishment; its failure to press its opinions to effect, or to control, in any significant way, literary activity.

II

The first, rather paradoxical feature to note, is that reviewing is said to be much improved over what it was in the inter-war years, and yet it is generally felt that reviews influence the sales of books much less than they used to. The point is made by Malcolm Oram, in an article, 'Do Reviews sell Books?':

> Many publishers maintain that times have changed in one respect . . . that although the general standard of reviewing is probably higher than it has ever been, the influence of the review on book sales has reached an all time low. (Aut Spring 74)

Or as Martin Amis, literary editor of *The New Statesman*, pungently puts it: 'the booktrade might well improve if the blurb-transcribing sots of yesteryear were reinstated' (NS 19.3.76). Suggestive conclusions may be drawn from the rule that the worse the reviewing, the better it serves the booktrade. Certainly in the 1920s, when Arnold Bennett could clear an edition with an approving adjective, and in the 1930s the general standard of critical journalism seems to have been dire. Nowhere is this more evident than in the way the best novelists, as a matter of course, ignored or despised it. The reviewers, as Virginia Woolf said, had nothing to tell the novelists. She contemptuously divided their criticism into two crude operations: 'Gutting' (i.e. summarising the contents of a book uncritically) and 'Stamping' (i.e. affixing a seal of (dis)approval on the book). There were also famous between-the-wars derelictions of critical duty—such as *The Times Literary Supplement*'s refusal to notice *Ulysses* (even at the behest of T. S. Eliot; J. Lidderdale and M. Nicholson, *Dear Miss Weaver*, London, 1970, p. 210). Orwell remembered the reviewing ethos of the time as a tobacco-laden old boys network:

Even more than at most times the big shots of literary journalism were busy pretending that the age before the last had not come to an end. Squire ruled the *London Mercury*, Gibbs and Walpole were the gods of the lending libraries, there was a cult of cheeriness and manliness, beer and cricket, briar pipes and monogamy, and it was at all times possible to earn a few guineas by writing an article denouncing 'highbrows'. (*The Collected Essays, Journalism and Letters of George Orwell*, ed. I. Angus and S. Orwell, London, 1968, i, 506)

Graham Greene makes the same points about the same formative period of his literary youth and the irrelevance of the ruling reviewers to serious writers:

The reviewing of novels at the beginning of the thirties was at a far lower critical level than it has ever been since. Gerald Gould, a bad poet, and Eric Strauss, a bad novelist, divided the Sunday forum between them. One was not elated by their praise nor cast down by their criticism. (*A Sort of Life*, London, 1971, p. 199)

'Middlebrow commercial consensus' seems to have been the flavour of the reviews of the time, and it was repudiated both by creative writers, and by critics like Q. D. Leavis.

The Leavises and the 'armed and conscious' resistance they inspired in *Scrutiny* undoubtedly had something to do with the breaking up of the middlebrow ethos of the thirties, with its characteristic blend of big-business advertising and star-reviewers. But the second world war had a lot more to do with it by cutting the main financial lines between the book producers and the newspapers. George Orwell found himself wondering in June 1944 'whether the book racket will start up in its old vigour after the war'. Then, Orwell recalled, the growth of advertisement, and particularly the 'screaming advertisement', led to a venal relationship between publisher and newspaper. Reviewers were habitually bribed and corrupted:

The literary pages of several well-known papers were practically owned by a handful of publishers, who had their quislings planted in all the important jobs.... Even reputable literary papers could not afford to disregard their advertisers altogether. It was quite usual to send a book to a reviewer with some such formula as 'Review this book if it seems any good. If not send it back. We don't think it's worth while to print simply damning reviews.' (*The Collected Essays, Journalism and Letters of George Orwell*, iii, 168–9)

As it happened the literary racket did not revive in its old vigour after the war. The revolution in advertising, effectively started by Gollancz in 1928 (Sp 19.10.56) which was instrumental in swelling the literary supplements of the newspapers was cut off in 1939; paper rationing, increased production costs and larger circulations meant higher prices for smaller space and less competitiveness between advertisers. A quieter style emerged, which survived the financial austerity that gave it birth. The London booktrade has never, in the postwar period, gone in for the intense advertising which flourishes in New York. In Britain there is nothing equivalent to *The New York Times Book Review*, half of whose forty-eight pages are customarily advertisements, and where it is common to see a book reviewed in company with a full page advert for itself which must have cost some twenty times as much as the reviewer is paid.

In postwar Britain the profession underwent a change in personnel recruitment. The expansion of universities created a new generation of academics with no prejudice against fiction reviewing. These were reviewers not obliged to support themselves by their literary journalism, and that much less manipulable. The 1944 education act, the growth in public libraries and a flourishing 'quality' press helped break down old stratifications and create a broader-based book reading population and a calmer, higher tone.

The purification of reviewing is a considerable achievement. For it was not simply a question of dictation by advertisers in the 1928–39 period. The very traditions of reviewing are corrupted, back to the earliest roots. It was a feature of the reviewing world of the nineteenth century, for example, that political and personal motives determined judgement. Reviews were lined up against each other and reviewers charged and hacked to command. Mr Escot, in Peacock's *Headlong Hall*, gives a jaundiced but essentially justified description of reviewing ethics at the time of the birth of the trade:

> I conceive that periodical criticism disseminates superficial knowledge, and its perpetual adjunct, vanity; that it checks in the youthful mind the habit of thinking for itself; that it delivers partial opinions, and therefore misleads the judgment; that it is never conducted with a view to the general interests of literature, but to serve the interested ends of individuals and the miserable purposes of party.

Lytton's fiction was attacked by *Fraser's* because he was a liberal and the magazine was Tory. Dickens was attacked by *The Saturday*

Review because he was considered radical and it was high Conservative. The reviewer in today's journal, however, is assumed to be above 'the miserable purposes of party'. *The New Statesman* will not, one may be sure, attack Kingsley Amis because he supports Black Papers on education—or if it does so, will present the criticism honestly in the education column. Nor, one would think, will it praise his fiction because his son is the literary editor. Puffs and vindictive hatchet jobs are, if not unknown, rare. (Boycotts less so, perhaps; but passive discrimination is hard to pin down). One may quote the testimony of a publisher, Anthony Blond, writing in 1971:

The reviewing establishment has been criticised as being cliquey, narrow minded, prejudiced in favour of Oxford and Cambridge and out of touch with popular taste; it may be all those things; it is also fair and totally incorruptible. (*The Publishing Game*, London, 1971, p. 63)

Finally, one may say, reviewing is less likely today to be lazy or intellectually dishonest by virtue of the booktrade's own monitoring of the reviews in the acerbic columns of *The Bookseller*'s Quentin Oates. This eponymous commentator is particularly savage on facile, pompous, stupid, trendy or pretentious reviews, and attention seems to be paid him by literary editors.

The general ethical improvement is less striking than the improvement in critical expertise. Partly this must also be due to the large-scale recruitment of university staff as part-time reviewers (a feature resented by the spokesman for the dwindling band of professionals, Auberon Waugh, who has selected the luckless Lorna Sage from the band of lecturer-critics for his asperity at 'humourless sub-academic rubbish'). The same recruitment has tended also to change the character of the editor from socialite bookman to trained academic, often of no less high-mindedness than the editors of learned journals. One may quote on this subject the assertions of two recent editors of leading journals, Karl Miller and Peter Ackroyd. Miller, whose career has taken him from *The Spectator*, to *The New Statesman*, to *The Listener* and, finally, the Lord Northcliffe Chair of English at University College London, describes how, in 1966, he refused the discipline of the general editor on the question of whether William Empson's reviews were 'incomprehensible'. Miller argues:

A properly conducted weekly need yield nothing in point of authority to any academic periodical, but it can only hope to keep its end up by cherishing difficult writers and by seeking out fresh talent in all its awkwardness—rather than sucking at another paper's oranges, or chasing after names and sages and scolds and pleasers and perennials and dependables. (*William Empson*, ed. R. Gill, London, 1974, p. 42)

It is evident that Miller is not entirely happy with the present state of reviewing, but the ideal he holds out as feasible is a loftier one than could ever have been conceived before the war. Ackroyd (Cambridge, Yale, literary editor of *The Spectator* in his twenties and author of the theoretical *Notes for a New Culture*) is more dogmatic, though no less idealistic. He goes so far as to suggest that the real vitality in English critical discourse is to be found not in academies, but in the columns of journalism. (Not, however, in the columns of *The New Statesman*, *Encounter*, *TLS*, *The New Review*—whose work Ackroyd sees as indicative of 'the death of the mind' Bk 6.11.76.)

Literary criticism . . . is now all but paralysed; this has nothing to do with book reviewers, who perform a useful public function and who, in any case, would never aspire to the dizzy ranks of 'the critics'. I am referring to those critics in the universities, who publish long articles in specialised journals, who write books about Henry James or Samuel Johnson, who, in short, are a cut above Grub Street and its environs. There has been nothing original from them in ten years. I have yet to read a contemporary academic critic who could write more intelligently, or read more carefully, than a good book reviewer. (Sp 6.3.76)

There are some false distinctions here—many university critics double as pin-money reviewers; Ackroyd himself is the kind of critic who writes books which are a cut above Grub Street. Grub Street itself is a cut above Grub Street nowadays. Nonetheless the protestation expresses, as does the quality of the average review in the top band of papers and journals, that present English reviewing is disinterested and much improved over its former self.

Why then, does it not operate as successfully as one would expect an improved critical establishment to do? A stern reply would be given by F. R. Leavis. The improvement is cosmetic only. Whereas complicity in the 1930s existed on the level of blatant hobnobbing (it was not a good idea, Frank Swinnerton wrote in 1932, for authors and reviewers to dine together *quite* so frequently; *Authors and the Booktrade*, pp. 110–11) in the 1970s it was more the complicity of an inert and timid coterie reluctant to take up the necessary adversary positions:

the occasional disinterested and real review, though it no doubt earns sporadic gratitude, doesn't at all tell against the total effect of concerted and conscienceless misguidance. In the BBC world and the weeklies (under which head fall the Sunday magazine-sections and the *Times Literary Supplement*) coterie reigns—in such conscious security that it feels no shame, or at any rate shows no sign of it. The case may be gross, but that, where the gross falsities are familiar and congenially directed, and, so, welcome to the coterie, is a recommendation. What offers itself as creative work would challenge recognition in vain if it were uncongenial to expectation and really, or at all profoundly, challenging—that is, disturbing to habitual complacencies and settled attitudes. (F. R. Leavis, *Nor Shall my Sword*, London, 1972, p. 221)

To some extent Leavis undervalues the improvements he himself has wrought by making this point for forty years. One may cite the testimony of Frederic Raphael, ruefully recounting his efforts to cash in on the Cambridge old-boy network in the 1960s:

After I had published half a dozen novels, not all of them derisively reviewed, I summoned my courage and dared to beard the brightest and best of literary editors in his glum office. He looked at me with the weary tact of those who have come a long way down the mountain to avoid any appearance of condescension. 'What makes you think,' he asked me, 'that you have any qualifications for reviewing fiction?' Like Aeneas, I stammered, prepared to say many things, said nothing and fled. As critics, the stern sons and daughters of the voice of Leavis have been as honourable as they have been unencouraging. (List 5.2.76)

Nonetheless some of the force of Leavis's indictment sticks. There is, it would seem, something essentially trivial and lightweight about the English review. It is, according to some, a national trait. Such is the view of Steven Marcus, commenting on his fellow contributors to *The New York Review of Books*, where the fiction reviews are commonly given to Englishmen: 'They write after dinner reviews. It's good cocktail party talk—witty, unserious, fashionable and stylish—but if you look close, there's very little to them' (Nobile, *Intellectual Skywriting*, p. 43). It is some defence, though not entirely convincing, that party talk is a tradition to some extent hallowed in English reviewing. Evelyn Waugh, for example, is found in the mid-1950s, resisting the 'trade unionist' tendencies of the new postwar reviewers, on the grounds that it was unEnglish to take reviewing seriously:

> In a civilised society everyone is a critic.... Even in the happiest days of the past it was only a small part of the population who fostered the arts and graces. That world still exists and is the proper milieu of the writer. In that world the most acute and influential criticism is uttered in private conversation by people with no identifiable qualifications. (Sp 24.2.56)

In other words the cocktail party, not the interminably expert columns of *The New York Review of Books*, is the proper *locus* of criticism. Waugh's views were not altogether fashionable when he uttered them, and they are probably unutterable today—at least in *The Spectator*. But the practice of many fiction reviewers retains much of the spirit of ultra-civilised amateurism.

III

A lingering attachment to coterie-dilettantism may account for some of the forceless nature of English fiction reviewing. But the main contributory factors are technical, and to do with the mechanics of current reviewing.

First, there is the fact new novels are reviewed so exclusively as *new* novels. There is usually no sense of context, no placing in order. The most considered and most informative reviews of 1975–6 were those on Powell and Raven's novel sequences, because their terminal novels could not, in critical conscience, be extracted from the series to which they belonged. Generally, however, the novel is examined in a disconnected, uprooted way which conduces to randomness and captiousness in the reviewer.

This combines with other technical features making for casualness and lack of real engagement. Editors and reviewers are, it would seem, free to make the selections of what they review. No-one instructs them. Yet, with up to two thousand new novels produced annually, the selection has perforce to be arbitrary and severe. According to the literary editor of *The Times*, from fifteen to twenty novels a week are received in the peak season; ten are sent to the reviewer; four or five are finally reviewed. The most important decisions as to the value of any novel occur invisibly, behind the scenes.

One can make similar deductions from accounts by another literary editor, and of a fiction reviewer, describing in more detail the process by which they arrive at their final short lists:

[Ian Hamilton. *Times Literary Supplement*] The books go on the main shelves in the main office, and the books that fall in my area come to me. That is, all the books that are literary books; poetry and fiction and so on. Each week, to take fiction as an example, one has say, twenty-five novels come in, and on a particular day, one browses through these. Clearly with novels, you can with some confidence eliminate perhaps half a dozen. (P. Firchow, *The Writer's Place*, Minnesota, 1974, p. 154)

[Jill Neville. *Sunday Times*] Often I am given a pile of between seven and ten books to sift through. At the very most I can choose four for the following fortnight. Riddled with fear that I might pass over something good, I first sniff them as if they were fish bought on a Monday . . . next I read the first and last pages of the novels still in the running, and if stimulated by these snippets I embark on the often uphill work of reading the book. This is where one earns one's money. Ploughing through page after page of an often worthy novel which, under normal circumstances, one would avoid, simply because it isn't the kind of thing one is naturally attracted to. (NF Jan. 76)

It is tempting to conclude that this pinsticking approach contributes to the alarming instability of the final judgements on fiction. One recalls the harsh comment of Angus Wilson, speaking as Booker Prize chairman, ill served, as he thought, by 'newspaper critics of novels'. Reading Wilson's strictures about the unsteadiness of reviewers' judgement, bear in mind Neville's comments on sniffing books like fish, or Ian Hamilton's casually tossing them on one side or the other:

I know how hard their job is for I have done it many times. But in general, as we saw the reviews appear of the books we were reading, we were constantly rubbing our eyes. Could this new weekly masterpiece really be the book that all four judges had agreed needed no discussion? There seemed behind this professional critical opinion some shadow world, some hierarchy that we knew nothing of. Of course it's natural and right to encourage in weekly reviews, and we who were judging had a fairer chance to say nothing. Novelists must be grateful to the ill-paid and overworked newspaper critics that their books sell at all. But a diet of overpraise interspersed with periodic vitriol is unlikely to produce a steady readership. (Bk 22.11.75)

Or a steady anything, one might add.

The multitudinousness of fiction leads to another much deplored feature of its reviewing, the group review in which four or five or more novels are lumped together in an unconvincing order of merit. The group review assumes in different works of fiction a generic homogeneity which, it may be objected, they cannot possess. The point is well made by Quentin Oates:

> No literary editor would dream of sending an assorted bunch of non fiction to one reviewer and publish the resultant round up with a general heading like 'Recent Non-Fiction'. Who would expect any critic to produce a readable piece somehow linking a life of Napoleon, a sex manual, a book on pig farming and a moving account of the girlhood of a cotton weaver. Yet that is what is happening with fiction reviews. (Bk 24.11.75)

Only in comparatively rare circumstances is a novel honoured with a solo spot. This means that there are more fiction reviews than any other kind—but the reviews are shorter. In D. H. and C. M. Nobles' *A Survey of Book Reviews: October–December 1973* (London, 1974), fiction came top in titles, with biography second and childrens' books third. But in terms of space, biography had 30 per cent and fiction only 17 per cent. And as a general observation it is evident that fiction very rarely leads the review pages. Traditionally it goes to the bottom or the end; a placing which clearly afflicts some reviewers who affect a desperate vivacity to compensate for their relegation. (This is particularly the case in *The New Statesman*, where the fiction reviewers come in like tail-end batsmen, determined to hit everything for six.)

The demotion of the fiction review, and its deprivation of full space has been laid to the fact that literary editors are out of touch with what the public wants. The fact that 75 per cent of loans from public libraries are of fiction suggest that a corresponding attention should be given to the novel in the review pages. 'There may be times', writes Malcolm Oram, 'when you feel forced to suspect that if serious literary editors were transferred to the sports page, they would happily choose to lead with the East African Croquet Championships' (Auth Spring 75). Literary editors ('far too literary editors', as they have been called) rise to the bait. In February 1976 David Holloway, Literary editor of *The Daily Telegraph*, declared as his principle:

What one is concerned about is printing a good quality of review. One cannot consider the saleability of a book when one is considering its reviewability. If a book is desperately specialist, it won't be done, but if even one in a thousand of our readers is going to enjoy that book we should review it. (Bk 28.2.76)

There can be few other sections of the *Telegraph* that aim to cater for a thousandth part of the readership.

The solo versus group review question is frequently raised in the trade papers, and the literary editors defend themselves. This is Derwent May, literary editor of *The Listener*:

I do think there is a case, with some novels, for long reviews—and of course, for proper and substantial critical essays on novelists as their oeuvre builds up. But the evidence is that readers don't usually want long novel reviews in newspapers.... On *The Listener*, in this last year, I decided to get away from the automatic reviewing of novels in the arbitrary groups produced by date of publication, and to send them out for review in batches more related by theme. However, I have decided to go back to the regular reviewing of the week's novels. This is partly because there is a news element in reviews—'What's out this week?'—that I think is important, though not all-important; and partly because I feel that the double scrutiny of the week's novels by both the literary editor, and the reviewer who makes the final choice, is a better way of ensuring that interesting novels don't get missed. (NF Jan. 76)

Even if one accepts the argument, one is left with a number of quite specific misgivings about the group review of the 'week's novels'. One is that it declasses the group reviewer and his normal material, since *really* important novels are habitually creamed off for other and better-known reviewers than himself. Every so often a novel is big enough to be treated like any other book, and one has a 'name' reviewing a 'name' (Raymond Williams on Solzhenitsyn, Kermode on Pynchon, etc.). This has the effect of downgrading the regular group reviewer (sometimes found at the foot of the same page) to hack status.

The group review encourages a manifest idleness and arrogance in reviewers; knowing he has only a few sentences the reviewer flagrantly neglects to do more than glance at the work in hand. The implication is that by simply mentioning the novel the reviewer has done something for which the author should be sufficiently grateful (he could so easily be one of the fifteen that weren't mentioned).

Linked with this is the reliance on blurb—rarely evident to the reader of the review since he is unlikely to buy a new copy of the book with the dust jacket on it. Compare the following review by Philip Howard of Frederic Raphael's *California Time* in *The Times*, 30 October 1975, with the blurb (written, incidentally, by Raphael himself). Here, as one can see, the author is leading the critic by the nose. The review here follows the blurb:

> Victor England, the great film director, returns to Hollywood to finalize arrangements for his next production. Everything seems propitious: he has a firm contract with a studio that owes him a substantial debt of gratitude and whose top executives are good friends of his. Why, then, is he left to languish in the grand hotel owned by Verdugo, which in Spanish means executioner? What is the relationship between Victor, who can write equally well with left hand or right, and Dr Jekyll and Mr Hyde, about whom he once made a film, a film which is showing on TV as he enters his suite? Who is the beautiful girl whom he sees in the lobby? ... Is Victor England a victim or a killer? (Blurb, *California Time*)
>
> ... Victor England (are we intended to see a symbol in the names?), the great film director, comes back to Hollywood to complete the arrangements for his next triumphant production. He has a cast-iron contract, and everything seems to be coming up roses. But then hints of menace no bigger than a man's hand-grenade insinuate themselves into the soundtrack and the periphery of panning shots. Why is Victor kept cooling his heels in a grand hotel, owned by one Verdugo (a name that, NB, means executioner in Spanish)? What are these repeated brief references to his film of *Dr Jekyll and Mr Hyde*, which sounds as if it excelled the great 1932 version by Rouben Mamoulian? Is Victor victor or victim? (T 30.10.75)

Anyone doing this kind of thing in an examination on literature would be disqualified for plagiarism. In reviewing it is condoned by the exigencies of the group review, which forces the reviewer to take short cuts. The pressure on a conscientious reviewer must indeed be fearful at times. In *The Guardian*, 6 November 1975, for example, Robert Nye was given the task of reviewing Martin Amis's *Dead Babies*, Bradbury's *History Man* and Moore's *The Great Victorian Collection*, in little over a thousand words. In other circumstances a leading novelist addressing himself to the work of other leading novelists would be a critical document of some importance. As it is, space forbade anything other than critical speedwriting.

The alternative to the group review is the not entirely satisfactory practice of the *TLS* and *The Evening Standard*. These journals give solo reviews of novels, but at the cost of an extremely arbitrary selection; though John Gross, editor of *TLS*, argues that 'they select themselves to a considerable degree' (PW 9.8.76), many neglected novelists would disagree.

In further defence of the group system it should be said that the fiction page of the *TLS* is the ugliest in the journal, made up as it is with a lot of little boxes, none of which intercommunicate. The desire to cover as many novels as possible (unlike the *Standard*, which takes only one a week, normally) again cuts down the space given *TLS* novel reviewers drastically.

Finally, in the consideration of technical matters, one may ask why is it that only new hardbacks are reviewed? Why do papers and journals not regularly review paperbacks? On the face of things this would seem to be a necessary service. More paperbacks are bought and read than any other form of novel and they arrive with bewildering rapidity and disorder. The reader-purchaser of the paperback is more at sea than the equivalent hardback customer. There is, for example, no assurance that the contents of a paperback are as new as its cover. Often it is in the interest of the paperback publisher to blur over any such embarrassing bibliographical facts and encourage thoughtless impulse buying. A glossy paperback may well enclose an old exhausted body resuscitated because the author has some current publicity. (Jack Higgins books began to rise from the grave in droves with the success of *The Eagle has Landed*.) It may be a confected book-of-the-film 'novelisation,' or a classic just out of copyright. More than most the paperback buyer needs direction. At best he will get a shallow consumer guide: 'Pick of the Paperbacks' (*Standard*) or 'Paperbacks of the Month' (*Times*) or 'Paperback Pickings' (*Guardian*), or, with a great deal of intellectual plumage display, 'Read All About it'.

One might complete the argument by saying that the fiction reader has, least of all, need for hardback reviews. Buying hardcover novels, Mervyn Jones observes, 'is an eccentric and antiquated custom, like snuff taking' (NS 3.12.76). His image seems borne out by the evidence of Ian Norrie, proprietor of High Hill Bookshop, Hampstead—a quality fiction reading territory if there ever was one. Norrie calculates that between 1957 and 1975 there was in his shop a progressive decline from hardback fiction comprising 10 per cent of total sales at the beginning of the period of 2.6 per cent in 1975. Meanwhile paperback sales (all varieties) had risen from 20 per cent to 51 per cent (Bk 15.5.76).

By the time most people buy a novel in its cheap reprinted form the review has been forgotten. Of all the disconnections which afflict fiction reviews, this seems one of the most serious. Literary editors' replies on this score are not altogether convincing. Ion Trewin, of *The Times*, maintains: 'we are a newspaper, our job is to write about new things, and new books should have first call on our space'. Holloway of *The Daily Telegraph* echoes him: 'newness is what counts' (Bk 28.2.76).

A more cynical explanation for the emphasis on hardbacks would be found in the fact that paperbacks are devised to sell without newspaper advertisement. Hence only hardback books are advertised in newspapers, and therefore reviewed—for the benefit mainly of libraries, a tiny band of bookbuyers and the advertising manager. An even more cynical explanation would be that the book represents a substantial part of the payment which the paper or journal gives its reviewer. If he gets from £25 to £60 for a review of four to five books (with a few others thrown in, simply as possibles) then the resale of the hardback volumes amounts to as much as half of the reviewer's remuneration.

IV

The most influential reviewer of novels in Britain today is Auberon Waugh. After a number of false starts in journalism, Waugh made his name as a reviewer in *The Spectator* and now does a one-novel-a-week star turn for *The Evening Standard*. His idiosyncrasies are famous; in an ethos dominated by dilute avant gardism, his taste in fiction is traditional and aggressively English. He is anti-experiment, and anti-academic—whether the academics be novelists or fellow reviewers. Irreverence is his trade mark. What, he asks in a review of *Humboldt's Gift* (the novel, incidentally, that Philip Toynbee hailed as the American *Brothers Karamazov*), do American novelists intend when they sit down 'to write 487 pages of sententious drivel?'

they are not aiming to entertain or divert us poor novel readers, but to improve us, to bludgeon us into a deferential attitude. Most particularly the book is aimed at students of American literature who are going to be forced to read it and take it seriously, whether they like it or not. Well, I am a free citizen of a free country, and this book is going into my wastepaper basket. (ES 7.10.75)

What, one may echo, is Waugh doing? In his valedictory letter in *The Spectator*, in April 1973, Waugh laid down his theory of 'reviewcraft':

The first aim of a reviewer, as with anybody who writes, is to be read ... you address yourself to the author, praising him for what is good in his novel, suggesting where there is room for improvement [Waugh is inclined to go somewhat further than this, giving schoolmasterly marks or medals for achievement] The great secret is not to ask yourself whether you approve of a book or think it good but to allow yourself to react to it, even if only with exasperation. The key quality in reviewing is not judiciousness or erudition or good taste, least of all is it moderation. It is liveliness of response. (Sp 28.4.73)

It is the failing of Waugh that in his unbridled 'liveliness' he often reduces reviewing to what Oates calls a 'blood sport' (Bk 8.5.76). His great achievement, however, is that he has a clear sense of what his role should be. Other fiction reviewers appear deeply uncertain on this question. Are they merely noticing books— bringing them to the attention of the paper's readers? Are they applying some critical-judicial-literary-historical-moral judgement? Are they responding, either as a superior or merely a representative critical sensibility? Are they writing an essay, of entertainment value in itself?

Because of these role-uncertainties the fiction reviewer is always prone to fall into a kind of shiftiness. Ian Robinson describes it well (he is thinking principally of *TLS* fiction reviews):

Take the case of reviews of novels. The commonest style is one of ironic defensiveness, a style which might tell us almost anything except whether the reviewer will commit himself to a novel or not, whether it matters or not. Whatever the novel turns out to be like, the reviewer's nakedness will be unrevealed. (HW May 72)

Waugh's code may be a brutal one, but it enables him to perform with confidence and directness in an area of writing marked by chronic uncertainty.

Commentators on reviewing tend to consider Waugh *sui generis*: is he the next Arnold Bennett? is he his father's son? But Waugh's primary significance is as the kind of reviewing Trade Unionist his father loathed; he has created for himself reviewing conditions of work enjoyed by no other (with the possible exception of C. P. Snow, who does a much more mixed bag of books). Waugh has a weekly column, in effect, which is his alone. This freehold enables him to sustain a public personality which is consistent and his own. Other fiction reviewers tend to serve either as distinguished visitors, or as part of a team appearing in print on a rotating basis. Members of these teams are overlaid by house style, in much the same way as leader writers. The 1975–6 *Guardian* team, for example (C. J. Driver, C. Wordsworth, N. Shrapnel), is more compassionate and easily 'moved' than the reviewers of the politically co-ideological *New Statesman* (V. Cunningham, J. Barnes, S. Clapp, J. Treglown). *The New Statesman* team presents a more brittle, academic and callous collective personality. At the bottom end of the field *The Sunday Express* will begin a review of *How to Save Your Own Life* in a style which is straight John Gordon: 'Don't be fooled by American novelist Erica Jong's wide-eyed innocent expression. She also has a mucky mind' (1.5.77).

Waugh is not constricted by house style and he glories in his freedom. He is captious about the single novels that he selects, occasionally dipping into sub-literary depths to review Jackie Collins or Jilly Cooper. He disobeys the tacit good manners of the reviewing profession, which enforces politeness (albeit frosty politeness). Waugh is mischievously familiar and calculatedly impertinent. Take the opening of his review of William Cooper's latest novel:

> William Cooper, at 66, is approaching the time when we must start considering him a Senior British Novelist. Before it arrives, I hope he will not take it amiss if I give him a word of advice which is also applicable to other Senior British Novelists, and that is not to write about passionate love affairs between men of over 60 and girls who are 40 years younger than them. Worst of all is to write about passionate love affairs between Senior British Novelists in their sixties and delicious young things discovering the first delights of sex. (ES 1.6.76)

Waugh has no compunction where literary sacred cows are concerned, indulging as he regularly does in attacks on what he, as the reviewer's plain man, conceives as pseud. (See, for example, the review of Bellow quoted above, or that on David Plante ES 6.4.76.) On the other hand he is capable of stout partisanship in the cause of the novels he admires. This was particularly evident in his support for Bradbury's *The History Man* (ES 11.11.75) whose mixed reception elsewhere Waugh saw as illustrative of the pervasive corruption of English reviewing.

Waugh's freehold on half a *Standard* page, every Tuesday, gives him time and length to deal with a novel fully. He reads carefully, not always a reviewing virtue (he is, for example, the only reviewer who regularly picks on sloppy editing). If there is a lesson to be drawn from him it is not that other reviewers should ape his cavalier pococurantism (as occurred disastrously in *The Spectator* when he left, and Tony Palmer took his place). A more useful lesson to be learned from Waugh is that it is possible for reviewers to free themselves from the machinery which at present largely controls and limits their activity. Whether they would all use their freedom in the same reckless way is another question.

The machinery, however, is by no means guaranteed to favour reviewing, even to the degree it does now. At some point newspaper and magazine criticism of fiction must face a major contradiction within itself. Publishers co-operate with it not because they want an expert, disinterested opinion on their books but because they feel that reviews help sales. Newspaper proprietors tolerate reviewing not because they want to educate public taste but because they think it attracts readers in the top advertising brackets. The somewhat misnamed 'early reviewing' controversy of summer 1977 (See Bk April–May 1977) suggested a growing inclination among publishers no longer to enforce the embargoes which prevent an early reviewer stealing the others' thunder. If a review is no longer news, because prior features in the press and media have upstaged it, fiction reviewing would have a hard time holding onto its newspaper space. And, on the whole, a hardheaded publisher might well feel that a colour magazine profile or an interview on *Tonight* is worth more than a few hundred words in a quality newspaper. At the same time reviewing may not have that much support in the increasingly cost-conscious world of journalism. As Peter Lewis (literary editor of *The Daily Mail*) put it in a letter of some indignation against 'early reviewing': 'If publishers persist in being greedy, by trying to back every publicity medium in the field, while favouring radio and television at the expense of the written word, Fleet Street may very soon lose patience and refuse to play second fiddle for their convenience' (Bk 16.4.77). Crushed between publishing opportunism and newspaper indifference, reviewing may have to retreat to the weeklies, monthlies and specialist journals.

* * *

The end of this section on 'Crisis and Change' is a good place to summarise some main implications; moreso as these implications throw a shadow on the next section, 'State Remedies'. There was unquestionably a crisis of some severity in the 1970s. Its general effect was to shake out distinctly British patterns and ways of doing things. Certain shelters under which the booktrade operated, like the library sale, the Net Book Agreement or the Traditional Market Agreement, have been rendered less safe (or, in one case, have disappeared). It is likely that the effect will be gradually to change the distinct British practice of a vast number of small-sale titles, nobly catering to a cultural mosaic of minority readerships. Whether this will take the form of a thinning of titles or a qualitative homogenisation (more coffee table books, more genre fiction, more show business biographies, etc.), is debatable. Recent figures would seem to suggest the second; but whichever, the general effect will be the same.

It is possible that the Net Book Agreement will not last, if the general bookshop system which is its *raison d'être* deteriorates beyond a certain point, or if it changes drastically from a stock-holding to a quick-turnover, low-stock business operation. In the judgement that 'Books are Different' in 1962 the law of the land determined that retail price maintenance in books was necessary to maintain the then current excellences of the British bookselling trade, as they were presented in court: large stock in hand, expert assistance, swift delivery. Since 1962 these features have been undermined by (1) the financial instability of smaller bookshops, (2) growing paperback trade, much of which is independent of traditional bookshops, (3) increases in delivery time on small orders, and surcharges, (4) a 'maximise turnover, minimise stock' imperative in a period of high inflation, (5) scepticism about the rule that 'stock sells books', and increasing faith that publicity sells books, and (6) antagonism between bookseller and publisher (see, for example, the President of the

Booksellers' Association's tart comments on publishers in his address to the Booksellers' annual conference in 1976).

A more general effect which can be expected is that the British literary-publishing-bookselling complex will be jolted at a somewhat faster pace along a path it was already committed to following. There will be an assimilation of British to other systems, where they are more efficient. It is likely, for example, that American editorial practices and book 'packagers' will figure more. New channels of supply will be set up, based on overseas practice. (See, for example, the great interest among the British trade in the German LITOS ordering system, and that country's wholesaling methods.) Where the British trade is actually weak, it may well be taken over. This could be the case, for example, in some areas of the mass-market paperback business, where America has led the way and Britain trailed. Another example was evident in October 1976, with the news that the German conglomerate giant, Bertelsmann (turnover £500m in 1975; ST 17.10.76), was about to penetrate the English market (ST 17.10.76). The weak point it chose for its assault was the book club market. This has always been an undernourished limb of the British booktrade, largely because the Publishers' Association tended to see the mail-order bookclub as a violation of the Net Book Agreement, and an unfair rival to the bookshop. Hence the British book clubs have been stunted as they have not in America (which already owns a chunk of British book club business) or in Germany, the land of their origin (where, incidentally, they collaborate with bookshops—unheard of in Britain).

The sections immediately following consider measures like Public Lending Right and the Arts Council grants programme. One weakness of these measures is that in most cases they are essentially preservative. However just and culturally benevolent, they aim to shore things up. PLR, for example, presumes that public libraries will continue to acquire new books in the same way as they have done in the past. Such presumptions are questionable, and render the success of these schemes questionable, even if they had sufficient money behind them—which they do not. A theme developed in the third part of the study, 'Trends Mainly American', is that the basis of the British book trade is now essentially unfixed, and shifting. It is these changes that will be significant in the future of fiction.

State Remedies

6 Public Lending Right: A Salary for Authors

If that's all you earn, why do it?
Schoolchild to novelist Paul Bailey, 1976

Every time I hear a library's burnt down, I'm very happy.
Novelist, Paul Theroux, 1975

Anyone casually following the issue in the newspapers might be forgiven for thinking that Public Lending Right is the single most important factor in the continuing creative health of English writing, and its postponement for over a quarter of a century a major cultural scandal, if not disaster. In the mid 1970s PLR was sufficiently a matter of national interest to warrant third leaders in *The Times* and *Guardian*, ill-attended but hot-tempered debates in parliament and the country's first ever 'Writers' Demo'. A major achievement was that a public notoriously indifferent to writers' welfare came to recognise what the letters PLR stood for. Whether they were reliably informed on the actual benefits of the proposed reform is something else. Support for PLR has been vociferous and *ad misericordiam*; resistance to it has often been malicious and childish. If the public's indifference was stirred, it was largely by rhetoric, entertaining enough in its violence, but seldom enlightening. In the first section of this chapter the theoretical argument for a salary for authors is examined; in the second some of the history of the PLR movement is reviewed; finally some estimate of the scheme's likely benefit in our present situation is attempted.

Authorship has always been a badly paid profession. Indeed rewards are customarily so low for the many, and so high for the very few, as to make it seem no profession at all, but a lottery. Well publicised surveys over the 1960s and 1970s confirm that a majority of authors earn under £500 p.a. from their books, and that income has actually fallen somewhat over fifteen years. Other hardships have aggravated the writer's condition. Sources of private income have tended to dry up. Authors' professional expenses have rocketed. The supply of freelance journalism has shrunk with the closure of many papers and magazines (and with any threatened closed shop for journalism a sizeable portion of it may be denied altogether). Edna O'Brien probably speaks for other novelists, even some who like herself are household names, when she says: 'the time is rapidly approaching when I won't be able to afford to be a writer' (NR Nov. 75).

There are, of course, a very few novels and novelists who make a spectacularly huge amount of money. But one fears that in some ways success may be as dangerous to talent as failure. There is, for example, something absurd in the 'fiscal savagery' of the tax laws which offer the suddenly rich writer the prospect of residing in Ireland (the nearest haven) or of paying 90 per cent of his earnings to the Inland Revenue; and that in spite of the fact that a book may have taken years to write and may be the last in a long line of previous failures—or worse still, a once and for all success. To be fair, supertax is probably the least of today's enemies of promise. But it does witness to the pervasive irrationality and inefficiency of authors' remuneration. We have a system which certainly drives a few successful writers out of the country but which, more seriously, drives a lot of unsuccessful (but not for that reason unworthy) writers out of business altogether. And authorship, though it has all the disagreeable features of the lottery, lacks even the unique good point of that venture. Lotteries are drawn on prescribed dates and one knows if one is a winner or a loser. Authors do not know. Late life, or even posthumous earnings may start to roll in up to fifty years after their owner's death, mocking previous poverty. Sylvia Plath for example, seems to have lived her last years in straitened circumstances and died in the same season as dismissive reviews of her first novel. Yet twelve years after her suicide we read:

> The poet and novelist, who committed suicide in 1963, gained posthumous success with her only novel, *The Bell Jar* (175,000 copies sold in hardcover, now available in a 1.5m Bantam printing), and with a collection of poems entitled *Ariel*. The latter has had an astonishing sale of 160,000 copies in the Harper paperback edition. (SR 31.5.75)

'Why should I write for posterity;' asks the author, 'what has posterity ever done for me?' Nowhere would this seem to be more true than in financial matters.

It is a feature of the novel, that unlike poetry and drama, it requires a huge and long investment in time and effort. David Storey, on the simultaneous performance and publication of *Mother's Day* and *Saville*, put it thus: 'three days for a play, ten years for a novel' (Obs 10.10.76). Novel writing, for that reason, is best undertaken as a career. English has no term equivalent to the German *Gesamtwerk* or the French *oeuvre*, but the 'total lifetime's production' of a novelist is what he comes to be judged by. Novelists are most accurately measured in large, years-long spans and periods. To support the author, what is ideally required is a steady and adequate income. And in the present conditions, while it is quite likely that a novelist's income will be steady, it will, on average, be a steady £300 a year.

A few fairy godmother stories are told, which bear out the desirability of life-long supportive income. Richard Hughes, for example, was famously slow in bringing out his novels—four in 50 years, and that many only because the novelist was 'urged' to publish his work in progress prematurely. Two sentences were apparently a good day's work (DT 30.4.76). His career was, as he put it, a race with the undertaker (ES 15.10.76). Hughes was allowed to develop at this vegetative pace by having had a lucky break early in his career:

> Not long after I left Oxford, a London publisher offered me a small fixed income provided he could have my first novel whenever it appeared. Then I fell ill and wasn't able to work for some time: so actually that first novel was *High Wind in Jamaica*, which he didn't get until seven or eight years later. But he was quite calm and happy about it, and I'm glad to think it paid him in the end.
> Q. That subsidy was enough to keep you?
> Hughes. Along with what was I was already making through book reviewing and amateur play royalties and so on. (P. Firchow, *The Writer's Place*, Minnesota, 1974, p. 206)

High Wind was a bestseller, as Hughes modestly intimates, and solved his subsequent money problems. It sold 25,000 in the first year and was taken (amid controversy) as one of the first (and more successful) titles of the Book Society (i.e. club). At one point it was making Hughes £75 a day, at a time when such a rate was extremely rare (ES 15.10.76). At the time of his death in 1976 it was still selling 100,000 a year in various forms (ES 29.4.76). *High Wind* will go on repaying Chatto and Windus's wise investment until 2026. Again, however, Hughes was beholden to favours;

Desmond MacCarthy printed the whole of the novel in his magazine. As Hughes later said:

> to have a well-known literary magazine suddenly drop all its usual features to produce just a single novel like that—well, it hit the public in the eye. I think that's one of the main reasons why the book was a best seller from the word go in England. (Firchow, *The Writer's Place*, p. 201)

Without such assistance few full time writers could have managed, as did Hughes, the following production schedule and survive: b. 1900, 1929 *A High Wind in Jamaica*, 1938 *In Hazard*, 1961 *The Fox in the Attic*, 1973 *The Wooden Shepherdess*, d. 1976. When he died Hughes left £17,149. The press was surprised at the smallness of the sum ('Only £17,149' was *The Evening Standard* headline, ES 15.10.76) and his agent was quoted as saying; 'it is very hard for a writer who doesn't produce a book a year to make a good living' (ES 15.10.76). Nonetheless it is extraordinary that Hughes managed as he did.

Other prewar cases can be found. That of Joyce and Miss Weaver, is, perhaps, the most famous. Between 1913 and 1923, this spinster spent thousands of pounds of her own money subsidising Joyce during his most creative and slowest working period. (See, e.g. J. Lidderdale and M. Nicholson, *Dear Miss Weaver*, London, 1970, pp. 223–6). But parasitism is not, when one looks at the probabilities, a feasible or commendable course for every novelist. Nor is it attractive to those who believe with PEN in 'The Writer as Independent Spirit'. Luckier was Joyce's contemporary, Virginia Woolf, who had her 'own' money to invest in her career. (She also had a husband and a half brother who were publishers, advantages denied Joyce and most authors). In *Downhill all the Way*, Leonard Woolf gives a graphic illustration of how slow earnings can be, even for a novelist who has achieved works of such magnitude as *The Voyage Out*, *Night and Day*, and *Jacob's Room*. Between 1920 and 1924 Virginia's annual earnings from her fiction were, as Woolf tells us; £106 5s 10d, £10 10s 8d, £33 13s 0d £40 0s 5d, £70 0s 0d (*Downhill all the Way*, London, 1967, p. 63). Virginia Woolf lived in the era when private incomes were commonly left for daughters, a source which, as Writers' Action Group's founder Brigid Brophy points out, has progressively dried up in the middle of the twentieth century.

Another example of the necessity of salary, stipend or regular handouts is evident in the early career of Graham Greene; though here the benefit is more oblique. After his first two novels had failed to get acceptance, Greene had his third try, *The Man Within*, accepted to his surprise by Heinemann. Historical romances were fashionable at the time, and the novel sold over 8,000. As Greene points out, this success was very fluky; especially when one considers that the first printing for his tenth (and vastly superior) novel, *The Power and the Glory*, was only 3,500. On the strength of *The Man Within*'s coup, Greene managed to 'blackmail' Charles Evans of Heinemann into signing a £600-a-year contract for three years. In the first instance this enabled Greene to give up his job at *The Times*. Without some such windfall he would have been unlikely to do so for 'no one on *The Times* was ever known to be sacked or to resign' (G. Greene, *A Sort of Life*, London, 1971, p. 171). And what the subsidised three years allowed Greene to do, perversely, was not to forward his career but to work out of his system a Conradian circuitousness which was taking him down an artistic dead end. His next two novels (*The Name of Action*, *Rumour at Nightfall*) were failures; expensive failures for Heinemann, instructive failures for Greene. They sold between a thousand and two thousand only. Greene concluded: 'there was nothing for me to do but dismantle all that elaborate scaffolding built from an older writer's [i.e. Conrad's] blueprint, write it off as apprentice work, and start again at the beginning' (*A Sort of Life*, p. 208). His fourth work was the entertainment, *Stamboul Train*, which saved his reputation with the firm by being taken as a Book Society choice; it also firmly marked the direction his future fiction was to take.

With hindsight one can see that the £600 p.a. allowed Greene to explore a cul-de-sac and turn around, in the minimum time. The whole process rested on a remote chance, however; a fluke sale for an immature work allowed him to lever a salary contract from the publisher. Without the salary there is a strong likelihood that Greene would eventually have found his destiny as the letters editor of *The Times*, unable in his spare time to concentrate on sweating out his stylistic infection.

The salary contract seems to have been fairly common before the war. Aldous Huxley had one with Chatto and Windus for his first novels, rather more easily got than Greene's since he was better connected. After the war it seems to have been uncommon; money was dearer and novels more plentiful. Indeed the salary contract has recently been thought to be positively eccentric. When he was given a three-year contract with Secker and Warburg in 1965 (£800 p.a. for two novels) B. S. Johnson was quoted as thinking that it was 'appropriate that an experimental writer should have an experimental contract' (M. Bradbury, *The Social Context of Modern English Literature*, Oxford, 1973, p. 166). Secker and Warburg has since made a six-year contract with Tom Sharpe in 1975, a more popular writer than Johnson ever was. Again the fact was presented by the firm as something unusual in the present age.

The most telling recent example of stipendiary patronage is that of Anthony Blond and Simon Raven. Raven had established himself in the early 1960s as a gifted novelist, but feckless in the best tradition of Bohemian authorship: expelled from Charterhouse, disappointing career at Cambridge, forced to resign his commission for gambling debts. The publisher Anthony Blond took his friend in hand:

> The routine was established by Blond's irritation with his talented friend's overspending and 'being a nuisance' in London. He offered Raven £15 a week to get out of town and start writing. For fifteen years the daily pattern has hardly varied. 'I live in a very small cottage,' Raven says, 'alone except for a lady who comes in and does for me. I rise at 8.30, form up at the desk by 9.30 and work until 1.30 in longhand. Then I lunch frugally off cold meat and a pint of beer.' (NF Apr. 76)

In one sense Blond's is an instinctively public school cum Oxbridge discipline: rustication, in a word, with the publisher as master. Raven was required to live, in a mild state of penance, 'more than fifty miles from the fatal fleshpots of London' (ST 6.6.76). He became, as he said, 'a remittance man', though after a while the 'fifteen crinklies' in the Tuesday post became an orthodox contract for the ten-volume 'Alms for Oblivion'.

What Raven had by this arrangement is almost precisely Virginia Woolf's ideal: a room of one's own and £500 a year. The result has been the near-million-word, ten-volume 'Alms for Oblivion'. A number of factors make any general application of this successful discipline unlikely, however. Blond is an unorthodox publisher, and personally friendly with Raven, as well as being his patron. (He commissioned and suggested the theme of Raven's first novel, *The*

Feathers of Death). Raven is somewhat unusual too, in apparently liking rustication. The autobiographical chapters of *The English Gentleman* (1961) reveal that he positively relished gating when at Cambridge, seeing his ability to abide by its arbitrary prohibitions as a mark of caste. Not all writers would be so pliantly masochistic. Most importantly, £15 was something in 1960; it is very little now, even if one were prepared to write in exile in Deal.

It is, one suspects, the steadiness and security of Raven's salary that was important, rather than the total sum of £5,000 (£500 per part volume), which eventually came to be paid: 'the main point was that he had the guarantee of a basic income for a decade or more to come' (NF Jan. 76). And as depreciation was making the amount impossibly thin, Raven landed the lucrative television commission for the Trollope Palliser serialisation.

Raven comes from a class for whom 'provisions' and 'remittances' are a normal part of life. A parallel can be found at a lower social level, occasionally, from the very different provisions of the welfare state. Alan Sillitoe, for example, would probably not have had the chance to embark on a literary apprenticeship had it not been for the fact that, while an airman in Malaya, he was hospitalised for a year in 1948, and thereafter received a disability pension of 45s a week which formed the basis of his income during the long years until *Saturday Night and Sunday Morning* (begun in 1948, turned down by three publishers) was accepted for publication in 1958. It promptly became one of the first English million sellers, in the unlikely company of the Penguin *Odyssey*, *Lady Chatterley* and *The Dam Busters*. Sillitoe published twelve books in the next ten years.

It is likely that any future support of this kind, if it comes at all, will have to be institutional. Nor should it, ideally, cost a writer his lungs or his freedom to visit the London he is writing about.

Oddly enough there is considerable resistance to schemes designed to give novelists an assured income. Often it springs from a common prejudice that, as John Fowles puts it, 'the more of the garret the writer gets, the better it does him'. Against the Hughes example, supporters of this Darwinian view might cite E. M. Forster who never completed another novel after getting his comfortable fellowship at King's College. Authors can indeed be forced into writing by severe external pressure. When he was told he had a bare year to live, Burgess turned out five novels in twelve months, and five of his best novels at that. Doubtless Skinner boxes could be devised that would get even a novel a year from Richard Hughes and the older Forster. Nonetheless there seem to be greater risks from universal hardship than from occasional slothful ease. Fowles provides from personal experience a vivid recollection of the quite inartistic exhaustion which afflicts part time authorship:

I can well remember, in the days when I had to teach for a living, the agonies of doing two different jobs; the impossible conflict between wanting to write into the small hours and knowing you had a nine o'clock class the next morning; of knowing when you get up that you could write all day, but must teach instead; and that most sickening experience of all, when you do at last have a free spell, of finding that the inspiration has gone. Of course you force yourself to write, and write badly. (*Public Lending Right*, ed. R. Findlater, London, 1971, p. 105)

People who cite the indomitable Trollope in this regard forget that he retired from the Post Office in the late 1860s to concentrate on editing and his novel writing. And it is particularly in the middle and later parts of his career, his prime, that a novelist needs to be able to reserve his energies. In the full strength of his youth a novelist can suffer heroic hardship, and his fiction may even be the better for it. The young unpublished David Storey supported himself by playing the toughest of physical sports, Rugby League. Without the experience there would probably have been no *This Sporting Life* (his first published novel). One could hardly expect the forty-four year old Storey to take to the field again, if his next novel fails. As John Brophy put it in his pioneer plea for PLR in 1951: 'except in his youth an author cannot use his powers to the full intensity in his spare time, after his nervous and physical energy has been used up on other tasks' (Aut Summer 51). These need not even be money-earning tasks. David Tribe points out in *The Author*, 1974: 'In a DIY age a greater proportion of the author's time is spent in domestic chores, whatever his social standing.' Trollope, one may recall, was woken up for his famous early stints by a servant with a cup of coffee. The Woolfs when they started the Hogarth Press, regarded their means as very modest. But they had two servants: 'Nellie the cook and Lottie the house parlourmaid'. Their combined wages were £76 1s 8d in 1917; Virginia earned £95 9s 6d from casual reviewing in the same year. Had she had to wash Leonard's clothes, cook his food and lay his study fire, it is likely that English literature would have been that much poorer for the housework. Of course many male literary careers have in fact been built on just such female sacrifices as Virginia Woolf was not called on to make. But even this morally dubious source of support is diminished in an age of women's liberation; only rarely can the modern author, like Shaw's Dubedet, use his wife's milk for ink.

Coming as we do at the end of a quarter of a millennium of romantic literature it is, of course, uncomfortable to think of creative writers demanding 'salaries' and tolerable working conditions with the kind of social conformity the terms imply. 'The exemplary modern artist', Susan Sontag tells us, should be a 'broker in madness' (*Styles of Radical Will*, London, 1969, p. 45). Whoever heard of brokers in madness complaining of wage differentials? There is a feeling abroad that novelists need life, not money, and poverty is one means of immersing them in the destructive element—on the cheap, so to speak. Lord Goodman answered this objection, rhetorically and elegantly, in *The Times Literary Supplement*:

> I heard a successful woman novelist some weeks ago in a radio discussion, airing the view that subsidy for authors would be a bad thing, because it would absolve them from the necessity of taking other jobs, thus reducing the world which they could observe and describe. This is a very arguable proposition. Its relentless logic would have left Dickens in the blacking factory and Bernard Shaw in the estate agent's office. But what is more apposite is that the advent of prosperity to both these great writers did not in any way reduce their activity or their quality; it merely gave them time to write. (9.10.70)

There is a converse, and largely invisible side to the chronic impoverishment of authors; namely that they do not join, or, having joined promptly desert the profession. It is, as Kingsley Amis points out, 'always much easier not to write a book than to write a book' (Firchow, *The Writer's Place*, p. 17) and any disincentive, however small, is potent. One example may be given, that of Auberon Waugh. In an angry attack on Gillian Tindall in *The New Statesman* (2.5.75) Waugh mocked the other writer for declaring that it was better 'for novelists to go out and do a job of work than to shut themselves up in an ivory tower with no experience of life'. Waugh's rejoinder, couched in barbed endearments, contained an explanation of his personal inability to write any more fiction:

No Gillian my sweet, it isn't true that all or even most novelists write better novels if they have to squeeze them in after returning from work in the evening or at the weekend. They don't have quite the same concentration on the job, you see, sweetie. I know it's different for housewives who seem to have quite a lot of time on their hands nowadays, but even if a fellow has the sort of employer who is prepared to allow him five or six months off whenever the spirit moves him to write a novel, he still has to support himself and his family for that six months, hasn't he my poppet? We're both reasonably well established for our age group—I'm a year younger, although you'd never guess,—but I don't think either of us can quite command a £1,500 advance before delivery, do you? I mean not for a novel? That's why I can't write any more novels, which I find a little frustrating because I would quite like to write some more and think they might get better with practice.

Waugh made a 'grand total' of £600 for 'my fifth and last novel' (Sp 1.1.76), which determined him to write no more. Elsewhere he has put his resolution in the form of a Lysistrata vow to publish no more novels until the advent of PLR.

One can take the proposition that novelists need some long-term finance, which is regular and sufficient, as established. Certainly writers themselves have long accepted it. The need for a regular income was a main reason why the Society of Authors advocated the royalty system in the 1880s. Royalties, unlike outright sale or half profits, sustain the author for as long as his book is on sale and mean six-monthly cheques over the period required to write the next novel. On the same track the Society favoured the 'minimum guaranteed advance' proposal in the 1930s. But this was doomed since it required the publisher to underwrite the author against the speculative chances of his work. It is one of the dead ends that the Society of Authors has commonly found itself in, trying to squeeze blood from a publishing stone.

II

Finding no comfort with the publisher the novelist turns to the public library. What he sees there is, to say the least, thought-provoking. Libraries spend up to £150m annually. They make over 600m loans annually of which some three-quarters are fiction. Public libraries give books a long shelf-life (and have their licensed suppliers harden the already hard covers to do so). Libraries buy their books at

10 per cent off, seldom buy duplicates, and above all, they issue them *free*. An author with ten books to his name, in a thousand library outlets, may conceivably have his works read $10 \times 1{,}000 \times 100 =$ a million times for, given an average price of £2 a novel and a 10 per cent royalty, £2000—spread out over a decade. The logic of this is put succinctly by Brigid Brophy and Maureen Duffy, two principal campaigners for PLR:

> A dramatist with an audience of 100,000 for one of his plays earns enough from it to live and function as a professional. A novelist with an audience of 100,000 borrowers of his book earns from it about £600. This means he can't function as a professional although he has a professional size audience. He is subsidising his audience. (ST 13.7.75)

The onus for putting this right falls centrally on the state which, since 1964, has taken responsibility for the library service. More particularly the Minister with responsibility for the arts is called to answer it. Whether he is able to do so is another question. One reason that PLR was so long in coming is, perhaps, that this figure is placed so ambiguously—a junior minister, answerable to three bosses. 'He just hasn't got the muscle' (Edward Hyams NR Nov 75) one disgruntled WAG member said of Hugh Jenkins. Even the normally decorous Society of Authors found this minister's inability to persuade his cabinet colleagues to keep his promise on PLR 'pathetic'. A general feeling formed in 1975 that what the newspapers called 'An Arts Supremo' was needed. Harold Lever and Lady Falkender were both tipped erroneously for the job—unduly hopefully as it turned out when the obscure Donaldson succeeded the soon to be obscure Jenkins.

Jenkins had particularly infuriated authors by assuring them to their faces and in a letter to *The Times* that a bill would in intro-
civil servants at the Department of Education and Science: 'the
sulting his masters first. Others were more inclined to blame the civil servants at the Departments of Education and Science: 'the minister's all right', Kingsley Amis was quoted as saying, 'It's the civil servants who are the shits' (NS 25.4.75). A. Alvarez was less generous, and even more exasperated in his language: 'the minister is a complete idiot. They're all a lot of fucking philistines' (NR Nov. 75). For his part Jenkins refuted the charge of impotence by maintaining that the delay was to allow 'field experiments' to get

PLR exactly right: 'I took a decision to solve the technical problems before introducing legislation, and that is where the delay has been' (NR Nov. 75). He may have been right. In authors' minds the months of delay would not have mattered were patience not exhausted by years and decades, even, of previous waiting. Jenkins could at least plead guiltless to the main offence, as could his well-meaning but equally inefficacious predecessors, Stevas, Eccles, Lee. Who then was to blame for holding PLR up for twenty-five years, in the face of general parliamentary approval? In the March 1976 debate Lord Goodman cast his aspersion against a mysteriously unofficial body of ill-wishers: 'It should be said that a great number of conscientious misguided unfortunate wretches in positions of influence but not of power have been able to prevent this legislation for twenty years' (twenty-five years, as Writers' Action Group corrected).

Whatever the reason, PLR has been inordinately long in coming to the UK. The scheme was devised as early as 1933 in Scandinavia and implemented in 1946 in Denmark (calculated on book stocks), 1947 in Norway, 1954 in Sweden (based on loans, not stocks), 1968 in Iceland (stocks), 1971 Holland (based on purchase of new books), 1973–4 Australia and New Zealand (stocks). Britain's timetable is less impressive, though doubtless more has been said and written about PLR here than anywhere else in the world. The first English champion of PLR was John Brophy, who ventured the idea as something of a daring novelty in 1951. In an open letter to *The Author*, Brophy suggested that public library borrowers should pay 1d over the counter in return for a 'cloakroom type ticket' (Summer 51). This rough and ready barter was quickly repudiated by librarians—who perhaps saw for themselves a grander role in life than that of cloakroom attendants.

Authors took to the idea of a library royalty and put forward a stream of initiatives and ever more sophisticated proposals. In the 1960s Brophy's scheme was adapted by A. P. Herbert, a gifted polemicist, who in his pamphlet, 'Libraries: Free for All?' suggested a 7s 6d annual subscription for all adult users, to go into a fund for authors' benefit.

Reader subscription was not on. It infringed the sacred principle of 'free' borrowing. Nor have librarians ever understood, or sympathised with the view that their institutions should directly support authors. They take particular exception to the assertion that libraries, which purchase up to 15m volumes a year, can be said somehow to exploit writers in the manner of some rapacious publisher from Gissing's *New Grub Street*. Libraries, in their understanding of things, encourage the book-reading, and consequently the book-buying habit. As the 1974 secretary of the Library Association put it: 'The Library Association cannot accept the view that the development of library services in this country is the primary cause of inadequate remuneration for some authors' (THES 18.10.74). Some authors respond to this in language less frigid, 'practically all librarians hate literature,' asserts Alvarez (NR Nov. 75).

The deadlock between authors and librarians, the one demanding a payment for multiple use, the other adamantly declining to pay up was to some extent cleared by the notion of a 'pool' (inherent in APH's proposal for an aggregate license revenue). Now, however, the envisaged pool is to be provided by the Treasury via the DES, not from readers' subscription. The pool has the compensatory advantage for the government of limiting their commitment to a controllable level (more lending, for example, would mean a lower division of the sum for each registered author). In 1975 the pool stood at a putative £1m rising to a somewhat more putative £5m. Servicing costs were originally calculated in 1974 at some £300,000 by the Technical Investigation Group. With inflation they had risen to something more like a half million, when the scheme was discussed in parliament in 1976. Since the nominal pool in these discussions was initially only £1m, the economics of the scheme were not impressive in view of the estimated 113,000 authors eligible for registration.

The account of Britain's long and devious progress to a flat-rate, loan-based PLR will make good reading, when Brigid Brophy and Maureen Duffy come to write it. One of the most interesting episodes will be the inside story of the formation of the commando WAG. This group was the first move towards a trade union for writers, in contrast to the professional association represented by the Society of Authors. For a long time authors had felt themselves in need of unionisation. Trade union language was already part of their vocabulary for talking tough. Visiting the Frankfurt Book Fair in the early 1970s, the novelist David Caute said he felt as out of place as a 'steel worker in a stock exchange'. Vivid though it is, Caute's image is potentially misleading. Writers are actually in the position of artisans rather than a labour force. They sell a finished product which they make in their own time and on their own premises. This makes it peculiarly hard for them to apply direct pressures or to combine; steelworkers can do this, novelists frequently can't since the conditions of their work disperse them into single, detached units. One of the great achievements of WAG was that it managed, temporarily at least, to overcome the problems of writers' combination. It accompanied an ideological position that was frankly proletarian; take, for example, an observation emanating from WAG in 1976 on the subject of contract reform: 'Publishers are the last remaining capitalists who can discard a used-up worker [i.e. author] or one whose work has lapsed from fashion without severance pay or a pension' (Bk 29.8.76).

In the first instance WAG's objectives were more immediate than the unmasking of class struggle within the booktrade. It was formed in 1972 specifically to get 'action' on PLR. It found itself at loggerheads with the Society of Authors from the first. The internecine struggle originally arose when the Society approved, albeit tepidly, the 1972 Eccles Working Party Report. This document advocated PLR to be operated by surcharge on library purchase of any new book. There were a number of advantages in the scheme; on the face of things it was simpler than alternatives. Publishers could collect, take their 25 per cent split, and pass the rest on to their authors with the royalty cheque (publishers were represented on the working party). The disadvantage was that the scheme made no allowance for authors of books already bought by the library; nor did it take into account that some books (notably novels) were borrowed much more frequently than others. Also it seemed to suggest that Library Funds might have to bear the cost of the surcharge.

Apologists alleged that the Society of Authors went along with the purchase scheme because it was important to get the principle accepted, and to argue over methods and details at a later stage. WAG disagreed; not just on the form of PLR, but with the common-front, conciliatory tactics adopted by the Society of Authors, the Arts Council and liaison figures like Lord Goodman. As they saw things, it was necessary for authors to confront the government and the publishers. To forestall any duping WAG insisted on formulating a just method from the start, without any doubletalk about principle. They repudiated the report, on the grounds that assessment from new book purchase 'disenfranchised' authors who had books already bought and in the libraries. Moreover purchase-based PLR favoured publishers—a party whom WAG have always suspected as the exploiting class. WAG wanted the Swedish loan based system. Similarly their campaign for it was distantly inspired by the Swedish authors' 'direct action' in 1969, when vast amounts of books were withdrawn by writers and their sympathisers with furniture vans. (This pressure was aimed at making the government renegotiate payment levels). Only Sweden of all countries operating PLR had a loan based system. And Swedish authors were, famously, the best organised, most militant and most selfish. The conclusion was irresistible; make trouble and you get what you want. Writers, as mobilised and politicised by WAG have, after 1972, almost unanimously come round to demanding the loan based scheme. The purchase scheme is discredited as a kind of establishment ruse.

History will determine what WAG's contribution to the implementation of PLR has been. Ideologically the group seems a response to Heinrich Böll's call in June 1969 for 'an end to humility' in writers, in his address to the first meeting of the German Writers' Union in Cologne. The French 'events' of the previous year had made direct action a more attractive option than it had been. In the short term and in England, however, there are those like the literary director of the Arts Council who are convinced that WAG's action has been counter-productive, interrupting the largely clandestine diplomacy by which things get done in the UK:

> The line I've taken, which has also been the Arts Council line, is that of course we approved but we wanted very much to get the principle of PLR accepted by the government, and to get some kind of legislation through and then worry about the method. This is where we parted with some of the representative groups who wanted to come to agreement about the method before getting agreement and legislation on the principle. What worried me was that there was a time when we might have got the legislation through but there was a lot of rather undignified squabbling among the different representative groups . . . while I think the actions of WAG have been well meaning, in the early days of the campaign they did some boat rocking among the various organisations concerned which very nearly sank the boat. And it was only when they were persuaded by someone more able than myself, Lord Goodman, to quieten down a little,

that actual progress was made. I don't myself, though this is a personal opinion, think they have been such a moving force as is sometimes contended. I think the Society of Authors were on the way to persuading the government to move on PLR. (NR Nov. 75)

The 1977 President of the Publishers' Association agreed: 'We should have had PLR by now if it had not been for the antagonisms the different factions have for each other' (T 31.3.77). Certainly WAG ruffled feathers. But not all the energy was directed towards feuding and mobilising fancy dress demonstrations in Belgrave Square. They have been instrumental in getting serious attention paid to the hardware required for their particular version of PLR. A common objection to the loan-based scheme was that it would be impossibly complex to monitor all the different loans made in the country's 11,000 outlets. Now it is conceded that within an 'acceptable' range of error and using a selected number of sampling points, a fair division of the pool can be worked out by computer from electronically captured data. A long way, it might be thought, from John Brophy's cloakroom ticket; but it is one of WAG's fiercest contentions that they have maintained Brophy's vision in something like its original purity.

There remains substantial resistance to PLR. One is sometimes driven to the belief that there must be an atavistic British suspicion of rewarding authors on the grounds that it will somehow corrupt their art. After the 1976 bill successfully passed its second reading, a violent correspondence was started in *The Guardian* by the founder of a spoof organisation called BAG (Borrowers' Action Group). The tenor of his argument can be gathered from the following letter:

Authors, like other underprivileged members of society who are too weak, sick or stupid to better their lot, are free to claim supplementary benefit. Why should a particular fund be formed for people (for there is no guarantee that they are currently writing) who happen to have written books? Books, like street lighting, and public lavatories, are conveniently shared gratis among a large number of people. Do we compensate the pocket torch manufacturer for loss of sales? Or pay the loo attendant a piece rate? (Grd 22.4.76)

This lavatory humour, one reminds oneself, after a quarter of a century's publicity on authors' expropriated rights; and in *The Guardian*, a paper which had always conscientiously reported the issues and arguments of what it once called in a leader, a 'debt of honour' to authors (Grd 24.4.75).

Apart from this residue of primitive antagonism, the more subtle objections of librarians remained, apparently indissoluble. They still maintain, as they always have, that publishers, who are free to fix book prices, should provide for their authors with larger royalties. For worthy authors whose work does not sell ('meritorious cases') the state should provide, via the Arts Council ('the soup kitchen,' as Maureen Duffy contemptuously calls it; (LAR May 75). Moreover libraries want to raise money for their own purposes (Bk 29.8.76). In this situation any kind of pressure, even the lateral pressure of having to provide the kind of books which are borrowed most (a natural concomitant of PLR) is to be firmly resisted as a dangerous drain on scarce resources.

Assuming that the objections of librarians are overridden, some longer-term questions remain. Will PLR be adequate? Will it return the immense amount of labour which has gone into getting it? Will the underlying argument turn out to have been wrong-headed? When APH coined the term he stamped it with the notion of abstract justice; tactically this line has been pushed by authors ever since: 'PLR is simple justice: it is neither welfare nor subsidy' as the WAG slogan puts it. As a result, a lot of time has been spent (or wasted) making a law as opposed to immediately implementing a privilege or a concession. The need to find time in a parliament with much bigger fish to fry has made for disastrous delay. It might have been better to do as other countries have, and bypass the legislative preliminary altogether; in other words take the money on whatever terms it is given. As it is, intricate problems of definition have arisen with a payment which is not quite royalty, nor quite copyright, but easily confused with both.

Another objection, is that PLR, especially when buttressed by the mighty apparatus of English law, might be consumed in its own administration, in the manner of a Dickensian law process. Inefficiency was one of the main objections of the Canadian Royal Commission, considering the introduction of PLR in that country. 'The most streamlined system', the report observed, 'could entail administrative expenses quite out of proportion to benefits' (p. 101). This objection has been elaborated very persuasively by an accountant, C. J. M. Hardie:

The first point is that if you want to help writers, and the government is willing to give £1m, this is a very odd and inefficient scheme, because it costs £400,000 which leaves only £600,000 for the authors. And if authors, on the whole, pay Income Tax at the same average rate as everyone else, a third of the £600,000 will go in individual tax payments. It is inefficient in two ways. Firstly it costs £400,000, and undoubtedly the cost will increase—it has gone up by 40 per cent between the first and second government reports. Secondly it is impractical to get £400,000, after tax, into the hands of the authors for an outlay of £1m. There are many alternative ways of getting money to authors, and plenty of precedents for payment of subsidies to the manufacturers of commercial goods. Bread is subsidised at the moment. (NR Nov. 75)

'The reason this inefficient scheme is being worked out', Hardie concludes, 'is because of a rather metaphysical idea about rights.' Bread subsidies, of course, need no laws to come into force; they are flexible, discretionary and immediate.

To the argument that PLR, once implemented, will mean only token payments, or payments reduced severely by the paraphernalia of working them out, authors have, of course, an answer. The first round of PLR is just a start. The money can be jacked up year by year. Events in Denmark in May 1975, when 3,000 authors extorted a higher PLR from the government by threat of direct action, would seem to bear out British authors' optimism. But Denmark has started thirty years ahead of Britain. They introduced PLR in 1946. They had 3,000 authors, cavilling at an 'unsatisfactory' PLR cake of £850,000 in 1975 (Grd 29.5.75). At the same period Britain had an estimated 113,000 authors, hungry for a distant future cake of £1m. It looks as if in this country we shall have something directly analogous to the Old Age Pension: a government dole which is always inadequate and in which every gain is simply a slight remission in a constantly eroding benefit. Meanwhile the struggle will take up all the effective energies of authors.

This last is a worrying possibility. For one of the really impressive achievements of the PLR struggle has been the mobilisation of authors. There was formed in 1975 an axis of the Society of Authors (Secretary, Francis King, founder member of WAG), the Writers' Guild (Council Member, Maureen Duffy, founder member of WAG) and WAG itself. This interlocking has made possible a united authors' front—as opposed to a cosy alliance between authors, publishers, agents and the state body of the Arts Council. WAG, which had no hierarchic structure, politicised authors, and made PLR an act of 'enfranchisement'. It was well on the way to being a writers' trade union. In 1976–7, with PLR crawling sluggishly through parliament, WAG efforts were diverted into the Writers' Guild (newly opened to 'literary' authors) and the campaign for a 'basic contract' between author and publisher (75 per cent of probable royalty of first printing in advance, scaled royalty rate, 10 to 15 per cent). On behalf of the WG Brigid Brophy launched an attack on the Whitford report on copyright as unfair to authors (Bk 7.5.77). 'Now', declared Brigid Brophy somewhat prematurely, 'there is a trade union' (T. 3.11.76). There wasn't. Though it is affiliated to the TUC, WG has under 2,000 members; but if there ever was to be one, PLR would have to be out of the way, firmly in the past, as either a victory or a dead letter.

III

It took twenty-four years to get PLR into the Queen's Speech, and another two years to get it to the committee stage. The leading campaigners, John Brophy and A. P. Herbert, died before catching even a Pisgah glimpse of it. A second generation of the Brophy family has been ten years campaigning, testing, setting up technical experiments, propagandising, and not, one suspects, writing novels. There is, as *The Guardian* put it after the 1975 writers' demonstration, a national 'guilt and a debt of honour' (Grd 24.4.75). It is, for the objective literary observer, irritating when one considers what might have been gained by faster and more immediate relief for writers. In Sweden they are now on second and third generation measures which should ensure a firm base for future literary activity. In 1975 our Minister for the Arts was talking of PLR as one might of some hare-brained novelty:

> There is something else that ought to be said. That is, when you are starting something new, you don't start very big. In other words, the Wright Brothers aircraft had to precede Concorde. As far as PLR is concerned, we're at the Wright Brothers stage. (NR Nov. 75)

Too true, except that the Danish Kitty Hawk flew in 1946; and it was not until 1976 that an enabling bill for British PLR was successfully introduced in parliament.

It is galling that PLR will be implemented at just that time when it can do least good. The libraries are no longer reliable buyers of books. The trend is to reduced or nil-spending, with Buckinghamshire blazing the trail. This might be borne if the PLR were lavishly implemented when it does come. But in the first instance the government went for the very lowest sum possible, £1m. And, as Lord Donaldson pointed out in the House, 'there would be very little for anybody' (DT 29.4.76). Indignant authors calculated that if they had to wait three years for their share of the million, they would actually be out of pocket when PLR gain was set against the recent (and immediately implemented) 8 per cent extra national insurance payment levied on the self-employed (T 2.6.76).

It was also galling to see the grudging spirit in which the abortive 1976 PLR bill was received. The second unopposed reading in the Lords, 5 April 1976, was accompanied by the most wretched auguries. In *The Guardian* for that day Robert Hilliard, Secretary of the Library Association, wrote a long, leader-page article, attacking the 'weaknesses of the legislation'—inconsistencies, problems of what to do with reference books, diminutive payments, excessive administration costs. In the debate itself, Lord Goodman, a long-time champion of PLR, did not rejoice in its imminence. The sum proposed was derisory. It would be better to give authors 'nothing' than this pittance. Lord Willis, another PLR stalwart, found the proposed amount 'shabby' and 'dismal.' No dates were vouchsafed by the government spokesman for implementation; only when 'resources' were 'available' would PLR come into force.

In its April 1976 editorial *The Library Association Record* fell on the bill gleefully, almost. It was 'hurried' (after twenty-five years); it was the thin end of a wedge ('it will not be long before the expenditure falls on library authorities'); it was inequitable ('Parliament is ... asked to legislate to confer public money on certain providers of material loaned by certain libraries'); it was procedurally erroneous ('being a money bill, the Lords would be in clear breach of Commons privilege by initiating it'). All these objections were ranged under the hopeful headline: PUBLIC LENDING RIGHT BILL DOOMED?

Surprisingly violent and efficient resistance was offered in parliament by recusant backbenchers. As the second reading of the bill approached, for example, Labour MP Michael English argued:

'Mothers without the support of the father of the family deserve public expenditure rather more than authors who are either prosperous or bad' (ES 6.7.76). English continued to oppose the bill in committee, making up a trio with Conservatives Roger Moate and Iain Sproat. The fierceness with which authors' representatives in the two houses pressed their case put backs up, disaffecting some old friends. The proposed cut-off point (i.e. ceiling payments for the most popular authors) and the attempted exclusion of foreign authors from the benefit irritated *The Times* sufficiently for it to deliver a punitive leader on the 'Authors' Equalization Grant' in May:

> The 'public lending right' in the course of being knocked into statutory shape in the House of Lords is beginning to look less like the translation into cash of a right which common justice warrants, and more like another state hand out—in the form this time of an authors' equalisation grant. (T 13.5.76)

According to *The Times* the 'equitable principle' on which PLR was founded and which was its strongest moral argument had been vitiated and 'wounded' by authors' (English authors') greed.

The second reading went through the Commons on 14 October by ninety-nine votes to nil; though the debate was almost sabotaged by MPs angry at the treatment of the preceding Seat Belts Bill. Another flutter was caused by the obstructiveness of Moate, Sproat and English in the committee stage. These opponents laid down nearly a hundred amendments during a period of considerable pressure on parliamentary time in the last weeks of the session. It was also a period when cuts in public spending were seen as a holy service to the country.

The deposed Hugh Jenkins commenting on the state of the bill, launched a covert attack on the faineant Minister for the Arts, in *The Guardian*, 2 November. 'Had I remained', he asserted, 'PLR would be on the statute book by now.' If PLR were lost at this stage, Jenkins said, 'with it will go a part of my faith in the parliamentary system'. Moate, Sproat and English held out to the end; on the night of 16 November they filibustered the bill to death ('like giggling fourth formers', Brophy observed. ES 17.11.76). 'Authors win on Lending Rights', proclaimed *The Guardian* headline (Grd 17.11.76), clearly sent in by a reporter who left before the end. They had not;

at 1.45am the lending right was lost for that session. PLR was not included in the Queen's Speech on 25 November.

The newspapers, at least, took the news philosophically. 1976 was, they concluded, a year for cuts, not increased burdens. 'The axe' as *The Sunday Times* put it, 'is mightier than the pen' (28.11.76). The future of PLR was, according to the same report, 'non existent'. The final twist of the knife for WAG came with the report 'Pricing or Taxing' published by the Institute of Economic Affairs in the same week as the Queen's Speech. This urged, persuasively, that a whole new system of user payments should be introduced to ease the financial pressure on councils. Among the suggested new levies was a 25p charge on every library book borrowed, to produce an estimated £150m—the money, of course, to go to the public purse not the author (T 29.11.76). Even that which the authors did not have was to be taken away from them, apparently.

It was, as it finally turned out, a tragedy of procrastination. What could have been done in 1966 painlessly could not be done in 1976. And what was done after 1976 would necessarily be too little and too late.

No one looking over the history of the PLR struggle could fairly deny that as a point of justice its case is unanswerable. Authors are victimised by the multiple use of their books in libraries, and this should be put right; if for no other reason than that refusing to pay up even a nominal amount creates a large grievance among authors. As Eva Figes put it in November 1976, claiming a symbolic reward:

> It is not so much the money involved—for a writer like myself the struggle to survive financially will not be resolved by a PLR payment... [But] due payment for the work done and services rendered is not only a practical necessity but a form of psychological feedback which we need to make us feel wanted and necessary to society. To deny PLR at this moment would be to fuel feelings of alienation to which writers are anyhow all too prone. (Grd. 9.11.76)

In passing, Eva Figes makes an important point about PLR—that its financial effect will be nugatory. For one thing the payments will be tiny to begin with and small at best. For another, libraries can no longer be relied on as the foundation for any long-term support policy. Thirdly, there is evidence from the US especially, that the cost of books is rising right the way through the manufacturing process. This goes back to the advance paid authors. In a 1976 American survey, covering 53 publishers and 116 books, it was revealed that 60 per cent of authors had advances of $5,000 or above and 22 per cent of authors $20,000 or above (NYTBR 4.4.76). In an article, aptly entitled, 'Some Hard Facts about the Economics of Fiction' in 1974, J. P. Dessauer reveals that for American first novels, advances are usually $2,500 to $5,000 and for established novelists, $15,000 to $20,000 (PW 5.8.74). For a novel to sell at the 1974 going rate of $6.95 and make money after an advance of $5,000 it must sell, it was calculated, 6,700 copies (NYTBR 28.3.76). Both the standard advances, and the required sales, represent a sharp increase over earlier levels.

It seems that literature is moving towards a high price equilibrium. PLR on the scale at which it will be awarded in Britain can only be a supplement to income; welcome enough, doubtless, as a token of goodwill but not of substantial value as an instrument of patronage. In retrospect PLR will probably emerge as a very small sideshow in the history of twentieth-century authorship.

7 The Arts Council: Subsidy for the Author

I believe if most men of letters were to be pensioned, I am sorry to say I believe they wouldn't work at all.
W. M. Thackeray, 1843

I couldn't go on writing novels and bring up a family without an Arts Council subsidy.
Eva Figes, 1975

Throughout the history of literature, and art generally, the state and its institutions have been major patrons. This supremacy was temporarily overthrown in Europe by the growth of the capitalist state in the seventeenth century. There followed—to foreshorten a long and complex process—the rich private patron and the commercially autonomous publishing and play houses, responsive to the tastes of their customers and the aspirations of their authors. These liberations are now inseparable from our conception of what literature is. By the nineteenth century the state as artistic or literary patron largely disappeared. But with the postwar welfare state it returned, and is now so firmly entrenched that once again we seem to be moving towards a state monopoly. Indeed, in some expensive activities like opera, we have already arrived. And, as is frequently observed, all art, including literature is becoming more expensive in proportion to its inability to increase productivity with generally rising wage levels. This is most obvious in the performing arts—no technology can reduce the size of an orchestra playing Wagner, nor can musicians be pegged to the payments of ten years ago. But, as we have seen, the same price rises are affecting literature. At the same time, private patronage for fiction has almost entirely dried up. A prize system remains, as a last and insignificant link between wealth and literature. The indirect patronage of fiction, whereby some novelists (mainly women) supported themselves by private means, had also dwindled to a negligible level.

In any general discussion of literature, the state as patron is certain to be invoked as a future inevitability; though, as the 1976 Redcliffe-Maud report on the arts points out, the manner in which state patronage will be provided for the unknown writer, who needs it most, 'is a problem that our society has not yet started to solve' (p. 58). Theoretically the problem defines itself as how to preserve artistic individuality and creativity in nationally owned or subsidised enterprises. Practically the problem more often defines itself as one of funds; put bluntly, there is seldom enough state money available for any kind of threat of gross interference to be posed. In this chapter the activities of the Arts Council, particularly their curtailed efforts for literature, are surveyed.

Originating as an idea among the Bloomsbury group, the Arts Council took embryonic form in the wartime Council for the Encouragement of Music and the Arts. Chartered as the Arts Council in 1946 it is, with the Third Programme (also founded in 1946), the Festival of Britain and the nationalisation acts of 1945–51 a monument to the nationally confident, if economically austere, post-war period. In the eyes of its architects, at least, the Arts Council was in the largest sense a political assertion. As Keynes remarked in May 1936: 'the failure of the nineteenth-century democracies to maintain the grandeur of the State is, in my judgement, one at least of the seeds of their decay' (*The Letters of J. R. Ackerley*, ed. N. Braybrooke, London, 1975, pp. 326–7). It was in this militant spirit that the Arts Council was conceived.

The Arts Council's direct support of literature began, to all intents, in 1966, following the initiative of Jennie Lee's white paper, *A Policy for the Arts*. This document observed: 'painters, poets, sculptors, writers and musicians are sometimes lost to art for lack of a comparatively small sum of money which would support their start in life'. Where the arts are concerned the Labour Party often appears materialistic to the point of vandalism. But one of the 1966 Labour Government's undoubted achievements was to turn attention to the wages artists earned as *wages*, in the same light as any other worker's payment. The artist was thus included in the state's work force. It was undoubtedly a philistine inclusion, though it had some enlightened consequences. The Labour Party conceives itself as the protector of the underprivileged, and it was probably necessary to demystify the artist to sanction socialist action. (Certainly it would have been harder to do while retaining the mandarin thinking of Keynes on the subject.) It was historically fortunate, too, that the white paper was delivered before the everlasting economic crisis, heralded in by the 1967 devaluation.

Before 1966 it had not been the Arts Council's prime purpose to help individual artists of whatever kind. Rather it supported the institutions that supported artists. Under the new dispensation the novelist, biographer and critic could, with the musician, sculptor and dramatist, look to the state as direct patron. Although it has always retained its preference for dealing with institutions and buildings rather than individuals, after 1966 the Arts Council would aim to provide more than equipment and opportunity. This was of particular significance to writers since they have none of the expenses connected with the performing arts and had missed the Council's benefits. Now they could legitimately expect them. But, despite the brave initiatives of the mid-1960s, the Arts Council seems to have done badly by the writer and not really to have advanced far beyond tokenism. This is most easily illustrated by comparison of the total annual revenue, the specific allocation for literature and, at the very end of the line, the amount which reaches authors in the form of grants-in-aid:

Total		*allocation to literature (England)*	*grants to authors*
1973–4	£17,541,961	£146,278	£41,500
1974–5	£25,068,785	£199,477	£47,800
1975–6	£29,089,106	£255,286	£35,600

It is possible to draw up what look like telling statistics here. The Department of Education and Science gives the arts about three-quarters of one per cent of what education gets; the Arts Council gives around one per cent of their disposable money to literature; the literature department of the Arts Council passes on some 15 to 20 per cent of its funds in the form of direct grants to authors. This would, prima facie, seem evidence of inattention to the cause of literature and, more particularly, authors. Nonetheless the singularity of literature's case needs to be considered together with the apparent meagreness of literature's slice of state patronage. Inspection shows that a larger percentage of what is given to literature finds its way to individual writers than reaches musicians or dramatists or ballet dancers in other sectors of Arts Council benefit. This is because the main institution of literature, the public library, is, unlike the opera house, supported by the local authorities. Arguably, then, literature gets its substantial patronage from another Treasury account, namely the rate support grant. As a non-performing art and an accepted social amenity (in the form of library books) literature has fewer housing problems and less contentious running costs than pictorial, musical or theatrical art. Moreover it has a large, commercially successful sector adjacent to it which has hitherto been willing to subsidise literary merit out of book-profits. This has not been the case with opera, for example, for many years.

Roughly speaking the fraction of the Arts Council patronage which does go to literature can be gathered under the following heads: (1) awards to writers and guarantees to publishers against loss; (2) subsidy for small presses; (3) subsidy for magazines; (4) subsidy for the institutions which house literary activity or which carry out promotional activity for literature (the National Book League, the Poetry Society, the Poetry Book Society); (5) educational activities (Writers' Tours, Writers in Schools). There is also an area of activity which does not appear in the annual accounts for which the Arts Council must be credited; it acts as a pressure group for good literary causes (like PLR) and has unpaid working parties studying aspects of the booktrade and literary situation. (Working parties in 1976–7, for example, were considering means by which distribution of quality literature could be assisted via Arts Council subsidised bookshops and a programme for financing the reissue of books which ought on literary grounds to be available.)

In 1975–6 the main divisions of Arts Council literary patronage broke down thus: £103,300 to institutions (the Poetry Society doing best with £28,000, the New Fiction Society second-best with £26,000); £26,600 to small presses (13 listed, Carcanet doing best with £8,000); £45,550 to literary magazines (10 grantees, *The New Review* taking nearly half the total with £22,000); £8,190 in grants to publishers (12 volumes benefited); £7,560 in creative writing fellowships at universities (2 fellows); £35,600 in awards to writers (35 listed); £9,705 on Writers' Tours and Writers in Schools.

The following sections survey the disposition of some £83,600 of the Arts Council money in 1975–6; namely the amounts which went to individual authors, and the subventions to *The New Review* and the New Fiction Society.

Grants to Authors

To use the phrase 'state as patron' suggests an aloof and impersonal machinery for 'artistic provision' (a favourite Arts Council-Civil Service term). In fact this is not how the Arts Council operates. Money for writers is dispensed on the advice of the 'Literature Panel' made up largely of the kind of person who might, were he not debarred by service, benefit himself. An unpaid group of a dozen or so authors, publishers, scholars meet quarterly to advise the director how to distribute money to a few dozen other authors, publishers, and scholars. In some ways it is tempting to think of the Arts Council as a microcosm of the British parliament. There is the House of Commons (the panel) which advises the Cabinet and PM (the finance committee and literary director) who take decisions which are ratified by the Lords (the Council) and ultimately the sovereign. Although the Council is fronted by the kind of titled and gilded people who would have been patrons in the eighteenth century, the initiatives come from the floor, from the artistic commoners who make up the panels.

Ideally the panel system should make for humanity and friendly expertise. Since they are not bureaucratic, members are as Lord Goodman puts it: 'uncoerced by rules and regulations of an academic and artificial character' (AC 1970–71). The panels are large, heterogeneous in composition and members are free to attend the meetings of the finance committee, which has executive power (though often they do not, one is told). Nominations for panel membership are taken from anyone within the organisation. The community of panel members and beneficiaries makes for flexible and humane patronage, but inevitably, perhaps, the very closeness of the literature panel to its beneficiaries has prompted suspicion and bitchiness (*Private Eye*'s question—'Is V. S. Naipaul authorising a grant for Margaret Drabble or vice-versa?').

In its early days the Literature Panel divided its support for authors into three categories: bursaries, maintenance, prizes. (Since then it has lumped them all together under 'grants' and withheld details of actual sums paid.) Bursary is a term usually applied to awards for young students; maintenance to assistance to the destitute or hard up; and prizes congratulate achievement. These divisions indicate the different and sometimes inconsistent tasks the Panel sets itself; to foster promise, assist work in progress and reward achievement.

Hence it is that any list of Arts Council literary awards is made up of names which mean something to an educated casual reader (Paul Bailey, David Caute, Charles Causley, in 1975–6, for example) and those which mean practically nothing. The Council is not rash enough to lay its money out on entirely unproved talent, however. To be eligible even for bursary-type grants writers need to have either a book behind them, or in front of them. They have to be sponsored by their publishers or by other 'responsible' professionals. The form of the Arts Council advertisement indicates the preconditions for assistance:

GRANTS TO WRITERS

On the recommendation of publishers, literary editors and other responsible members of the literary profession, grants may be awarded by the Arts Council to writers who are British subjects . . . who have normally had at least one volume published or have had a body of work published in critical magazines; and who are currently engaged in writing. The main purpose of such grants is to enable writers to buy time to complete the projects on which they are engaged.

The rules ensure a certain minimal proficiency. What the Arts Council requires is business references and collateral in the shape of one book achieved and another contracted for. This cautiousness does not mean, as it would in business, that large sums of money are involved. It appears that the average award is around £1,000. This is neither wage nor even an adequate supplementary benefit. All that one can say is that it is about double the normal amount earned by the novelist: a double pittance.

The amount of money given directly to writers has remained oddly static while the Arts Council fund generally has risen. In 1970–1, for example, some fifty English authors shared £33,950; in 1975–6 the number of authors had shrunk but the £35,600 disbursed was much the same. The annual reports indicate that the Council is not hopeful of ever having much of a kitty for the direct support of writers and their publishers. Nonetheless, in his 1975 jeremiad on the state of novel publishing, Peter Owen suggested that the Council should take on itself to underwrite the whole production of quality fiction, just as it undertakes to support opera totally: 'the problem of ever-increasing costs—firmly linked with higher prices and reduced sales in a vicious circle—can only be solved, in part at least, by making available to publishers substantially more money in the form of grants through the Arts Council' (Grd 4.7.75). It is, perhaps, not so wild a suggestion when one considers that the Council's past justification for giving literature such a small crumb of a small slice of a small cake is that: 'a great deal of literature is produced by the normal commercial processes, and by publishers' willingness often to use part of their resources to subsidise serious literature' (AC 1973–4). That willingness is under threat, as we have seen.

What then would be a utopian programme for the underwriting of literary production? Assuming the Arts Council gave £5m to it (which is less than the Opera gets, and what it was hoped the government would expend on PLR), small editions of some 3,000 works could be guaranteed (going by 1975–6 subventions to publishers). This would cover every new work of fiction and volume of poetry, good, bad and awful, published in a normal year. There is, of course, no chance of its happening. In 1977 the Arts Council grant was declared to be pegged for three years and in these circumstances literature might well have to reduce its expectations.

Whatever the future the Arts Council suffers present criticism of its panels' manner of operation. In 1977, for example, *The Guardian* gave front-page prominence to allegations that the panels were 'castrated' and incapable of exerting their will against the bureaucracy of the Council (2.5.77), or its 'oligarchic' tendencies, to use Hugh Jenkins's much publicised term (T 16.4.77). Charges of nepotism and an insipid or 'safe' choice of beneficiaries are routinely and often spitefully made. Nonetheless, one's feeling about the panel system, at least insofar as literature is concerned, is that it has not had a chance to operate at full throttle. It works with small sums necessarily divided into what are, in terms of patronage, minute sums. Small as they are, these awards are fiercely competed for. The panel thus finds its efforts absorbed by the self-deforming task of distributing too little among too many. Disappointment in the majority of applicants naturally converts to resentment and automatic charges of favouritism and corruption. Given a realistic fund there is every likelihood that the panel system could run efficiently and less invidiously. But to expect a realistic provision is, in the present climate, unrealistic.

Before examining institutions patronised by the Arts Council it is worth considering more closely its dedication to the 'separation of powers' or as Redcliffe-Maud calls it, the 'arm's length' principle. It is at once a strength and a weakness of the Arts Council that it does not transmit 'policy' or any 'ideology' of art. It does not venture its patronage but puts itself in a position to be solicited, preferably by an intermediary (see the foregoing 'Grants to Authors' advertisement.) Nor, in any direct way, does the Arts Council expect results; no-one, that is, has to produce a novel or return their grant. The remote and non-interventionary nature of the Arts Council operation can be handily illustrated by its support of the Poetry Book Society. The Arts Council finance committee makes a decision, annually presumably, to support the Society; the Society's selection board makes its independent choice from commercially produced volumes which have been selected, in their turn, independently by the publishers. Some of these volumes (if they are by Carcanet, for example) may have had prior indirect Arts Council support from some award to the press. At no point does the Arts Council visibly use its economic lever to influence what the publisher chooses to publish, or the selection committee to select.

At times the arm's length principle must require heroic self-restraint. In the much publicised affair of the Poetry Society in 1976, for example, the Arts Council was bitterly attacked by officers of a society it was supporting with a £28,000 annual grant. Prominent members of the Poetry Society were, as *The Times* correspondent put it 'ravenous to bite the hand that feeds them by showing an almost pathological hostility to the Arts Council which is the Society's principal patron' (1.6.76). In the end, of course, and in a blaze of unwelcome publicity, the Arts Council did exercise some discipline, as it did elsewhere at the same time, over the wayward Institute of Contemporary Arts. But in both cases the action was awkward and reluctantly undertaken.

The admirable features of the Arts Council arm's length principle are evident enough and can be traced back to a post-war distaste for the cultural commissars of the totalitarian states. As Michael Davie puts it: 'the basic principle of State Patronage of the Arts in Britain is that politicians must have no say in arts policy whatsoever' (Obs 27.2.77). This means that the Council and its political representatives cut a very poor figure when obiter dicta on policy are required. This embarrassment was evident in the conference of European Ministers

Responsible for Culture, held in Oslo in June 1976. Whereas Scandinavian ministers could confidently declare that art had a role in their social-engineering programmes, and could be directed to a 'firm political objective' the English minister could only deliver himself of 'muffled reservations' (ST 27.6.76). Muffled reservation was very much the tone of the authoritative Redcliffe-Maud report a month later. There must be, the report warned, 'no ministry of culture or promotion of the arts through Whitehall machinery'. The arm's length principle was essential—by which was entailed a deliberately broken circuit between the state decision-makers and the state dispensers of patronage, between the state dispenser of patronage and the ultimate beneficiary.

This aspect of the Arts Council's practice needs to be borne in mind while one considers the two cases that follow. Both have provoked controversy and pressure on the Arts Council either to cut off its grant or to interfere with editor's and selector's prerogatives. Although when pushed to the absolute limit the Arts Council will do the first it will never, apparently, do the second.

The New Review

In this section we turn to the most expensive of the literary ventures which the Arts Council has undertaken, *The New Review*. Consideration of this journal also takes in another controversial Arts Council issue, that of 'centralisation.' In effect this means 'centralisation on London'. A frequently deplored feature of the Arts Council has been its favouring of the metropolis, at the expense of the regions. To its provincial enemies *The New Review* is a diabolical compound of a London-based, elitist, expensively subsidised magazine. And even within London it is accused of being monopolised by a clique. The anger *The New Review* inspires has made it the most controversial literary monthly since *Blackwood's Magazine*.

The New Review was, as the name suggests, an upgunning of *The Review*. Ian Hamilton founded the earlier magazine in the early 1960s. The Arts Council had been generous to *The Review* and in 1974 agreed to be even more so to its successor:

The Council agreed fully to subsidise the new monthly literary magazine *The New Review*, edited by Ian Hamilton who for many years had edited the quarterly *Review* (a poetry magazine). *The New Review* was successfully launched in April 1974, and seems likely to establish itself both nationally and internationally as the leading British literary magazine. (AC 1973–4)

Practically, what this meant was £12,500 the first year, £19,000 the second and £22,000 the third. Such sums from public funds ensure scandal. ('Arts Council gives £25,000 to *New Review*' was headline material in the *Standard*, 12 May 1976.) From the beginning *The New Review* was attacked; notably by Auberon Waugh and *Private Eye*. In reply to the above entry in the Arts Council report, Waugh argued:

It is not true that *The New Review* was successfully launched. In fact they are already selling off back numbers at half price. The main point about the magazine is not that it is any better or worse than any of the other publications struggling to make ends meet in the dusty recesses of Pseuds' Corner, but that apart from being more expensively produced it is *exactly the same*. The same writers write about the same people just as boringly as they have always done. (PE 10.1.75)

It would seem that even some of the Literature Panel were of Waugh's mind. One wrote persistently in protest to the magazine itself. *Private Eye*, again, reported one of the confidential meetings of the panel in its issue of 11 July 1975. Unless the report is pure fiction (which might be the case), the leak must have come from a disaffected panelist:

At the last panel meeting in March, Hamilton attended to 'exchange views' with members. Elizabeth Thomas expressed the views of many panel members that *The New Review*'s editorial base was 'small and restricted with the same flavour as the former *Review*'. Alexis Lykiard hoped for a diversification which would allay the 'feeling commonly expressed that "the same old people" were contributing to *The New Review*'. Tom Maschler observed that 'sales were a little disappointing and that since many people did make a charge of cliquishness against the NR there might be some truth in this criticism'.

Cliquishness here means, as it usually does, London cliquishness. *The New Review* is seen as another and more extreme *London Magazine* (the other main magazine beneficiary of the Arts Council). The attack on this feature of *The New Review* was countered by one of its best known contributors, Clive James, in a letter to *Private Eye*, shortly before the above piece:

Your organ has been guilty of many transgressions in its time, but furthering the aims of an Arts Council cabal hasn't previously been one of them. The members of this cabal don't want *The New Review* brought down so that they can redirect the money towards a better magazine, always supposing that they could produce such a thing. They want *The New Review* brought down so that they can redirect the money towards those talentless regional poets who run in and out of Peak District pubs with carrots stuck up their noses in order to raise the consciousness of the indigenous fauna. (PE 30.5.75)

It is not clear whether the enemy within that James refers to are the cantankerous members of the Literature Panel. It is just as likely that he is thinking of the general change of policy accompanying Roy Shaw, appointed as Secretary General of the Council in summer 1975. Arnold Wesker describes Shaw's Peak District background in a *Sunday Times* profile, at the time of his appointment:

His northern background was 'very ordinary working class—not cultured working class like yours'. His first university was the Sheffield public library; his initiation into the arts came from the wartime dispersal of theatre, ballet and opera productions into the provinces. (ST 29.6.75)

After Shaw had been in office six months the Council released a reorganisation plan; effectively this would devolve the Council, in line with other devolutions in the pipeline. Shaw was quoted as saying: 'We are aware that for a long time there have been criticisms that arts money and activities have been focussed on the capital, and we want to be seen to be serving as effectively as possible the whole country' (T 30.1.76). The provincial pull would appear, in 1975 at least, to have been stronger than the metropolitan. All this took place against a large social and political commitment to devolution. And in mid-1976 there appeared the long awaited Redcliffe-Maud report which endorsed a decentralisation of arts patronage to the regions (though it left the issue somewhat fudged by insisting at the same time that the Arts Council should retain a 'key role' in a 'gradual' dispersion of power).

This left *The New Review* doubly attacked. On the one side it was accused of being the creature of a 'clique of conceited and untalented oafs . . . which nobody wants to read despite its vast annual subsidy' (PE 30.5.75). On the other its disproportionately large share of Arts Council money (half of the total given to literary magazines in

1975–6) would seem to have been contrary to new devolutionary trends. Hamilton himself gallantly argued in the tenth issue that the Arts Council only paid something like a sixth of his monthly bills: 'indeed, on balance,' he observed, 'it might be argued that the Arts Council gets more credit, or blame if you like, for the whole project than it could possibly be said to have earned' (NR Jan. 75). He might also have said that *Encounter*, founded in 1953, reported as facing a 1975 deficit of £60,000, was no advertisement for free enterprise. Was it not better to be subsidised by the Arts Council than by *Encounter*'s hoped for angel: 'Mr Leon Levy, a New York philanthropist... who is described as an investment company executive who is president of the Oppenheimer Fund Inc, and chairman or director of several Oppenheimer organisations' (ES 26.11.75). (Sir James Goldsmith was nominated for the same role in October 1976 ES 15.10.76. Presumably either Mr Levy or Sir James would have been preferable to the CIA connection which led to the earlier resignation of Spender and Kermode from the editorship.) As a matter of literary history Hamilton pointed out:

> It is not an accident that no literary monthly has been founded in this country for over 20 years, although half-a-dozen well-supported blueprints have been toyed with—none of these came to anything, it was always contended, because the capital required to launch something on this scale would be around £75,000. *The New Review* was launched, last April, on a tenth of that amount. Work that one out. (NR Jan. 75)

What one could work out was not entirely in Hamilton's favour. With a retail cost of 90p, later reduced to 75p, and a circulation of 4,000 a month, *The New Review* sales revenue was probably around £20,000 a year. The few advertisements the journal carried can have added little more. The Arts Council seemed, on the face of it, to be carrying considerably more than a sixth.

One could put this in context: *Encounter* at its height had a sale of something over 20,000 (Bk 8.9.73), though in 1975–6 it too had financial problems. In 1977 Emma Tennant's *Bananas* (with an Arts Council grant of £950 an issue, ES 17.2.77), had a 1976 circulation of 4,000. Hopes of a rise to 10,000 when, in January 1977, W. H. Smith agreed to stock it, seem not to have materialised. 6,000 was claimed in February, but even at this Tennant was not sure she could go on.

Encounter, *The New Review* and *Bananas* could all three claim that they were, however, unlucky to have been launched in peacetime. For some reason war makes for flourishing conditions for magazines—some might say the only flourishing conditions. The first world war coincided with one of the most ambitious waves of literary periodicals Europe has known. And in the second world war *Penguin New Writing* went as high as 100,000 copies per issue (i.e. more than *Private Eye*, or of *The New Statesman*, *The Listener* and *The Spectator* combined in the mid-1970s). *Horizon* reached about 50,000 reputedly. Both *Horizon* and *Penguin New Writing* closed in the early 1950s for failing readership. The conclusion seems to be that literary magazines' good times are everybody else's bad times.

Given the general inclemency, *The New Review*'s mere survival was a kind of achievement; and the Arts Council's dogged loyalty is another. But it is not enough simply to exist in an environment hostile to literary magazines without going under. The strength of Hamilton's case must stand on the quality of the contributions to his magazine. These can speak for themselves. Since the concern of this book is with fiction I list novelists and short story writers who have touched *The New Review*'s coin: Theroux, McEwan, Gordimer, Bradbury, O'Brien, Jacobson, King, McGahern, S. Naipaul, O'Faolain, Drabble, Bainbridge, Trevor, Storey, et al. Whatever is said about *The New Review* now there is no doubt that it will be much consulted by future students of literature.

Was the Arts Council right to back *The New Review* to the hilt? It is one of the paradoxes of the British literary situation that money should have been the primary issue. In Canada in the 1970s there was money and will enough to set up a first-class literary miscellany on the lines of *Encounter* or (by implication) *The New Review*. 'Such a publication is sorely needed,' the Canadian Commission on publishing reported. All that was lacking, the same report glumly observed, was the literary talent to spend the money on. London had no shortage of publishable material; all it lacked was the money. Of the two countries, Canada would seem to be the poorer in real terms.

There are, nonetheless, things to be regretted about *The New Review*. Historically it is comparable to *Penguin New Writing*. What Lehmann did, with spectacular success, in that journal was to hybridise the little magazine and the mass-market paperback. *The New Review* attempted a similar hybridisation; though in its case it crossed the little magazine with *Playboy*, taking in the revolution in magazine merchandising which that chic journal had started. Indeed, at times *The New Review* looked like *Playboy* without the nudes (if one discounts the February 1977 cover of David Hockney and R. B. Kitaj. 'David Hockney', Atticus revealed, 'dyes his hair'; ST 20.2.77). It adopted the long interview, the feature article, the appeal to sophistication, the large glossy format, the artisitc illustration. It aimed, as Ian Hamilton put it, to express the 'growing journalistic concern with culture' (Grd 17.9.76).

Unfortunately *The New Review* failed journalistically. It seems never to have found bookstand space and thus never had a chance to try its appeal on the open market. Smith's took a very small batch, but never, apparently gave it a proper run. Other retailers would not touch it. One never saw *The New Review* well displayed. What it was left with was what it was least suited for—library subscription by largely academic institutions, in whose reading rooms it cut a strangely garish figure. The Arts Council compounded this mismatch by donating copies to public libraries (in a covert attempt, it was spitefully alleged, to bring circulation figures up to respectable levels).

The worst mistake the Arts Council seems to have made is to give money for production without making any effort to lend expertise in distribution. *The New Review* was simply not seen by many of the people who might have bought it. Seconding a professional circulation manager to *The New Review* might have been a worthwhile Arts Council investment.

The New Fiction Society

The New Fiction Society is one of the most imaginative schemes of patronage for the novel ever devised. Its expensive and dubiously successful career is a real setback to the Arts Council's future activities in literature, and will discourage any other bold schemes.

The New Fiction Society was, as its name implies, a book club set up under the new relaxed dispensation of the post-1968 period by which new fiction could at last be provided at discount prices by clubs. It was, in fact, very early in the field and competing with the world-wide giant, Literary Guild. As Martyn Goff, director of the NFS, put it with some justifiable pride in 1976:

> The only other simultaneous fiction book club is the New Fiction Society. Whereas the Literary Guild is a highly profitable activity run on the

sharpest and toughest commercial lines, the New Fiction Society is a non profit making set up backed by the Arts Council and run by the National Book League. While the Literary Guild has editors with one eye always on the balance sheet, the NFS has David Hughes and an advisory panel; and their job is to make sure that the new and the young and the more serious get a proper showing. Dinah Brooke, John McGahern, and Ian McEwan are not likely to be seen on any mass book club's list on their present form. All have been chosen by the tiny New Fiction Society. (Grd 28.1.76)

On the face of it the NFS represented an admirable half-way house of fiction; a commercial outfit with intellectual responsibility; a club which would patronise the sales of quality fiction on those fringes where it most needs stimulus. The aims of the NFS were, as originally conceived, ambitious. 'The New Fiction Society has been sponsored', the 1974–5 Arts Council Report announced 'in order to increase the sales of new fiction.' A new class of reader would be educated into buying and so reducing the price of the new novel. At the same time the NFS intended, equally ambitiously, to patronise the new novelist as well as the new fiction.

As its first advertisements put it, NFS would become 'a society of booklovers whose *combined demand* for good fiction will enable publishers to reduce prices and encourage talented new authors'. In its earliest projections it saw itself helping the unpublished talent to publication. The non-conformist spirit of the club was evident in their defence of not having selected the 1975 Booker Prize-winner:

Members have wondered why the NFS did not offer the winner of the 1975 Booker Prize, Ruth Prawer Jhabvala's *Heat and Dust.* It was carefully considered, but in the end struck us as a very gentle and low-key book, verging slightly on the tedious, a work of old-fashioned formal elegance that broke no new ground in either construction or content.... The selection of *Heat and Dust* by the Booker judges confirmed to us that the NFS was seeking out a much more vigorously contemporary fiction. (NF Jan. 76)

The Arts Council seems to have gone overboard for the NFS. In 1974–5 the report records an award of £34,500; almost half the sum allocated to the subsidy of all institutions, and £10,000 over the foreseen limit in 1974. In 1975–6 the subsidy stood at £26,000, about one-tenth of the literature grant.

The NFS took out national advertising. (It is estimated that between £1 and £4 have to be spent to recruit every subscriber to a bookclub). A striking full-page advertisement in *The Observer*, 28 September 1975, took the form of a quiz of eight questions under a gallery of somewhat ghastly portraits ('3. Is this a working-class novelist? 4. Is this the new James Joyce?'). The advertisement concluded:

The English novel is alive and well. If you can answer the questions above, you probably know where. But it is possible that less than 0.1 per cent of the population could get all the answers right.... Nowadays, unless it is your job, it is difficult to keep up with the main currents of good writing. The New Fiction Society has been founded for the thoughtful reader, who, like Lord Goodman, 'can't churn a way through the hundreds of novels that are published each year in the hope I will alight on the right one.'

It is a cruel joke on the NFS that despite this expenditure on advertising space it should have ended up with an enrolled membership of .004 per cent of the population, some 2,000. When it began in 1974, it was reported 'They are aiming at a membership of 10,000 in the first three years' (Aut Autumn 74).

The fact that it seemed unable to pass 2,000 members accounts for the subsequent throes of the NFS. Its obstinately unexpanding membership was an insuperable problem and utterly confounded its original high aims. The Poetry Book Society can pride itself on the extra few hundred sales its membership represents. Hundreds make all the difference in the sales of slim volumes, whose normal print run is 1,000. This is not the case with novels, especially the attractive, middle-market novels the NFS eventually came to favour, after their initial good intentions about worthy unknowns. The most they could ever add was 2,000 to the total sales, and the actual achievement was often only three or four hundred (600 of Robert Nye's *Falstaff* was a record in January 1977)—what difference would that make to Iris Murdoch or Malcolm Bradbury? Nor with 2,000 members making four selections a year could they cover costs. Selling at discounts of 25 per cent without corresponding market enlargement meant impossible economics; unless, that is, one saw the NFS as part of the Arts Council's general cultural philanthropy, a dignified way of giving money away in good literary causes. As it was, in January 1977 the NFS stated that since October 1974 it had sold 13,000 volumes at a cost of £60,500 to the Arts Council. It would have been cheaper to buy the novels at full price from a bookshop and give them away to passers-by at Piccadilly. As the Literature Director put it to the Society in a letter of April 1977. 'Your 2,000 members cost us £25,000, or £12.50 each [i.e. per year]. Or, to put it another way, we are paying £25,000 to sell 8,000 books, i.e. more than £3 per volume. This doesn't make very good sense, does it?' (NF April 77). In order to attract a wider range of readers the NFS was obliged very soon to lower its sights in spite of its original ideals. This let it in for the unkind criticism that, as Ian Robinson put it:

> It is a perfectly ordinary middle-brow-fiction book club.... In October 1975, they were offering works by Lawrence Durrell, Muriel Spark, Doris Lessing and Malcolm Bradbury, as well as a special offer of signed works by Kingsley Amis, Iris Murdoch, V. S. Naipaul and others.... All I wonder is why these writers, having made considerable successes in the market, also need the helping hand of the Arts Council. (THES 12.3.76)

Robinson overstates here; one can make a list of NFS selections which would never have had a look in with commercial bookclubs. Had Robinson been a member in March 1976, for example, he would have been offered *Survivor* by Marc Brandel, *The Last Summer of the Men Shortage* by Geraldine Halls as April choices; *The Survivors* by Simon Raven, *A Lavender Trip* by Sasha Moorsom as May choices. Nonetheless members made the same point as Robinson in letters to the Society magazine, calling attention to the original pledge: 'we will help new (and unpublished) authors who are members to make contact with publishers.'

Had it succeeded in its pure, or even in its semi-commercialised form, the NFS might well have transformed the character of the patronage of fiction in this country, creating a book club which could take over the role of the public libraries at a time when those institutions were failing in their support of the novel with minority readership. As it was it foundered on the stubborn resistance of the British reading public to actually buying new fiction—even at a discount and with all the attractive extras which the NFS threw in. The failure (or at best equivocal success) of so intelligently conceived a scheme is a sobering fact to anyone drawing up blueprints for future literary patronage of a directly interventionary kind.

Both *The New Review* and the New Fiction Society represent major gambles by the Arts Council Literature department and it is regrettable that neither can be scored as an unalloyed success. Both, in spite of their under-rated achievements have given ammunition to enemies of the Arts Council. It is likely that bad publicity may have encouraged the known tendency of the Arts Council to protect itself by dividing its patronage into uncontentiously small parcels, devolving decisions about donation wherever possible to regional authorities or intermediate institutions, and playing safe wherever possible. There may well be no 'New' anything for a while. Such a tendency can only be further encouraged by the fact that the Council's funds are pegged in the foreseeable future to mid-1970s levels. The thinking of the Council's policy-makers seemed similarly pegged and cautious. Speaking in the debate on the arts in the Lords on 15 June 1977 Lord Donaldson, the Minister, concluded: 'This was not a moment to make too much fuss about getting an awful lot of money. What they had to try and do was hold what they had' (T 16.6.77).

'The period of restraint' which the Arts Council annual report for 1975–6 foresaw effectively put out of any consideration the imaginative schemes of literary patronage which had been shown to work elsewhere. Such measures as the tax-exemption for writers of 'cultural merit' (Ireland), the block purchase of approved novels for donation to the libraries (Norway), the extension of copyright to raise revenue for cultural purposes (France), a Writers' Co-operative Publishing House (Sweden) were all relegated to that indefinite future period when Britain should have reached the sunny uplands of economic prosperity.

8 Campus Writers

1956: Nabokov, who in 1940 tried and was unable to obtain an academic position in England, is proposed for an important chair at a Great University. After a heated debate the proposal is defeated: 'Gentlemen, even if one allows that he is an important writer, are we next to invite an elephant to be Professor of Zoology?'
Nabokov: His Life in Art, A. Field, London, 1967, p. 11

A running theme in Peter Firchow's book on English literary conditions, *The Writer's Place*, (Minnesota, 1974) is the relative merits of the American 'free enterprise' system of patronage via the university, and the semi-socialist British Arts Council. When it is put to him the English writer, as canvassed by Firchow, seems in two or three minds about the advantages of more university employment. Pamela Hanford Johnson approves:

America has been awfully lucky to have patronage through the academies, awfully lucky. I've done some of this work myself in America. Americans are very generous in looking after their writers. We haven't done so at all, or only on a very small scale and that's why we're really down to BBC television and journalism. It would be very valuable to a lot of writers here if they had more university patronage. (Firchow, pp. 217–18)

V. S. Pritchett, a writer who has always enjoyed a connection with London journalism, demurs. For him the campus entails a limiting kind of intellectual provincialism, a benign prison camp which keeps the writer away from the reviving metropolitan air:

For prose writers, playwrights, novelists, I think the university is dangerous, because the university is a specialised community. It is quite unlike the outside world.... Artificial worlds have a sterilising effect on writers. (Firchow, p. 280)

Kingsley Amis shares the antagonistic view, declaring himself 'a little suspicious of any closer ties between the academic setup and the literary setup' (Firchow, p. 21). His objection is in line with his well publicised distaste for academic expansionism, and his phobic fear of takeover by intellectual trendies. A more indignant argument is often heard elsewhere from artists less financially successful than either

Amis or Pritchett. Academics, they point out, make their living from creative writers—shouldn't they be prepared to pay something back?

To begin with, one would make a distinction between the various capacities in which universities can 'employ' writers. In America, for example, most operate full-time as writers teaching writing in universities (e.g. the late Theodore Roethke, whose career was entirely subsidised by the various academies in which he taught); others have a sabbatical or honorary arrangement with universities, entailing little or no teaching load (e.g. Vonnegut, who had two useful years at Iowa, which enabled him to get *Slaughterhouse 5* into order); still other writers are employed by universities in incidental connections (e.g. Nabokov, who was a Fellow of the Museum of Comparative Zoology at Harvard when Edmund Wilson induced an American publisher to take an interest in *Bend Sinister*); finally there is the side benefit of the single public reading, or tour. American universities are generous in the number of paid visits which they sponsor. They are also generous in the scale of payment. The going rate in 1976–7 was $150–$400, plus expenses. A writer with an air timetable can put together an itinerary which will bring him $2,000 or so for a month's work.

Where they are teachers American creative writers may, or may not, actually teach creative writing. Most can, but not all want to. Saul Bellow, for one, has strong feelings on the subject.

Q. Are you teaching now?
S.B. Yes, I teach at the University of Chicago. I teach literature there. I don't teach writing courses.
Q. I see it's important to you to make the distinction.
S.B. Yes, because I don't like teaching writing.
Q. Is there a profound reason for that?
S.B. It makes me too unhappy to read some of the inept things.

(PW 22.10.73)

Bellow indicates a certain inclination to bite the university hand. Nonetheless, either as teachers of writing, or of literature, or in simply honorary and visiting posts, there is a long and still growing tradition of American writers supporting themselves on generous university stipends. A random list might include: Malamud (Bennington), Kosinski (Wesleyan, Yale), Joyce Carol Oates (Windsor), Heller (CUNY), Berryman (Minnesota), Barth (Buffalo), Wilbur (Wesleyan), Hugo (Montana), Hawkes (Brown), Lurie (Cornell),

Doctorow (Sarah Lawrence). No survey of American authorship can ignore the all-importance of education dollars in the writing of modern American fiction and poetry.

The historical explanation for the close collaboration between American writers and American academic institutions is hard to disentangle. One cause, certainly, was the impetus given by Sinclair Lewis's speech on the award of the Nobel Prize, in 1930. Lewis arraigned what he felt was a disastrous divorce between creativity and criticism, pointing to the complete absence of any 'living' element in university English. 'Our American professors', Lewis observed, 'like their literature clear and cold and pure and very dead.' Lewis proposed an invasion of 'the secure blankness' of the American college by living writers, and his call was generously answered in the next forty years. Now there are plentiful courses, programmes, workshops, conferences and seminars: and every English department of any substance has its writer in residence. The recruitment of writers was given an added boost by the vast educational boom, and the money it generated, in the 1950s and 1960s. Saul Bellow, who as we have seen is no friend to the system, recalls his own 'surrender' during this boom period:

> I don't think I had more than $3,000 or $4,000 a year until I was in my late forties. Before I took a job at the University of Chicago, I filed a tax return of $6,000 or $7,000 in 1962 or 1963. It really didn't make much difference. Writers were swallowed up by the institutions in the fifties and sixties. They couldn't hold out against them. Universities had so much money to spend during the great educational boom at the postwar period. Anything resembling an independent literary life was simply wiped out and you had the choice of going into one of the media or going to a university. I thought a university was the better choice. (Grd 10.11.76)

Britain had no boom equivalent to America's. Nor have British educators, unlike American, thrown off their doubts about the teaching of living literature, whether as a subject or a skill. Our English professors still prefer their literature cold and clear and pure and very dead. And although we admit a very few famous writers on an honorary basis (E. M. Forster at King's, for example), and a smallish number of supremely ambidexterous writer-critics can hold jobs on their purely academic qualifications, British universities will not touch creative writing. Hence the majority of creative writers are no use, surplus to educational requirements. More so in a period when austerity forces departments to fight for the renewal of every teaching post—posts that they regard as vital to their function.

The educational ideology behind the British boycott of campus writers is expressed authoritatively by David Daiches, writing forty years after Lewis. What is remarkable is not that his opinion is unadventurous but that in other respects Daiches was a main architect of the most progressive English course in modern university history, namely that at Sussex, the most publicised of the new universities. He is far from being an enemy to experiment and eclecticism—or even Americanism, come to that (he spent a large part of his career at Chicago):

> My own view is that, in the first place, I am very suspicious of 'creative writing' courses, having the old fashioned view that you cannot teach 'creativity' and that a potential poet or novelist of any quality will learn his craft by reading and writing and talking without regular formal instruction. Most 'creative writing' courses in America that I know of, whether conducted by well-known writers or by routine academics, are simply courses in what we would call practical criticism, or even in simple composition, and have nothing to do with creativity.... Poets and novelists can make splendid contributions to the understanding of literature at a university but not, I think, by teaching formal courses in how to write poetry or novels. (Aut Spring 74)

In a characteristically utilitarian way, Daiches is thinking principally of what use writers can be to the academy. Against such cold reasoning British writers often assert that they are in possession of a mystery which mere academics can never communicate and which students are eager to share. Peter Redgrove, a poet who has taught in American (but not British) universities, contradicts Daiches on this point, maintaining that practising writers can inform and enthuse students in a way denied to cerebral critics:

> Very few jobs in the universities, schools or colleges of education are occupied by people who are primarily writers, employed for their qualities of imagination. It is an anomaly, a flaw and a paradox in our educational system. Why must our universities be full of critics, critics, critics? Nobody would dream of learning about painting from anybody who was not a painter, or about sculpture from somebody who had never sculpted. (Aut Summer 73)

However sympathetic one may be in principle, one must point to places where Redgrove's views fall down in practice. The point about novelists and schools can be shortly disposed of. Whenever schoolteacher-novelists have any success, like John Fowles, William Golding or Evelyn Waugh, they get out of schoolteaching as quickly as they can and they never go back. In *A Sort of Life* Graham Greene recalls his terror at going to Sackville Street to 'pawn' himself to the schoolteaching profession. A slave in the Constantinople market would not have been more fearful:

> I had a horror of becoming involved in teaching. It was a profession into which you could so easily slip, as my father had done, by accident.... Had he been afraid of feeling the trap close, as I was now? I wanted nothing permanent I explained in near panic. (*A Sort of Life*, London, 1971, p. 153)

It is only in universities, with their thirty-week year, their four-day week, their ten-hour weekly teaching load and their regular sabbatical term, that the writer can sustain a double role. But the pressure on university English posts is incredibly fierce. Jobs at a reasonably thought of department will attract hundreds of applicants, most of them highly qualified candidates with up to three degrees and a list of publications in learned journals. Any writer has to make a dauntingly good case for consideration.

II

This is a question of patronage which can only be answered in terms of national educational preferences. If we are to have universities playing a much larger part in the support of living writers, we must justify their existence in universities. And this comes down, as Daiches assumes, to the desirability of the Creative Writing courses which the majority of American writer-professors run and which put them legitimately on the college pay roll. British educators have always distrusted such courses, for the reasons Daiches gives. But as in other spheres, scorn of Americanism is no guarantee against following the leader, which that country increasingly is. Already many British English departments have adopted the American course credit system in place of the examination, which was one technical barrier to Creative Writing here. (Finals in Creative Writing would be Kafkaesque). We may then reasonably examine

Creative Writing not as some exotic academic barbarism, but as a future possibility which may perhaps have some incidental benefit for our writing profession. What, then, is Creative Writing and could it happen here?

The most famous 'program' in Creative Writing was begun at the University of Iowa in 1931, under Paul Engle. According to Engle it was 'a part of the whole American idea . . . that any university can teach anybody anything' (*Teaching Creative Writing*, Library of Congress, Washington, 1973 p. 7). It is not the British idea. British authorities (and authors sometimes) have reserved for Creative Writing a satirical contempt, equating it as Anthony Burgess does in *Enderby's End* (1974) with 'courses in soul cookery' and the 'whorehouse of progressive intellectual abdication'. British satire gains added force from there being no clear American opinion on the subject. Some less idealistically national defences than Engle's are offered. One commonly heard is advanced by Theodore Roethke, talking to an English interviewer in 1960:

> The English [Roethke] knew, tended to deride such classes, but the idea was not to manufacture poets, no more than essay-writing is to produce essayists. To make people write poetry was to give them an insight into poetry which could be more profound than learning about poetry through critical writing. (A. Seager, *The Glass House*, New York, 1968, p. 270).

This sounds suspiciously like the traditional arguments put forward in favour of Latin and Greek as gymnasia for the growing intellect. Some such rationalisation is probably inevitable. American professors are acutely embarrassed by the necessarily minute success rate of their Creative Writing courses (i.e. the estimated 1 per cent who actually become published creative writers, compared to, say, medicine's 90 per cent who become practising doctors). There is the other uncomfortable fact that these Creative Writing graduates are being produced at a time when magazine outlets are fast disappearing and publishing houses shortening their lists. Nor does Roethke's argument hold up that most Creative Writing students have no long-term writing ambitions. One reason given for the current difficulties of the American novel at a 1975 conference was just the 'huge bloating mass of fiction' excreted by the Creative Writing courses which swamps every publisher in the country, making it that much harder to pick genuine talent from drilled, soulless competence (PW 10.11.75).

A more cold-blooded, though more tenable way of regarding Creative Writing is as an educational masquerade—a rip-off for the author. A few American writers are brazen enough to make this claim. Kurt Vonnegut, for example, observes that a Creative Writing stint enables a writer to 'dry out' on a good salary. It serves as an occasional sanatorium for a notoriously hard-living profession. Vonnegut, however, is a wilful heretic on the subject (NYTBR 14.4.74).

An equally radical, if more constructive, critic of present Creative Writing is the anarchist Paul Goodman, whose writing is immensely influential, especially among students in America. In his book *Community of Scholars* (New York, 1962) Goodman claims that the appointment of creative writers reflects a failure of nerve on the part of the college system. It arises from a desire to 'pep up' courses 'as if the ordinary faculty feel that there is a creative life to which the students should be exposed', (p. 137) but which the authorities have to import from the outside. Goodman presents the process as a kind of vampirism, the dead institution feeding itself on the vitality of the living writer. Goodman conceives of a thorough-going transformation of the college, to make it a proper community for living writers and scholars.

Uncertainty among the Creative Writing teaching profession was manifest in a symposium held in the Library of Congress, 1973, entitled, 'Teaching Creative Writing'. No single, persuasive rationale of the subject emerged from the discussion. What did emerge, however, were a number of increasingly pressing worries about its future. Creative Writing classes are extremely expensive, in terms of cost-effectiveness. Creative Writing only works if the class is small, meets regularly and for longer than one-hour periods. Intimacy and informality are of the essence and these cost money. Creative Writing requires more than its fair share of eminent and therefore top-salary teachers. Eminence has the other drawback that little Creative Writing pigs are overawed into squealing like the old boar. This and other pressures help create those two much cited features of the Creative Writing system, institutionalisation and homogenisation. The stereotyping and deadening effects of Creative Writing are often thrown in its American teachers' faces. Universities have an unfortunate tendency to appropriate their subjects of study. The hermetic effects of MFAs (Masters of Fine Art) teaching MFA literature to aspirant MFAs has often been deplored.

There are, then, misgivings, even in the land of Creative Writing. Nonetheless after forty years the subject has reached the point in the US where it can no longer be sneered away. It can even deliver its ultimatums to the sceptical. As the distinguished Stanford Creative Writing Professor, Wallace Stegner, puts it: 'whether we like it or not, that is where it is—most contemporary fiction and poetry have come out of it' (*Teaching Creative Writing*, p. 65). If we believe him Creative Writing is the largest employer and, repulsive thought though it may be, manufacturer of novelists and poets in the US, and will remain so.

We may return to the original questions. First, is Creative Writing a desirable innovation for the British system, bearing in mind that its advantages can work two ways, for the student educationally and the writer-teacher financially? Secondly, assuming Creative Writing to be desirable, can it be implemented? As regards the first question, British writers with direct experience of Creative Writing find themselves in a state of some perplexity. It is not a subject on which opinions are easily clarified. William Golding offers a typically ambivalent response from his experience in 1962 when, as a campus cult hero, he taught in America. His sarcastic essay, 'Gradus Ad Parnassum' describes in some detail the 'embarrassing farce' of an allegedly typical Creative Writing class. The ludicrous and painful episode is given with all the force of thoroughly indignant English common sense. Golding's sensibility as a teacher as well as novelist is injured, we feel. But the novelist has a troublesome afterthought:

> Yet . . . the good in the method is obvious too. How can one convey a sense of the thousands, the hundreds of thousands of students who found in these classes a high road to the enjoyment of prose and poetry, a glimpse of the creative process? How can one go against the testimony of dozens of talented professional writers who all claim they were helped, produced even, by creative writing classes? (*The Hot Gates*, London, 1965, p. 156)

Having spent a year in America, Golding confesses: 'I still don't know what to think.' It is likely that he knew better what to think about Creative Writing classes before he left England. Other opinion would seem to confirm Golding's. Creative Writing is often ridiculous but may well be worth giving a try.

The second question as to whether we can actually implement Creative Writing is somewhat easier to deal with. In the present situation it is impossible that universities could afford to give the experiment a fair trial—even if there were a wholehearted sentiment in favour. Over 1975–7 most English departments had posts frozen when they fell vacant, and in some cases disestablished altogether. It is hard to see how an innovation which is expensive in time and money, not to say dubiously educational, could be put forward in this quinquennium or the next. More so since conventional wisdom is that the era of innovation in university teaching has come and gone. Nonetheless it is worth noting that it was in the early 1930s, during the worst of the depression, that Creative Writing got started in America. It seems possible that in times of hardship authors have trouble freelancing and are drawn to the institutions, initially on the institution's terms. Once in, courses are relatively easy to introduce on a casual basis, and they tend to become formalised in course of time. Something of this kind may happen in British universities over the next ten years, but at so slow a rate that it will certainly be overtaken by faster moving developments in the booktrade and the profession of authorship.

III

There is already a small corps of campus novelists in Britain—probably as many as there are novelists in publishing or in the BBC and many fewer than there are novelists in journalism. A list of full-time university-employed novelists would probably not include many more than David Lodge, Simon Gray, Gabriel Josipovici, Malcolm Bradbury, A. S. Byatt, Angus Wilson, Iris Murdoch, Dan Jacobson, J.I.M. Stewart, Rachel Trickett. With the exception of the recently retired Stewart, who continues, in one of his guises, the Dorothy L. Sayers tradition of elegant frivolity, all these novelists are serious. They are also academics who hold their jobs primarily by virtue of scholarly and critical achievement well above the average. In this last section, the present condition of the British university novelist is considered, in the presumption that it will not materially change in the near future.

Since the death of E. M. Forster the best known of the university novelists in this country is Angus Wilson, who has been a don for fifteen years. Wilson started late as a novelist (at thirty-five) and late as a university lecturer (at forty-five). Although he was invited to East Anglia, Wilson can be said to have earned his university place by academic rights; he is a distinguished critic, particularly of Dickens. But his conditions of employment are honoured ones, and might be thought near sinecure. He is a professor and has leave two terms in three (the average sabbatical entitlement is about one term in ten); and lives forty miles off-campus ('The Book Programme', BBC 2, 2.3.76). His teaching duties are very light, and take the form of a single seminar. Wilson, as he well might be, is 'grateful' for 'the kindness of the university' for whom he is as he over modestly puts it, 'a very minor celebrity'. He concludes: 'if one is going to be forced to do these things, I think perhaps it is better to teach at the university than it is to do very frequent reviewing or to be in the television world or to be in the editorial world of publishers' (Firchow *The Writer's Place*, p. 343). Wilson's opinions have to be taken in the context that he is, in a sense, *emeritus*. East Anglia treat him as they do because he is a very major celebrity. More typical are Malcolm Bradbury and David Lodge, who write directly in the tradition inaugurated by Kingsley Amis in *his* university days (Swansea, 1949–61). Bradbury and Lodge are campus novelists through and through, having spent practically the whole of their post-adolescent lives in universities. Not surprisingly, academic life has provided the setting for much of Lodge's fiction and all of Bradbury's in such acclaimed novels as: *The British Museum is falling down*, *Changing Places*, *Eating People is Wrong*, *Stepping Westward*, *The History Man*. Bradbury and Lodge's fiction is so closely linked with their academic experience that it often partakes of the *roman à clef*. Certainly Bradbury's first novel was a reverberating subject of gossip at Leicester (his first university and, none too mysteriously, the setting of *Eating People is Wrong*), for years after he left. So too with *The British Museum is falling down*, and University College London. One imagines that Lodge's *Changing Places* was pored over with some eagerness at Berkeley and Birmingham, and *The History Man* at East Anglia.

All these novels display an ingroup jokiness, a sense of shared jests among a coterie. The British campus novel easily converts to a kind of privileged literature, fully appreciated only by a few in the know.

One still, for example, meets academics who remember the work in progress *Lucky Jim* being read aloud to them by the author. *Lucky Jim*, which is dedicated to Philip Larkin (then a librarian at Leicester) has a number of jokes which, again, are only obvious to someone who knew Leicester in its University College days. (Doubtless a thesis will be written one day about that unfashionable institution's role in postwar fiction: it figures centrally in the fiction of Bradbury, Snow and Amis and in the poetry of Larkin.) Clique interanimation remains an essential part of the campus novel, whose authors regard themselves as part of a fraternity writing for each other. The dedication of Lodge's *British Museum*, for example, is to Malcolm Bradbury, 'whose fault it mostly is that I have tried to write a comic novel'. (Bradbury returned the compliment by dedicating *Possibilities* to 'my friend' Lodge.) The same novel has an extravagant number of donnish parodies of fiction—most clearly picked up by fellow teachers trained in dating exercises. Intertextual games are common in the academic novel, both here and in America.

All this has to do with a large objection: is the university, per se, a stultifier of fictional talent? Bradbury's three novels are, on the face of them, only as various as the turns of his career. *Eating People* is set in a University College (Leicester, where Bradbury was a student, 1950–53), *Stepping Westward* on an American campus (Indiana where Bradbury was a visiting professor, 1955–6), and *The History Man* at a new university (East Anglia, where Bradbury has been since 1965 and where he is now a professor). Three more various academic settings it would be difficult for a British academic to find. Yet, one asks, is there enough variety within universities as a whole, even if one were to go from Patrice Lumumba to Bob Jones via the Sorbonne? The answer might, of course, be 'yes' if one were actually talking about universities. But where the university novel is concerned 'university' tends to mean the English department, traditionally the quietest and most self-engrossed corner of the university.

David Lodge bears out this last point. Writing a mock 'Don's Diary' in *The Times Higher Educational Supplement*, Lodge expatiates on what is his most recent fictional theme: that the English English department (unlike the American) is a very undestructive element in which to immerse:

Monday. Intended to rise early to prepare today's teaching, but stayed up late last night watching trashy film on TV and overslept in consequence. No time for breakfast, let alone preparation. Bluffed way through tutorial at 10; 11–12 coffee and gossip in Common Room. Bluffed way through seminar at 12. Drank too many beers at lunch and fell asleep in chair afterwards. Late for lecture at 3. Stumbled through old dog-eared notes, almost as bored as students. Drove home with splitting headache, kicked dog and quarrelled with wife. Somehow one cannot imagine it in the THES though I daresay that in a campus novel it would not seem wildly improbable. (THES 6.2.76)

Certainly not improbable in Lodge's campus novels which deal with just such minor self-defeats, self-betrayals and lapses. But is it, one asks portentously, the stuff of fiction? Is there not a lack of necessary tension in the academic lifestyle? One may return here to the metropolitan V. S. Pritchett and quote his reservations in full:

Artificial worlds have a sterilising effect on writers. They begin to think of life in terms of specialised communities. There have, of course, been a number of rather good 'academic' novels, though awfully small in their scope. The curse of academic life is the watchfulness of one academic on another. Writers can be as bitchy as they like about one another, but they've got the whole of London or the whole of England or the whole of Europe to be bitchy in, and it does not really matter. But in academic life, the infighting goes on day-by-day, inch by inch, hour by hour. Their jobs depend upon it, the whole organization encloses them.

There is, of course, one great compensation which goes a long way to answering such objections as Pritchett's. The English university teacher-novelist is forced to become an expert in the theory of his craft. Novelists testify to the value of enforced critical expertise. As Lodge puts it:

As an academic critic and teacher of literature with a special interest in prose fiction, I am inevitably self-conscious about matters of narrative technique, and I believe this is a help rather than a hindrance. I certainly think that my criticism of fiction gains from my experience of writing it. (*Contemporary Novelists*, ed. J. Vinson and D. L. Kirkpatrick, London and New York, 1976, p. 833)

Antonia Byatt argues that her academic tasks are actually necessary for her fulfilment as a novelist:

I discovered, when I tried to give it up to write more, that I couldn't write if I wasn't teaching. I now teach at University College London . . .

the novelist Dan Jacobson who has just joined the department says he feels here part of a tradition, and that all this thought and talk is good for his writing. (T 9.6.76)

Bradbury echoes Byatt on the necessity of teaching: 'I couldn't, myself teach if I didn't write: I'm very doubtful if I could write if I didn't teach.' His reasoning is much the same as the other novelist's: 'Teaching is a relief because . . . it is human in intense ways, a line of primary relationship . . . I also feel the need to link criticism with creation, teaching and reviewing with the run of public cultural debate' (THES 5.3.76). One may have some doubts about the shimmering rainbow of staff-student relationships and it is easy to see how the Byatt-Bradbury belief in critical-creative reinforcement could in less sensitive hands lead to what Gore Vidal calls 'plastic fiction'. Nonetheless there is clearly a powerful defence here to allegations of dessication and sterility.

The argument then has two sides. The campus limits the actual fictional territory of writers at the same time that it widens a certain intellectual awareness. With this in mind one may consider one of the finest of university novels, Raymond Williams's *Border Country*. Williams's novel records the alienation and encapsulation of the self which the university produces in its more sensitive inmates. It is only when he returns home to his dying father that Matthew (Will) Price recovers a sense of personal reintegration by 'measuring the distance he has travelled'. And in writing the novel Raymond Williams is, one suspects, undertaking just such a measurement for himself. Williams, as one would expect from his critical writing, has a powerful grasp of the ways in which the academy obstructs the integration of province with metropolis, traditions with modernity, self with community. In essence the novel is a demonstration of how someone like Matthew Price (and by implication Williams himself) could never write a novel like *The Rainbow*; yet *Border Country* is, paradoxically, one of the nearest things to *The Rainbow* which modern times have produced.

The notion of the border country, of being uneasily between two worlds, is central to Williams's thought. In this respect one can quote the testimony of a colleague, more frankly Marxist than Williams: 'His particular social transition made him an extraordinarily "typical" bearer of some of the classic contradictions of the social formation: proletariat/bourgeoisie, region/metropolis, rural/urban.'

To which one could add 'university/outside world' (T. Eagleton, *Criticism and Ideology*, London, 1976, p. 24).

The divided nature of the campus novelist is a study by itself, and it is subject matter to which the self-conscious university novel is constantly returning. Malcolm Bradbury candidly admits to being 'schizophrenic'. Hence it is that his novels, all of which he conceived of as satirical of the new universities (university colleges, the American campus, 'new' post-Robbins universities), never seem to have conflicted with Bradbury's zeal and effectiveness as an educationalist in just those institutions. He joined a new university, at a time when the heat was strongest (this may be one reason why no fiction was produced between 1966 and 1975). He was instrumental in setting up one of the first American studies courses in Britain. His latest novel, *The History Man* shows the influence of his interdisciplinary activities, particularly his love (and latterly love-hate) affair with sociology. Bradbury is the most distinguished of modern literary sociologists with *The Social Context of Modern English Literature* (1971) to his credit and another collaborative scheme with the sociologist Bryan Wilson projected. The interdisciplinary ideal, again, was a formative element in the make-up of the new universities.

Yet, when one reads the novels—particularly *The History Man*—they seem an elegy for the destruction of old humane 'liberalism' by the 'cannibalism' represented by the new order, particularly the new order of universities. Taxed on this, Bradbury affirms that there is a mutually reinforcing benefit from positive action and negative reflection. It would require a peculiarly modish approbation of his own term 'schizophrenia' to accept this at face value. One is left with the constant sense that Bradbury is creating literature in the face of what he memorably calls the 'sense of absent literariness' in modern university life (T 7.8.76), its lack of what should be central to it, and is no longer. This, it would seem, is Bradbury's border country: the liberal university behind, the barbarous campus in front.

David Lodge, Bradbury's partner in campus fiction, seems to have solved his problem differently, by a kind of guarded, retreated pose. For him the university has seemed a kind of refuge. His whole career has been served in the rather staid, municipal surroundings of Birmingham. He seems remarkably firm minded about the way in which freedom has to be balanced against the administrative responsibilities which come with promotion. For a long time he was one of the most distinguished critics in England, yet one who was, surprisingly, not a professor. Only recently has he taken a personal chair (which carries less administrative duties). One cannot know, but it would seem likely that for the last ten years Lodge could have had any number of professorships in England or America, had he so wanted. But what he admires and covets most in the university set up is the provision of free time; the fact that one can avoid pressure and write novels and critical books, turn and turn about:

I am one of those who think that university teaching is a privileged profession though as the privileges are earned by a certain sacrifice of libido in youth and of income later I do not feel guilty about it. One of these privileges is being paid (however inadequately) to read and re-read great books. Another is certainly the sabbatical or study leave.... It is not only a question of having time to write, but of having a *continuous* span of time free, in which one's own work can develop a rhythm and thrust that can hardly emerge in something put together like a jigsaw puzzle in odd moments. (THES 6.2.76)

The advantages, to sum up, are time and a high level of theoretical discourse on the nature of fiction constantly about one. The cost is paid in psychic division, controllable schizophrenia, financial and emotional impoverishments. The cost, if we are to credit the novelists themselves, is not exorbitant.

In contrast to some of the other areas examined in this book, it is unlikely that there will be a close assimilation of British and American practice with regard to writers and universities. It is just possible that over the next decade British universities may move more towards American patterns and hence open up a wider gap for Creative Writing. But the possibility is diminished by the fact that American higher education flourishes in a much more expanded condition than Britain's—teaching anybody anything. Similar expansion seems remote here. Britain will continue teaching a select few students a select few subjects.

The British university will continue, in all probability, to offer a niche for a modest number of creative writer-critics. And the fact that they are professional critics and teachers will tend to establish them as importantly thoughtful practitioners. Their significance will not be in their number—which is unlikely to rise above a score—but in the links they make between theory and practice and the intellectual self-awareness they bring to their craft.

Trends, Mainly American

9 Paperback Revolutions

You pay nothing for my book, Sirs. You only pay for the binding.
Nineteenth-century advertisement

Anyone over the age of thirty has lived through an age of paperback revolution. Indeed it might be more precise to say he has lived through several. Penguins, established in 1935, were a notable starting point. From America in the 1950s came the higher pressured mass-market paperback, sold by saturation methods. At the same time and in the same place the quality paperback emerged, a form aimed at the growing college readership. Both these innovations have been adopted by the English booktrade; and even Penguins, the great originator, have sacrificed some of their individuality and conform to styles which would once have seemed barbarously American.

According to Publishers' Association figures, British paperback sales in 1976 were 150m, representing a value of £75m, on the home market (Bk 14.5.77). The British paperback accounted for some 30 per cent of booksales. In America in 1974 it was announced that for the first time more soft than hardback books were sold (NYTBR 15.2.76). We are used to paperbacks and one of the first questions a layman of the 1970s is led to ask about new novels is why they are expensively *not* in that form. Why, for example, should a new novel, which is normally read only once, be produced in a form which will long outlive its reader? (Libraries calculate that their hardback is good for some 150 issues.) A hardcover novel looks in better shape after fifty years than its owner is likely to. Why should fiction not appear first, rather than last, in cheap disposable paperbacks, low enough priced to be bought on thoughtless impulse? Why should one have to wait until a novel is distinctly un-novel and all reviews forgotten before one can afford to buy, say, three a week—which is what the public library regards as normal consumption? The questions are sharpened by the fact that the last twenty years reveal the paperback as a form peculiarly congenial to the novel. In *The New York Times Book Review* paperback bestseller list of 1975, of the sixty-six titles listed two-thirds were fiction, and the three 'supersellers' of the year were all novels (*Jaws*, *Fear of Flying*, *The Other Side of Midnight*; NYTBR 7.12.75). On a slightly loftier level, one could point to France and its rational tradition of publishing a book first in soft-back.

The trade's answer on these issues would seem to be sympathetic, worldly-wise and hopeless. In 1934 Geoffrey Faber observed: 'the experiment of issuing new novels at low prices in paper covers has been tried again and again; always disastrously' (*A Publisher Speaking*, London, 1934, p. 135). 'It has been tried,' says Anthony Blond, 'and it has never, never worked' (*The Publishing Game*, London, 1971, p. 85). Clive Bingley concurs: 'no firm has so far succeeded consistently in marketing successfully long-run low-priced novels or general books in paper covers unless they have first been issued in hardcover' (*The Business of Book Publishing*, Oxford, 1972, p. 26). The experiment is still tried from time to time, however. A recent venture which illustrates both the underlying aspirations and the apparently inevitable disappointments was the 'Midway' line, launched in Britain in 1973. This intended 'quiet revolution' was brought out under two imprints: Quartet Books (formed by ex-Granada employees) and Wildwood (formed by ex-Penguin employees). The project got the following lukewarm welcome in *The Author* (writers are generally reluctant to see the sum on which their royalties are assessed brought down):

All those dismayed at the diminishing market for new fiction will have been watching with interest, and some misgivings, the Midway experiment—the publication simultaneously with the hardback edition of a 'quality' paperback at approximately half the hardback rate. Quartet Books (four ex-Panther executives) published their first six midways in association with Hutchinsons in May, at prices from £1.25 to £1.50. At about the same time Wildwood House (two ex-Penguin directors) launched three titles in midway editions (priced at 95p to £1.10) in conjunction with hardbacks published by Secker, Hamish Hamilton and Deutsch. . . . It is too early to judge whether the experiment is successful. (Aut Winter 73)

The experiment in fact failed. The best one can say is that it has been tried again and still 'has never, never worked'. In Autumn 1974 *The Author* reported:

Disappointing news of the first novel-publishing year of Quartet Books and Wildwood House, aimed at enthusiasts for new fiction who couldn't afford (or wouldn't pay) hardback prices. Quartet launched a Midway edition of originals in soft covers: now it has had (for the time being) to cut titles to a handful with obvious commercial potentiality. Wildwood launched cheaper editions of new fiction published by other hardback houses: they have now jettisoned the project. The sales are depressingly low. Reporting in *The Bookseller* (July 6) Malcolm Oram disclosed that even a highly publicised novel such as Elizabeth Mavor's *A Green Equinox*, one of the four books shortlisted for last year's Booker Prize, sold under 1,000 copies of a Wildwood edition of 4,000 at £1.10: while it sold out in hardcover from Michael Joseph at £2.50 on a first printing of 2,500.

One can contrast this poignantly with the advertisements with which Wildwood launched their project in April 1973:

The Wildwood House fiction scheme was devised to encourage readers, writers, critics and booksellers to take new fiction as a serious contender on the shelves—to make new fiction more available, visible, accessible, and we hope profitable. Look for the distinctive Wildwood House covers which we hope will soon be a familiar draw to readers everywhere. (Bk 7.4.73)

The causes of the Wildwood failure are not easy to disentangle. But they could have saved themselves some trouble by looking at the first major midway experiment, that which took place in America some twenty years earlier. In 1950 the large and well-established firm Simon and Shuster proclaimed their intention to publish new novels in hard and soft covers simultaneously, at $1 and $3.50. They began with a batch of five of their new titles, to be brought out in tandem 'Essandess Readers' Editions'. Richard Simon argued: 'I have always felt as a consumer that books cost too much.' At the same time he noted: 'If we were to bring out a new book at only the lower price [i.e. $1] the public would feel that there must be something wrong with it' (PW 14.1.50). The two-tier Essandess combination would, it was hoped, make for a rational division of sales. The figures expected were 10,000–20,000 cloth, 25,000–50,000 paper covers. And since Simon and Shuster controlled and profited from both forms they would seem to have been on firmer ground than Quartet or Wildwood. Otherwise the scheme was conceived in exactly the same terms as the later experiment: 'Simon and Shuster has launched this project in the belief that... the potentially increased volume of sales will more than compensate for the author's lower royalty and the bookseller's lower per-unit profit'

(PW 22.4.50). The underlying commercial belief was that high prices for new fiction had left an underutilised sector of the market—the Essandess cheap editions would create purchasers where none had been before.

Trade opinion was, as *Publishers' Weekly* reported, 'divided.' A survey was taken and it broke down thus among booksellers: 44 per cent in favour, 25 per cent opposed, 16 per cent felt it was too early to judge, 15 per cent felt that it all depended on the book as to whether dual publication worked or not. (This last 15 per cent, the smallest group, proved right—which perhaps says something about trade wisdom.)

Simon and Shuster publicised favourable responses prominently. One was from a Californian who said that he could never justify books costing 'as much as the hat I wear for a year. . . . But now you have a cost commensurate with a necktie' (PW 22.4.50). The Essandess idea was favourably received by the universities, and may quite likely have laid some of the ground for the 'quality paperback' which Anchor launched so successfully in 1953, when Jason Epstein took an even bigger leap in the dark. Altogether there was vast interest and publicity in 1950 for this new cheap form of novel. The economic principle behind the scheme was widely and intelligently discussed in the trade and its journals. And Simon and Shuster did all they could to whip up similar interest in the general public. They put $50,000 into their advertising campaign, and took a full-page advertisement in *The New York Times* (17 April) to explain the experiment to potential purchasers. There was, of course, substantial bookseller resistance to be overcome. ('How can we survive', one dissenting bookseller asked, 'on a $1 item that may become a *substitute* for a $3 item unless we can *triple* our sales?' PW 15.4.50.) Nonetheless the first five titles got a good launch and there was no appreciable boycott.

From the first one title did outstandingly well. This was *The Cardinal*, by Henry Morton Robinson. It had advance orders of 158,000 soft and 85,000 hardcover and eventually went on to sell 435,516 and 152,879 respectively (PW 15.4.50), topping the best-seller list of 1950, and holding a position there in 1951. But the Essandess experiment depended on the success of all five if it were to pioneer a new pattern. Everyone had expected *The Cardinal* to be a smash hit, and the publishers had put it in as a frontrunner. The fact that the other four did not move was much more significant to the success of the experiment. Booksellers, always the weakest link, were annoyed to find libraries buying cheaper editions and strengthening them. Without the promised recruitment of new purchasers trade confidence in the scheme eroded. Though they tried, Simon and Shuster found it impossible to get the soft version sold through alternative newstand outlets, as was normal with mass-market paperbacks in the 1950s. The scheme, in short, failed, and the publishers blamed an anachronistic distributive system for the failure.

Nonetheless the Essandess experiment can be seen to have had one lasting effect on the American booktrade. It was obvious from *The Cardinal*'s individually huge sales that dual editioning could work where the title was a 'hot' property. The midway form came to be reserved for surefire novels. In this context we can understand Viking Press's later successful exploitation of the scheme with *Gravity's Rainbow*, by Thomas Pynchon, king of the American Campus in the 1970s. Viking brought out a tandem edition of the novel, printing 9,000 hardcover at $10, 75,000 softcover at $4.95. The sales were, apparently, good on both fronts. Bantam were encouraged to give $369,000 for the paperback rights (PW 7.5.73) and in April 1974 followed up with a 'true' paperback at $2.50. By 1975 there had been four printings and 290,000 copies were in print. Cape, who brought out a belated *Gravity's Rainbow* for the English market, followed the original Viking marketing with a paperback at £1.95 (c. 5,000 printed?) and a hardback at £3.95 (c. 2,000 printed?). How they did is not clear, but the estimated size of the English printings give some clue to the feasibility of dual publishing here. The British market and publishing institutions may be, in absolute terms, too small to handle a simultaneous softback, even of surefire successes. This is the view of Peter Owen, in a letter to *The Bookseller*, 7 July 1973:

> Sir ... I should like to comment on the suggestion that long novels should come out as paperbacks, selling at 75p or £1. With current costs, in order to achieve this economically, a minimum print order of about 12,500 would be necessary. Most hardback publishers do not have the distributive facilities to sell paperbacks to specific outlets and the conventional booksellers certainly could not assimilate such a large number of books.

It might also be argued that even the continental market was not big enough—except for the really guaranteed bestseller. The

Gravity's Rainbow experiment was not repeated on any significant scale until *Gulag Archipelago* in July 1974 when Harper and Row did 185,000 at $12.50 and 1,750,000 paperback at $1.95, both of which editions sold out simultaneously (NYTBR 21.7.74). But Solzhenitsyn would have sold in 1974 (the year of his exile) if his work had come out in Victorian three-deckers or monastic scrolls. No generalisation can be made from that example.

There remains a fund of optimism in the British booktrade on the subject of midways. In mid-1977 the small house of Allison and Busby had another try, with six novels in a dual edition at £4.50 and £1.95. There were a number of hopeful aspects; first, the scheme was modestly conceived. Secondly, the firm had both editions working for it (as Quartet, for example, had not), and the 'library' hardback edition was realistically highly priced at £4.50 (55p above the normal price). Among the first half-dozen authors at least two had a following (Michael Moorcock and Alexis Lykiard). Finally, Allison and Busby had £5,500 assistance from the Arts Council (T 4.6.77).

II

There are, it will be clear, a number of reasons which continue to frustrate ventures such as Essandess and Wildwood, or more radical schemes to switch entirely to paperback form. In Britain, particularly, the discouragement of libraries using paperbacks has also played a part. If the discouragement were relaxed arguably libraries might go in for more multiple and mixed ordering (one hard and five soft, instead of two hardbacks, for example). Another factor is the absence of conscientious paperback reviewing. At the moment authors do not feel really published if their work appears only in paper covers. Hardback remains, as one commentator puts it, 'an ego trip for authors because of reviews' (Bk 7.4.73). Press prejudice against noticing paperbacks is a factor which operates equally in America and Britain, and the invisibility piques those few quality novelists whose work does appear only in paperback. One can cite the case of Kurt Vonnegut:

Mother Night [Fawcett, 1962] and *Canary in a Cathouse* [Fawcett, 1961] and *The Sirens of Titan* [Dell, 1959] were all paperback originals, and *Cat's Cradle* was written with that market in mind. Holt decided to bring out a hardcover edition of *Cat's Cradle* after the paperback rights had been sold. The thing was, I could get $3,000 immediately for a paperback original, and I always needed money right away, and no hardcover publisher would let me have it. But I was also noticing the big money and the heavy praise some of my contemporaries were getting for their books, and I would think, 'Well, shit, I'm going to have to study writing harder, because I think what I'm doing is pretty good too.' I wasn't even getting reviewed. (*Wampeters, Foma and Ganfalloons*, London, 1975, p. 307).

In America, as Vonnegut proves, paperback originals are not uncommon and can be by major writers—though there are probably not many Vonneguts lurking in the drugstore racks.

Why not, then, go the whole hog? If publishers multilaterally abolished the hardback novel (as they abolished the three-decker in 1894) reviewers would surely be forced to notice new paperbacks. Addressing himself to the question of a second 'total' paperback revolution, Malcolm Cowley voiced the persuasive opinion that such a transformation would have apocalyptic consequences: 'the system would collapse, some other system would take its place since books are a necessity of our culture, but first there would be a period of anarchy during which all the bookish professions would suffer' (*The Literary Situation*, New York, 1955, p. 116). There is some warrant for these gloomy forebodings in past American literary history. In the 1840s, unscrupulous publishers produced pirated versions of novels as supplements to newspapers. Although the practice was stopped by intervention of the US mail, the immediate effect of the drastic price drop was unsettling and destructive in the extreme.

Cowley's apprehension of the paperback deluge fits neatly with the cherished conservatism of English publishing, which insists that hardcover publishing allows editorial freedoms and authorial excellences which the paperback, with its large-sale imperative, would not. The hardback is a kind of governing elite of the world of fiction. This belief was expressed by Sir Robert Lusty, an elder of the publishing world, addressing the Worshipful Company of Stationers and Newspaper Makers, in the annual Livery Lecture, in 1974:

Should publishing ever be confined to what can be done only in paperback it would be pop publishing of the most deadening kind. One of the major glories of book publishing, which must never be surrendered, is that it, almost alone, operates the media through which new creative talent nearly always finds first expression. No other media can achieve its ratings or its viability with so small an audience. That is why it is vital to publishing and to creative expression that the attainment of at least economic balance should be reached by editions much smaller than have become necessary today. (Aut Winter 74)

An area of confusion here, and a confusion relative to the Wildwood issue, is that 'paperback' is an imprecise term. Clearly 'midways' are not the same as Lusty's 'paperbacks'. What was hoped for in the Midway experiment was the creation not of mass-market products, but a modest reduction in the price of new novels with a corresponding modest increase in sales. One might borrow American usage to express this distinction. There, paperbacks are customarily divided into two categories: 'mass-market paperbacks' and 'trade paperbacks'. The first are, generally, fiction and wide-appeal books designed for non-bookstore sale, at rock bottom prices. The second are quality and specialist paperbacks designed mainly for bookstores; they are usually non-fiction (though some experiments in novels have been attempted in 1977; PW 20.2.77). Despite the emphasis on novels, Wildwood clearly aimed at the British equivalent of the trade paperback market.

III

Although paperbacks are a relatively modern form, little regarded in this country until forty years ago when Lane began to sell his uniform Penguins in Woolworth's, the issue they raise is a perennial one. Since 1832 English publishing of the novel has been marked by a reciprocation in which new novels are produced in a first form which is expensive and conservative in make-up, but capable of being experimental and adventurous in content. Meanwhile reprints (or 'nearly new novels') are, as regards titles, safe-choice unadventurous works which appear in a form that is strikingly innovative in marketing and technology—like the paperback.

This polarity was established when Colburn and Bentley introduced their reprint series, The Standard Novels, at 6s apiece, in 1832. This set a production sequence which lasted for sixty years. The new novel invariably appeared at 31s 6d, in three hardback volumes, and sold in relatively few numbers to libraries (though it was a Victorian joke that there was *once* a man who was reputed to have bought a three-decker for personal use). The reprint, following at two years or so, sold in large numbers, originally at a fifth of the three-volume price, to purchasers rather than institutions.

The hardback new novel, designed for the bookshop and trimmed down to one volume, made something of a comeback with the Net Book Agreement of 1898. The establishment of the 6s–7s 6d novel over the next thirty years laid the ground for a repetition of the reciprocal pattern in 1935, when Penguins appeared at 6d. Lane's series was given a boost by the war, representing, as it did, the most economical adaptation to the stringencies of wartime regulations. Penguins had a very good war. Just before its outbreak they had launched an ambitious series of more than 160 'Specials'. Sales were immense and on them the Penguin wartime allocation of paper was assessed. The war also muffled a growing resistance among publishers to licence Penguin reprints to compete with their own backlists and the abiding dislike of booksellers for any cheapening of the produce on which their discounts are calculated. One may contrast this with America where de Graff's Pocketbooks were given reprint licences at this time on the stipulation that the 25 cent editions should *not* be sold in bookshops (W. Jovanovich, *Now Barabas*, New York, 1964, p. 31). This accompanied the characteristic American pattern by which their paperbacks sell like magazines, in drugstore racks and newstands, strictly rationed as to the time they can occupy space. In England things were quite different for Penguins. They were free to mop up vacant space in the bookshops—not only that, they were welcomed. Other factors helped Penguins during hostilities to upgrade themselves as an institution. They were portable and easy to post, which made them the ideal wartime book. One would like to think, too, that their very uniformity made them that much more attractive to a nation in uniform. A number of commentators noted Penguins' propaganda value in preparing the nation for combat by a judicious selection of titles.

Booktrade history suggests that since the beginning of the industrial revolution there has been a certain polarity between the expensive new novel, and the cheap reprint, with each diverging into a separate identity and function. Penguins, however, may be said to have blurred this polarity. It was not just that they were successful; their outstanding feature was the way in which they, as reprint, usurped the market territory of their opposition, the new hardback book. Penguins' bookshop presence was their distinction; and this may well have come about from accidental factors, like the war and the way in which it dissolved certain resistances. Whatever the reason, Penguins came to enjoy a privileged status; their large sections were in effect, sponsored bookshops within bookshops. What gave them unprecedented success and cultural influence was less that they were revolutionary, in the common sense of the term, than that they became extremely orthodox. They were no longer Woolworth's 3d and 6d book: indeed they very quickly discarded that degrading image. They were paperbacks which sold just like hardbacks. The psychology of buying, handling and reading Penguins, especially in the period 1940–70, is interesting to recollect. There was no sense of dealing with an inferior object when, in a bookshop, one turned from the latest novel to the latest Penguin. Indeed, one might feel one was going up in the bookworld. Penguins' extraordinary intellectual respectability was most evident in the *Lady Chatterley* publication. Because it was put out by Penguin one could carry it openly in the early 1960s. (I remember at the same period being asked at Smith's newstand if I would like my New English Library *Carpetbaggers* decently wrapped up.) Penguins were kept and displayed by owners as proudly as hardbacks—while many an intellectual would have been ashamed to have had a row of Four Squares or Corgis on show in his living room. It was indicative in 1959 when an enterprising firm marketed a kit for converting one's Penguins into hardbacks (extremely ugly hardbacks, incidentally). Penguins even sold like hardbacks, from a backlist up to 4,000 strong. Penguins still have an unusually long life in metropolitan bookshops; they are not displaced by the latest batch from Harmondsworth, but take their place in an alphabetically ordered, exclusive bookstand. It was claimed in 1977 that 80 per cent of Penguin sales were still from the backlist (Bk 14.5.77).

When Penguins went to America, where they had a huge success, they repeated the English pattern by forming a base in campus bookshops, by far the most respectable bookshops in America. Over 50 per cent of their product is exported, and everywhere they go they take moral precedence over lesser paperbacks. In England Penguins' pre-eminence was founded on two main advantages: they had no need to fight for rack space; secondly they were under less than normal pressure to sell out or get out. (Up to half of American paperbacks are returned after an average rack life of fifteen days.) Nor did they need to advertise. Even their covers could remain modestly unillustrated, while other paperback imprints were forced to scream for attention. Finally the orthodox nature of Penguins' merchandising meant that they were free from the bane of paperback production, the need to have a smash hit every three months. A Penguin could wait on display almost as long as a hardback to find its discriminating buyer. And that buyer would, probably, seek it out methodically from the catalogue and the alphabetical system of arrangement, or by browsing undistracted by the promiscuous display of naked bodies or strident self-advertisement.

Penguin's hegemony led to authors and publishers vying to be their clients; even if, in some cases, it meant less money. In 1948 a consortium of the best quality publishers (Heinemann, Hamilton, Faber, Chatto, Joseph) joined to give Penguin first refusal of all their titles. This privilege was shored up by the exclusion of American books and influences, and the tight hold which Penguin, with the rest of the British publishing industry, held on the old imperial markets after 1947.

Penguin's position as market leader has been challenged in the last fifteen years on a number of fronts. There was the relaxation of the embargo on American quality paperbacks, books of marked intellectual adventurousness. There was the increasing importance of subsidiary rights to hardback publishers, which rendered them less high minded as to their disposition. Penguin have never, it would seem, led the field in the sums paid for the rights of bestselling titles. This was fair enough for as long as the paperback revenue was not vital to the first publisher; they could lease to Penguin and enjoy the compensatory glory of cultural benefaction. By 1975, however, things had changed. Now the paperback tail increasingly wags the hardback dog. 'For most general trade publishers', Malcolm Oram observed in 1975, 'the real "profit" comes not from home sales but from overseas and subsidiary rights sales.' The same authority quotes Cape as saying that 'if we had no share in subsidiary rights we should go out of business'. In Cape's case the subsidiary revenue comes to 10–15 per cent of their annual income, and the house is responsible for a sizeable amount of the new quality fiction published in this country (Aut Autumn 75).

The growing importance of the paperback market, as it passed the 100 million copies sold annually in the mid 1960s, 150m in the 1970s, and came to occupy over 30 per cent of the market has created eroding pressures for the old, genteel Penguin style. No one firm, however large, can monopolise that scale of business. Competitors have been thrown up and Penguin, in competing, has shed many of its unique features. There are now other mass producers in the field: Pan, Corgi, Panther, N.E.L. Pan, for example, came into its own with the Bond books in the early and mid 1960s. These regularly sold a million in paperback, and twice as many in America. (Pan claimed ten out of the first eighteen million-sellers in Britain were Bond novels.) In 1965 the Bond books sold 6m of Pan's 21m. They were, in a real sense, a breakthrough comparable in some ways to Lane's, thirty years earlier. Hitherto the million-sellers in paperback had been largely haphazard, lucky shots, sex soap operas, or long servers. (The first five were: *Lady Chatterley*, *Peyton Place*, *Saturday Night and Sunday Morning*, *Dam Busters*, *Odyssey*, Sp 8.5.64) The importance of the Bond books was that they revealed a new reliable market for a certain kind of book that was not trash and could be marketed as a 'brand name' (i.e. 'the latest Bond'). Pan's role was made easier for their not being encumbered like Penguin with any great cultural accountability. (Other lines, like the 1976–7 Panthers, seemed more inclined to meet Penguin on Penguin's traditional middle-high-brow territory.)

Evidence of Penguin's change is to be seen in almost any mid 1970s bookshop. Penguins no longer monopolise the most interesting titles, they no longer have smugly uniform covers which force the purchaser to read rather than scan, their new titles display is often more prominent than their old stock, in some cases they no longer have pride of place among the paperback racks.

Another factor affecting Penguin in this period was the author's growing demand for a higher share of his paperback earnings. This demand fell in the first instance on the hardback publishers, though it was transferred to the paperback licenser—especially in cases where the paperback licenser did not pay top prices. The traditional 50–50 per cent division had been under pressure since its inception in 1966. In 1975 it was announced that the authors had succeeded in making the division a matter of private negotiation with a norm of 70–30 per cent in the author's favour. In America, meanwhile, 100 per cent had already been achieved by one author (Susann, for *The Love Machine*, PW 2.4.73). There was no reason therefore to suppose that the 70–30 per cent division would be the last concession demanded.

This change in profits division accompanied a change in the hardback-paperback alliances. 'The country's paperback industry', Oram reported, in 1974, had undergone 'a flurry of expansive activity unmatched in its 38 year history' (PW 14.1.74). In the economic jargon of the 1970s, firms 'verticalised.' This was done by hardback firms starting their own paperback lines, or mutual incorporation. Though less violent in Britain, this repeated an American sequence of somewhat earlier when big conglomerates systematically acquired paperback subsidiaries (Random House/Ballantine, Simon and Shuster/Pocket Books, Harcourt Brace Jovanovich/Pyramid).

The new astringent and competitive conditions, together with a formidably organised opposition, will presumably serve further to bring Penguin into line with other paperback producers. Presumably, too, they will make more use in future of the Allen Lane hardback imprint along the lines of the Viking-Penguin combination in the US.

IV

The modern mass-market paperback is cheap not solely, or even mainly, by virtue of its intrinsic make-up (its paper back, perfect binding and imperfect paper) but because of its place in the production and marketing sequence. In this they display a whole range of differences from the hardback novel. Paperbacks, unlike hardbacks, are racked in a way which invites invidious comparison (up to 500 are visible, cover upward, at a decent Smith's outlet). Thus they compete in price with each other, and find floor levels more readily than hardbacks. Though there is no standardised price, competition keeps paperbacks at minimum cost—6d in 1935, 2s 6d in 1955, 6s in 1970, 40p in 1974, 60p in 1975, 75p in 1977. Selling at 75p the paperback will need to clear 15,000 to warrant a £1,000 advance to the author (Bk 14.5.77). Every title must be in some sense a best-seller. Selling and selling quickly are the primary aims. In this respect the paperback firms' activities are essentially different from those of the hardback publisher. More effort goes into selling and less into cultivating authors or improving manuscripts. Paperback firms spent an estimated £2.5m on advertising in 1977 and showed every sign of following the American pattern of exploiting the media to encourage sales. The aim is to spread up and down the market, overriding tight-knit readership groups. The bookshop and the library are not the main targets. What is aimed at is the American condition of the ubiquitous sales rack attracting a wide spectrum of purchasers.

A row of hardback novels on a shop shelf presents an uneven sight; some are differently sized, some of markedly inferior physical quality; a glance at the inside cover reveals that some are cheap because they are priced at the levels of years ago. Any new hardback novel is the consequence of a large number of single, individually considered decisions as to paper, type, proof correcting, publication dates, price, length of time in print. It is conceivable that we might have hardback novels all manufactured to the same size and typeface, on one quality of paper, with standardised cover styles, minimal handling of proofs, the resulting books all to be published once a month to fill standing orders from retailers. In other words a hardback standardised in just the way that the paperback is standardised.

Objections to this proposal are easy to envisage. It carries to an extreme the 'spawning' theory of publishing. It also exaggerates what has been called the 'cannibalism' of some forms of modern publishing in which fiction has no permanent existence, each monthly wave of books ruthlessly exterminating its predecessors. Many publishers might think that the costs of standardising new quality novels might be higher, in terms of the 'quality', than any returns in cost benefit.

V

The paperback sector is the most active in the current booktrade and what happens there will have consequent effects on the whole field, and thus on the future shape of fiction; to this extent 'revolution' is still the right word. In Britain we are, it would seem, committed. France is still in a position to resist the paperback revolution (see J. M. Bourgois—'the paperback revolution has not yet taken place in France' Bk 26.6.76). Arguably she would be right to resist; it has been asserted that the mass-market paperback is disastrous for French literary culture because its booktrade has no efficient means of distributing it (PW 5.3.73). What has happened, allegedly, is that paperbacks threaten to swamp bookshops, there being no wide bore marketing channel to bring them to the drugstore, corner shop or newsstand outlets which flourish in Britain and America. This has led the French publisher Jerome Lindon whose Editions de Minuit publish Beckett, Robbe Grillet and Butor to 'declare war' on paperbacks as 'corrupters of youth' and debauchers of bookshops. 'I think avant garde literature is going to suffer,' he says. More particularly the 2,000 or so copies of his softback Editions de Minuit will be overwhelmed by an avalanche of cheaper, meretricious fiction, confusing the discriminating buyer. (French literary culture is dominated by the élite 13 per cent who buy 75 per cent of French books. It is essential that this élite should remain loyal to their traditional reading matter; Bk 26.6.76.)

No substantial British publisher is in a position to declare war on paperbacks. Most have decided to join what they cannot beat. It is also the case, however, that Britain no longer leads the paperback field as it did in 1935. It is America which now makes the running, and it is to America that one must look for auguries of the British future.

Although they are nowadays drawing closer together there are important differences between the traditions of British and American paperback publishing. The American firm Pocket Books Inc. was formed by Robert De Graff in 1939. De Graff seems to have begun with the perception that 'book reading and book buying are two vastly different propositions' (PW 22.4.39). He wrote to *Publishers' Weekly* in April 1939 that:

> I notice you quote from the *Times Literary Supplement* that there are about twenty readers to a book. This is a good average, but I have been told by owners of circulating libraries that it is not unusual for detective stories in particular, to go out 50 or even 100 times. Has anyone ever considered publishing a special cheap edition for this market, which people would buy instead of lend, that would not interfere with the sale of regular editions?

From the first de Graff aimed at separation, rather than complementation. He also aimed at the popular, and as he perceived unexploited, end of the market.

De Graff was a publishing innovator. He had been in cheap reprint publishing for at least fifteen years before he launched Pocket Books. And he seems to have been the first to apply market survey techniques to the question. In 1938 he sent out 25,000 letters and questionnaires to book and magazine readers all over the country to see what they wanted. Fifty-two titles were provisionally offered, from which ten were selected on the basis of advance orders. The initial ten were: *Lost Horizon*, *Bambi*, *The Murder of Roger Ackroyd*, *Wuthering Heights*, *Enough Rope*, *Wake up and Live*, *Topper*, *The Way of All Flesh*, *Five Shakespearean Tragedies*, *The Bridge of San Luis Rey*. These came out in June 1939, at 25c. To them were added, later in the year: *The Good Earth*, Maupassant's Short Stories, *Showboat*, *A Tale of Two Cities*. There is a superficial resemblance to Lane's original ten—but with the addition of a broad streak of vulgarity and ingenuous, self-improving high-mindedness.

De Graff spent months of experiment with covers, paper and so on. He decided eventually on eye-catching covers (unlike Lane's sober Penguin uniform). Huge publicity was arranged and a controlled launch of the project in New York. From the start it was observed that twice as many re-orders came from newstands as from bookshops. This is how the breakdown went in the first New York period:

	Order	*Re-order*
Newstands	8,150	15,285
Drug and Cigar Stores	2,980	10,500
Bookstores	6,245	8,658
Jobbers	6,730	5,450
Departmental Stores	15,050	4,705
Specialist Book Stores	1,910	1,735
Rental Libraries	3,350	5,150
5 & 10 cent stores	1,000	100 (PW 29.7.39)

Following his early experiments de Graff inaugurated a sales method which was quite different from that of Penguins, who were already on the way to being institutionalised in bookshops. The de Graff technique is described, with some distaste, by Malcolm Cowley as: 'the saturation method.... Instead of being widely advertised the product is simply placed on sale, but in the largest possible number of outlets, and usually in impressive quantities, until it has been displayed to every potential customer and the market is saturated' (*The Literary Situation*, p. 103). It worked from the first. Pocket Books sold 10m in 1941 and doubled the figure in 1942. The saturation method which is still standard practice in America means that a customary 50 per cent of American paperbacks die mutilated, their covers torn off for return markers. (The sales average of the large firms ranges from 35 to 69 per cent of their total production, with Bantam claiming the lowest returns: PW 31.3.73). As Jovanovich says: 'each competes desperately for display space at the newstand or drugstore, and each is held in stock only briefly with a life cycle scarcely greater than that of a fruit fly' (*Now Barabas*, p. 30). *Publishers' Weekly* estimated in 1975 that the average duration of the paperback's shelf life was fifteen days (31.3.75). In Britain estimates of the main paperback firms' returns from retailers were estimated at 6–12 per cent. The British rate would thus seem to be a quarter, or less, of the American (Bk 14.5.77). In June 1977, however, it was noted that paperback returns in Britain were rising fast, although this was blamed on the recession rather than American saturation techniques (Bk 4.6.77).

As Cowley noted, what the American paperback represented was an invasion of territory previously held by magazines. The paperback competes with the magazine in terms of immediate illustrative appeal, recurrence and monthly novelty. It has, however, the advantage of a huge copyright backlist whereas the magazine has to come up with new features all the time. In the long term the irresistibly expansive paperback may be said to have conduced to the death of the American middle-market magazine—a loss which Cowley particularly regrets and which he sees as having cut the ground from under mass-appeal quality fiction (PW 17.9.73).

Others have taken exception to the American paperback industry. In 1956 Penguin Books regarded the waste-maker aspect of the American operation with a kind of snooty loathing:

> American paperbacks are said to have totalled 250m. But a further 80m were left unsold on the newstands and were returned to their publishers ... several million paperbacks had to be written off as 'premature returns', a trade euphemism for parcels returned to the publishers without ever being opened in the drug store or news stand. This cut-throat competition continues in one segment, and that the largest, of the American paperback industry, and will doubtless end with the elimination of the weaker members of the pack and the stabilisation of a handful of big operators making a good thing out of a noisome commodity with which, by comparison, the 'horror comic' is as innocuous as a parish magazine. (*The Penguin Story*, Harmondsworth, 1956)

There remains something profoundly offensive about aspects of the modern American paperback scene. There is, for example, the degrading use of authors as 'brand names'. This is the more irritating when the name is not that of the author of the novel in question, but a more famous writer endorsing the product. The consumers of paperbacks in America are nowadays often regarded as no more rational than Pavlov's dogs. Ballantine's version of Heller's *Something Happened* (a subtle and difficult novel) came out in a variety of three different coloured covers. It was discovered that the red cover sold better than the white or blue (NYTBR 2.11.75). For a while there was a palpable preponderance of red covers among would-be best-selling paperbacks. Covers generally have developed ever more ingenious gimmickry, and a walk through the paperback section of an American bookstore can be a dazzling experience. Most American paperbacks have computerised Universal Product Code markings, which they share with supermarket toilet rolls and cracker packets. The justification for the UPC marks is the growing importance of the supermarket to the paperback trade. Gothic fiction, sold via these outlets, is a major paperback category, and according to surveys 'the average hardcore Gothic reader . . . is a woman over thirty' (NYTBR 11.5.75).

Ruthless merchandising is not the whole story. American paperback firms have recently moved to reduce the waste in their distributive methods. Bantams, for example, have undertaken not to force feed their independent distributors (PW 31.4.76). In other ways Bantam, who are the market leader with over 20 per cent of paperback sales, have set out to improve themselves. They have led a trend towards backlists for, especially, college course authors. Increasingly American mass paperback houses, *The New York Times* reports, are reissuing and keeping in print the works of 'latter-day writers of high reputation' (NYTBR 14.9.75). In this practice American firms may be seen as coming closer to the old Penguin model while Penguin itself, ironically, moves closer towards their aggressive salesmanship.

One of the most interesting developments in the American paperback scene since the war is the evolution of the 'quality paperback' in the early 1950s. This is credited to Jason Epstein, then a Doubleday editor in his twenties. Epstein admits that Penguins were originally in his mind, 'but with unique features' (P. Nobile, *Intellectual Skywriting*, New York, 1974, p. 85). The main difference was that America, unlike Britain at that time, had a vastly expanding college population, with a chain of campus bookshops to service it. Norman Podhoretz, a contemporary of Epstein's, testifies to the innovativeness of Anchor Books, and their importance to the intellectual life that was forming in America at that time:

> Jason Epstein ... had been driven to start Anchor Books at Doubleday precisely by his unhappiness with the kind of stuff the firm regularly published and by the will to find a way—a commercially viable way it had to be—of exploiting his best 'liberal arts' talents. The brilliant solution ... rested on the perception that those ancient American enemies, commerce and culture, were on the way to being reconciled by social and economic change; or, to put it more concretely, that the growing population of the colleges, which on the one side was creating so much dissatisfaction, was on the other side creating a profitable market for serious and difficult books. (N. Podhoretz, *Making It*, New York, 1967, repr. 1969, pp. 161–2)

Discussing his career twenty years later Epstein claimed that the lines of distinction that he had helped draw between the 'trade' and the mass-market paperback have become 'increasingly obscure over the last ten years.' He went on to say that trade paperback is no longer a separate category (PW 16.12.74). Quality, he implied, was no longer confined to a top, narrow stratum of paperback book production.

Reading the trade journals in America and Britain it seems that no one can guess whether the hardcover novel has a future in a book world dominated by the mass-market paperback. Can the novel, in its diverse and traditionally published forms, co-exist with the paperback blockbuster, earning advances of half-a-million dollars, selling 10m copies in a few years and with a final revenue sufficient to justify the purchase or setting up of whole new publishing houses? Some possible futures may be tentatively advanced:

1. Hardcover novels will dwindle to 'library edition' status, or to privately printed collectors' items.
2. Hardcover fiction publishing will become more of a screen for paperback issue, taking on more of the functions of talent scouting and market testing.
3. A balance will be struck, keeping the two sectors in equilibrium, the paperback largely 'bankrolling' the hardback side of the industry, allowing it a relatively free hand to cater for various minority reading groups.

4. Hardbacks will be forced into a more competitive relationship with paperbacks and will be obliged to bring their costs down, either by production and distribution changes (e.g. midways and standardisation) or by some technological innovation.

5. A large, hitherto unexploited market for quality fiction will be uncovered, which will meet the minimum threshold requirement for paperback profitability. This might be an optimistic deduction to be drawn from the remarkable success of Melvyn Bragg's 'Read All About it', which had its first series in 1975. Although first put out by the BBC at an unpromising and unfixed hour this programme quickly proved itself capable of attracting an audience of millions interested, it would seem, in good paperback reading. By 1977 the National Book League had set up a scheme which would co-ordinate *Read All About It* selections with bookshop promotion (*Book News*, Spring, 1977). Similar optimistic deductions could be drawn from the introduction of paperback review sections in newspapers previously indifferent to cheaper literature (notably *The Times*, in April 1976).

In the future in Britain much will depend on the new, and potentially revolutionary, Viking-Penguin merger. This takeover by Britain's largest paperback house of one of the most prestigious American hardback publishers promised new permutations of British-American, hardback-paperback publishing. It is appropriate to finish with Penguin-Viking's stirring manifesto, issued immediately after the merger. If the future is as they see it, then it is rosy indeed:

The creation of VIKING-PENGUIN Inc. is more than a merger. It is also a portent. It is the way by which quality publishing can flourish in the years to come. PENGUIN and VIKING recognise that the forum for English language publishing is not the United Kingdom or the U.S.A. but the English speaking world. PENGUIN and VIKING have both long recognised—and now by their merger they emphasise—that the old rigid distinctions between hardcover publishing and paperback publishing are becoming obsolete. PENGUIN and VIKING know how to publish every kind of book, in any appropriate form or shape, in every part of the world—and how to sell these books everywhere. (Bk 15.11.75)

10 Packaged Literature: Book Clubs and Genre

Ever since the eighteenth century reader-combination has been a standard response to the excessively high-priced new book. The first massive manifestations of the combining impulse were the vast circulating libraries of Victorian England. A main factor in their hegemony was the exorbitant price of new fiction, higher than it has ever been before or since at 31s 6d. Interacting with the guinea and a half peak-price were the recent concentration of readers in huge urban areas, and the dramatic improvements in transport, communication, delivery and advertisement systems in the nineteenth century. Fiction was suddenly convenient to supply and inconvenient to afford. Commercial libraries and book clubs need advanced communications and an organised mass market; they also need a high shop-price for books, which drives customers their way. One can trace their prosperity in a direct line with technical innovation, from the penny post in 1839 to the Honeywell computer of the Book of the Month Club in the 1970s: prosperity which has never been threatened by any competitive price reductions in new fiction.

Libraries operate by multiple usage and bookclubs by the economies of scale which are guaranteed by the pre-purchase contract which every member must sign. Nonetheless they may both be taken as products of the same technologically mature cultural environment —the booktrade, we may say, in its industrial phase. As reflected in the books they issue their main characteristic is that they have a sure apprehension of their readerships and homogenise them into vast units, with confirmed tastes and predispositions. Like-mindedness among subscribers is what ensured commercial libraries', and what ensures bookclubs' profits. Hence they encourage like-mindedness. In this they differ from the modern public library which tends, on the contrary, to heterogenise its members and to maintain a diversity of minority readerships. The public libraries have no commercial interest, and can defy their patrons' majority appetite for purely popular reading matter. Viewed historically we may see that the large commercial library of the nineteenth century was superseded not by the public library, but by the large commercial bookclub of the twentieth century. In modern times Mudie would have run a book-club. He would not have found the task very different from what he was used to. Both the commercial circulating library and the book-club are packagers who will flourish when books are easily accessible but more expensive than consumers would like. The only difference is that in modern conditions, where postal delivery and mail-order have the edge over personal collection, the bookclub is the dominant form. Short of some drastic technological revolution the bookclub seems likely to maintain its dominance for the foreseeable future.

It is a feature of the subscription libraries of the past and of present day bookclubs that they foster a commercially protective intellectual timidity ('Mudieitis' as the Victorians called it). The spirit of fiction has often been depressed by their insistence that the author defer to family readership and supply the average member with what he demands. Nowhere is the bookbuying customer more right, and his taste less resisted. Examples of the 'play safe' philosophy are seen in any number of current advertisements. The following, for example, appeared in *The Bookseller*, 14 April, 1973:

AMERICAN MISCHIEF. Alan Lelchuk. Most praised, Damned and Talked About Novel of the Year. Book of the Month Club Selection in America. A Rare Event for a First Novel.

Rare because first novels are riskier than those by established, brand-name authors. Other 'rare events' cynics would say, are the selection of overtly high brow novels, novels with genuinely contentious political themes or any work which may be feared to disturb the somnambulistic reading preferences of the mass reading public.

II

The leader in book club activity is, again, the United States; though the book club idea seems to have originated in Germany after the first world war, as an ingenious commercial exploitation of shortage. The American book clubs had a somewhat similar early history. Although formed a couple of years before it, their breakthrough came in 1929 with the calamitous depression. This had the effect of stripping out a large part of the American bookselling network, while generally the demand for books remained unchanged as it always does. Britain was never as badly hit as the US and the unbroken continuity of British bookshops has meant continued inhibitions on cut-price selling. America in the early 1930s found herself a continent without many bookshops or many inhibitions on how to sell books. This cleared the way for unrestricted mail-order and organisations like The Literary Guild which now, unironically, advertises itself as 'America's Bookshop'. Or, as Harry Scherman of Book of the Month Club put it in the late 1930s: 'the bookclub uses America's 40,000 post offices as book outlets'. The robustness of the American bookclub is in a sense the measure of the puniness of the American bookshop.

The American Book of the Month Club was founded in April 1926 (its great rival the Literary Guild apparently began operation in December of the same year: there is, however, some doubt about dates here, see C. Lee, *The Hidden Public*, New York, 1958). BOMC's techniques were founded partly on German precedent, partly on Scherman's previous experience in the book mail-order business (where he sold 48m volumes of The Little Leather Library). Scherman was essentially an entrepreneur. His inventiveness and imagination were devoted not to the selection of books, but to their distribution. To make up for his editorial inadequacies he hit on the brilliant and everywhere imitated idea of a panel of hired judges. These judges were selected to reassure the customer, while at the same time representing the whole range of club membership. In this way the first panel was composed of: Dorothy Canfield Fisher (woman novelist, representing the sex which has always made up a large portion of bookclub subscribers), Heywood Broun (nationally known columnist), William Allen White (country editor, to represent the Midwest taste; provincials have always figured largely in bookclub membership), Henry Seidel Canby (former Yale Professor, the touch of class), Christopher Morley (bestselling essayist, playwright and novelist).

Harold Guinzburg, the head of Viking Press, had similar ideas for the Literary Guild, though his board was rather higher toned (it included Carl Van Doren and J. W. Krutch—internationally known literary scholars). The Guild, however, was slower to take off than BOMC and Guinzburg was eventually obliged to sell it off to Doubleday under whom it has become a bookclub giant.

At the end of its first year BOMC had 60,000 members (a period, incidentally when subscribers were obliged to pay their own postage);

900,000 members in 1946; 1.25m members in 1976 (IHT 20.4.76). In the year ending June 1975 BOMC earned $4,352,861 on 12m books taken by its membership. The BOMC spends $12m a year on promotion, advertisement and circulation. It is reckoned that $12 must be spent to recruit every single member. The membership is probably solidly middle-class, middle-aged, middle-America; the stodgy heart of the reading public.

It is instructive to look back at *Publishers' Weekly* for 1929, to see the fears which the American booktrade felt at the growth of the clubs. By this time the general reaction, initially passive, had become savagely hostile. American publishers attacked the 'jury system', the emphasis on 'single books' which they felt would impoverish and stereotype literary taste. The bookclubs, it was felt, imposed mendacious standards: 'there are no "best books"' it was asserted. Literature does not compete with itself like other products. Extreme exception was taken to the criticisms of bookshop service in bookclub advertisements. And the American Booksellers' Association, especially, objected to the 'centralising of power' by the clubs; power which, it was feared, would wrest a large part of the booktrade away from its traditional and responsible operators.

Looking back on the occasion of its fiftieth anniversary, BOMC was by no means ashamed of itself. The board chairman Alex Rosin declared, on the contrary, that his club had done much 'to avert an intellectual famine in this country' (IHT 20.4.76). Certainly the impression given by present bookclub activity in America is one of healthy competitiveness, with profuse choice for the discriminating consumer and no great regimentation of taste. (The situation is somewhat less healthy in the UK where one bookclub group, Book Club Associates, dominates). American clubs offer large discounts. They are remarkably swift in responding to, or anticipating, good critical opinions. Thus, for example, a fortnight after Paul Theroux's *Family Arsenal* received an approving review on the front page of *The New York Times Book Review*, a full back-page advertisement for BOMC offered it at 25c, as an inducement bonus for new subscribers. The general service offered by the large clubs is fairly indicated by a 1976 advertisement for the Literary Guild, which has always been the stronger of the big two on fiction:

You get top bestsellers at up to 40 per cent off prices of publishers' editions.... You enjoy even greater savings on Bonus Books—up to

80 per cent off publishers' edition prices. You never have to buy a minimum number of books a year. (NYTBR 1.2.76)

The same advertisement offers any four books out of twenty listed for $1. Many of the titles are those currently on *The New York Times* hardback bestseller list, elsewhere in the supplement. Looking at the Sesame's cave advertisements which decorate the back and middle-spread pages of *The New York Times Book Review* it is hard to see American bookclubs as starving the reading public of titles.

III

In Britain bookclubs have always met chilling resistance from the Publishers' Association. When the Book Society was started in 1929, with a guaranteed sale of about 10,000 copies per book in the early 1930s (F. W. Swinnerton, *Authors and the Book Trade*, London, 1932, p. 134), it was seen as a barefaced attempt to rob booksellers of their easy business—'that section of our turnover which is compensation for all the non profit making business we must do' (R. J. L. Kingsford, *The Publishers' Association*, Cambridge, 1970, p. 134). The same objections were null in America, where trade associations had lost much of their combined power after the slump.

The Book Society was less offensive than its American counterparts in that it operated simply as a mail-order bookseller, selling its special editions in conformity with the Net Book Agreement. In general outline, however, it followed American precedents (it had, for example, a selection committee, headed by J. B. Priestley and Hugh Walpole). The major British innovation in the field occurred with Gollancz's Left Book Club, founded in 1936, which profited by the political excitement of the era and rose to a membership of some 60,000. More orthodox clubs were set up at the same period by the Readers' Union and Foyles. It was, in fact, Foyles' eagerness which precipitated disciplinary action by the Publishers' Association when they rashly brought out a 2s 6d club edition of an H. G. Wells novel immediately after conventional 7s 6d publication. This led to the association insisting that special book club editions should wait 'at least six months after first publication'. There followed increasingly tricky restrictions on prices, delays and discounts, settling down to a normative 7s 6d/2s 6d ratio and a twelve month delay for fiction, with a bar on first publication in any book club edition (See Kingsford, *The Publishers' Association*, pp. 134–8).

Until 1968 no English bookclub edition could be issued until this one year delay elapsed, with the exception of religious and political items. In 1968 simultaneous publication was finally allowed, with a 35 per cent club reduction for fiction 25 per cent for non-fiction. Nonetheless the majority of British clubs still tend to be reprint oriented. Effectively the only simultaneous fiction clubs in 1976 were the Literary Guild, the Mystery Guild and the New Fiction Society. Looking back over the fifty years one may draw the deduction that British book clubs, and their market, has tended to fall into American ownership (and latterly German) simply because trade organisations persistently stunted domestic evolution out of loyalty to the traditional bookshop system. And where the British trade has been most passive and inert, foreign penetration has been most effective. This is seen vividly in the case of World Books/Literary Guild, currently the largest 'British' bookclub. Up to the 1960s the parent of this British bookclub was the Reprint Society, owned entirely by British publishers: Collins, Cape, Chatto, Murray, Macmillan and Heinemann. This had been profitable enough, one gathers, as a receptacle for the consortium's bestselling titles. But when things began to go wrong in the 1960s: 'they reacted defensively, and with true publisher's caution. Instead of examining the causes of the decline the publishers concluded that television was taking away their members, and when a buyer appeared, the Reprint Society was sold' (Grd 27.1.76). The buyer materialised as the multi-national Literary Guild (W. H. Smith and Doubleday, otherwise Book Club Associates). After a battle with Robert Maxwell's British BOMC, the Literary Guild emerged as the country's single large simultaneous club, able to take advantage of the licence which the PA issued after 1968 (World Books retained the original reprint function, providing an outlet for the Literary Guild unsold books). And, of course, the Literary Guild is closely modelled on its American namesake. By the tenth anniversary of its parent, W. H. Smith-Doubledays' Book Club Associates, Literary Guild had sold close on 6m volumes (Bk 6.3.76). In the same anniversary year a cloud appeared on its horizon with the news that the massive German Bertelsmann operation was going to buy into the British market, bringing with them the techniques pioneered in Europe (including co-operation with bookshops). The efficiency of these techniques was attested by the fact that German book clubs' membership is at least four or five times as high as that in Britain (Grd 28.1.76). The scene seemed set for a new era of competition. As the *Sunday Times* reported in January 1977:

A shake up in the British book club business has followed hard on the heels of the news . . . that Germany's giant Bertelsmann company is to establish a book club operation here. The British Printing Corporation has agreed to sell the four book clubs run by its Purnell Book Services subsidiary to Book Club Associates, the group jointly owned by W. H. Smith and Doubleday. BPC does not conceal that the threat of more intense competition triggered its decision. (ST 30.1.77)

For the moment the Literary Guild is the largest UK bookclub dealing in new fiction. Its style is described by Martyn Goff (who runs the smallest, hence the slight acid tone):

The Literary Guild is the main simultaneous book club offering fiction as well as nonfiction. Over the past 12 months (i.e. 1975) which comprise a 13 cycle series of choices, they have selected six works of fiction against seven non-fiction. Actual sales of novels are comparable to non fiction, a Literary Guild choice may well add 50,000 to either. Occasionally it chooses a mildly highbrow novelist like Iris Murdoch, but what their readers really seem to want is Alastair Maclean or Frederick Forsyth. Even in the case of such popular writers, the order from Literary Guild has a real effect on the title's publication: it is probably larger than the whole of the rest of the printing which means that it will have a substantial downward effect on the publishing price. (Grd 28.1.76)

Goff is right to stress the other downward effect which is exerted on quality (especially in that damning phrase 'mildly highbrow'). Book clubs assume home and hearth stability in their subscribers (an address and some degree of contractual responsibility is essential). What they aim at is tacitly communicated by their advertisements. Customarily these display prosperous, commuter-belt breadwinners, with literate wives and intellectually curious children. A prominent Literary Guild advertisement in 1975 in the Sunday colour supplements showed avuncular Frank Muir, engagingly bourgeois, surrounded by books which, one was sure, decorated a front-room somewhere in Gerrard's Cross. Others showed two-car families, standing in the gardens of their mock-Tudor houses.

A lot can be learned from such pictures and the cultural ideology which underlines them. The book clubs (especially the Literary Guild) do not offer that much of a bargain for the limitations they impose. Why do close on a million people belong to the book clubs, then? A likely reason is the anxiety which most people feel in shops where choices involving taste are concerned. One can quote Margaret Drabble's justification for belonging to a book club: 'it enables one to make little leaps into the unknown—and without the panic of choice that sometimes brings one out of shops (more often clothes shops than bookshops) empty-handed' (Obs 28.9.75). The book club is equivalent to the mail-order catalogue—one can make choices in private; moreover it sanctions those choices by pre-selection through the committee of experts, whose main function is not to advise (in the manner of *Which?*) but to reassure; hence Frank Muir and his pipe. Such comfort figures and panels are an important part of the bookclub psychology. In this way the bookclubs occupy a cultural plane which is totally insulated from the review which presupposes individual decision making. There is a strong drive towards automatism; £7m spent on advertising each year (Grd 28.1.76) conditions readers into making the proper, unison responses. This, if anything, is the culturally sinister feature of the book club habit—that it is a habit, not a free intellectual act. The defence usually put forward by the clubs, that the bookworld has become too large and complex for the individual to cope with single-handed, is belied by the public libraries. These have a huge and bewildering assortment on open display—yet patrons browse quite happily for hours; and usually they have little idea what they want before they go in. It would seem that the book clubs appeal to some mysterious neurosis of modern consumerism; where purchase is concerned we want to have our range of choice taken away from us rather like the chorus in *Murder in the Cathedral*.

IV

Another feature of the increasingly 'packaged' nature of all fiction —including the quality novel—is the advance of 'genre' or the categorised product. By 'genre' is meant such familiar forms as Science Fiction, the detective novel, Gothic etc. Genre in fact takes in a majority of the novels sold in this country. Genre is a capacious term covering many levels of quality. At one extreme there is the Woman's Weekly Romance Library at 10p a volume—comic books without pictures. At the other extreme there is near-classic literature by writers such as Greene, Hemingway, Chandler. It will help in the first place to identify some of the main features of genre. It is popular; it is profitable; it is formulaic. Characteristically the genre writer thinks of the market first, his artistic ego second. Spy-thriller writer Alistair MacLean (21 books in as many years, estimated world sales 128m in 1976) declares as his credo: 'I don't write for myself. I write for my public' ('The Book Programme' 4.5.76). Genre often has an initiated and devoted public who organise themselves as fans (viz. the 'fanzines' published and circulated among devotees of science fiction). It is marked by mechanical reproduction. One thinks of John Creasey's 560 books in forty years. 'Carter Brown' (i.e. Alan G. Yates) a sub-Spillane male-action writer, has a master-contract to produce six 120-page novels a year. Barbara Cartland has 160 or more titles to her credit. Robert Silverberg, a science fiction novelist, made himself a dollar millionaire before the age of thirty by his prolific writing. John D. MacDonald is credited with 65 titles and sales of 67m. It is for such writers, as Kurt Vonnegut (sometime sf novelist) points out, that the electric typewriter was invented. Not for the genre novelist the agonies of composition or the luxury of second drafts.

Genre incorporates a high ratio of familiar to strange elements. Habitually it eliminates the bewilderment associated with avant garde and experimentalism. It specialises in books without shock. The consumer of genre likes what he knows. If, as Ezra Pound says, the modernist's motto is 'make it new' then the genre author's motto is 'make it the same'. The stereotyping tendency was brought to its highest pitch in such productions as *Ellery Queen's Mystery Magazine* (offering what it called the *crème du crime*) which made a practice of heading every story with the 'editor's file card' which gave Author, Title, Type (e.g. Crime, Detective, Suspense, etc), Locale, Time, Comments. Genre fiction is, characteristically, convention-governed. Plot automatism is common, increasingly so as one goes down the scale into pulpier depths. One knows there will be ultimate detection, marriage for the heroine, defeat of the bug-eyed-monster. There is a soothing quality to much genre fiction; a high incidence of what Q. D. Leavis calls 'living at the novelists's expense'. Occasionally there is some pseudo-daring and Wilbur Smith's male-action novels are banned in South Africa, for example, or James Bond is accused by Tass and *The New Statesman* of deep cultural depravity. But generally the material is bland, despite its claims to unbearable excitement. Similarly genre may have a superficially impressive specialised knowledge as in Dick Francis's racing stories, or Peter Benchley's underwater melodramas. But in the event there will be nothing to task the reader's capacities. Genre's blandness goes together with its international acceptability. Often it is of multi-national origin. 'Carter Brown', mentioned earlier, is an Australian living in England, writing detective stories set in the United States, largely printed in Hong Kong, and bestsellers in Europe (especially West Germany). James Bond was probably Britain's best-ever literary export.

V

For most of the last 150 years there has been a fairly distinct gap between quality fiction and genre. Clearly there have been occasional convergences: Thackeray and the silver fork novel, Wilkie Collins and the early detective novel, Graham Greene's 'entertainments', for example. Some writers of what we would normally think of as quality fiction have cold-bloodedly interbred with the lower form particularly in America. Raymond Chandler, when he was fired from his job in the oil business in 1933, at the age of forty-four, set out to learn how to write detective fiction. As his biographer M. MacShane tells us, for five years Chandler made a precarious living as a writer for *Black Mask* and other pulp magazines. As late as 1938 three stories he sold to *Dime Detective* earned him only $1,275—about one-tenth of what he earned as an oil executive. Not until spring 1938 did he begin to write his first full-length novel, *The Big Sleep*, on which his subsequent reputation was founded. Chandler went on to win golden opinions from respected literary critics and could even speculate on joining Faulkner, Steinbeck and Hemingway (all of whom had some connection with genre as well) as a Nobel Prize-winner. He did not, of course. But his achievement as a novelist is acknowledged and this achievement is securely based on his voluntary apprenticeship in the lower ranges of genre,

There are contemporary English novelists who can also be cited in this context. Kingsley Amis has frankly stated his interest in genre:

I lament what I take to be a trend against the genres. It might well be agreed that the best of serious fiction, so to call it, is better than anything any genre can offer. But this best is horribly rare and a clumsy dissection of the heart is so much worse than boring as to be painful, and most contemporary novels are like spy novels with no spies or crime novels with no crime, and John D. MacDonald is by any standards a better writer than Saul Bellow, only MacDonald writes thrillers and Bellow is a human heart chap, so guess who wears the top grade laurels. (*What Became of Jane Austen?* London, 1970, p. 69)

'One day', Amis wrote in the early 1970s, 'I may tackle a straight science-fiction novel and a straight detective story' (*Contemporary Novelists*, ed. J. Vinson and D. L. Kirkpatrick, London and New York, 1976, p. 44). He soon did so. In fact his raids on genre are pretty well comprehensive. He wrote a James Bond book, *Colonel Sun*, in 1968; a ghost story, *The Green Man*, in 1970. In 1973 he produced a 1930s detective novel, *The Riverside Villa Murders* and in 1976 a straight science fiction novel, *The Alteration*. He has also ventured into the television world with a script for *Softly, Softly*, the police series. He still has the romance and historical novel left, though these specifically feminine forms he may prefer to leave to Elizabeth Jane Howard (who has written for *Upstairs, Downstairs*).

Amis seems to be working from his own preferences and prejudices in embracing genre. In America the situation is more acute, and the choices to some extent forced. Some young writers actually claim to have turned to genre because all other avenues are blocked off. Barry Malzberg, the brightest of the young science fiction writers is a case in point. His bitter recollection is worth quoting at some length:

I realised by June of 1965 that it would be impossible for me to make a career in what was my field of choice: as a literary writer. The quarterlies were impenetrable, the coteries omnipresent, the competition murderous, the stultifying control of the publishing houses' literary editors absolute. If I was ever going to achieve an outlet as a writer of fiction I saw I would have to go to the commercial markets, the mass or genre markets that is to say, and while partially converting myself to the strictures of category fiction *sneak in* my literary intentions. Science fiction was what I chose because from the outset science fiction seemed to be that field where one could sell stories of modest literary intention with the least amount of slanting: one could, if one touched the base of stricture, be paid a living wage for somewhat ambitious work.... Almost from the beginning I was a 'success.' (FSF Apr. 76)

In ten years' writing Malzberg has 23 novels to his credit, under his name and that of M. O'Donnell. A *sine qua non* of sf 'success' is rapid production.

If public libraries reduce their indirect patronage of general quality fiction it is likely that many young British writers will be obliged to follow Malzberg's practice, 'sneaking in' their literary intentions while deferring to the strictures of those genres that admit some literary qualities.

11 Independent Publishing

You must know that what protects you is neither your great humanity nor your great art, but your mercantile value to world corporate enterprise.
Warning message from the American *Small Press Review* to Alexander Solzhenitsyn on the publication of *Gulag Archipelago*

The man with his own press is a part of America's literary heritage. The US remains the prime exemplar of the more resolute forms of authorial independence considered in this chapter. What Britain does in this field tends to follow what is observed to have been done across the Atlantic.

The notion of self-publishing is itself a rather slippery one, since no-one can take on *all* the functions involved in publishing. I take 'independence' here to be not primarily a matter of getting printer's ink on the fingers, or of peddling one's literary wares on the pavement; though these sometimes come into it. Finance is the key element. If the conventional publisher has one inalienable function, it is as a provider of risk capital. The fact that the necessary capital and risk are so high in the case of the novel explains why it has been largely a monopoly of commercially orthodox producers and, therefore, so prone to various commercial prostitutions. (There is no poetry equivalent to the detective novel, the pornographic novel or the western romance.) Despite the financial problems, however, there have been and continue to be brave experiments in the independent publishing and self-publishing of fiction, some of which are considered here.

Notable American self-publishers in the nineteenth century were Walt Whitman (he personally set up the 1855 *Leaves of Grass* and distributed the work), Washington Irving and Mark Twain, who published the bestseller *Huckleberry Finn* in 1885. Later American naturalists were often forced to self-publish by the timidity of commercial firms. Stephen Crane's *Maggie: A Girl of the Streets* was published by its author with a borrowed $700. In 1905–6 Upton Sinclair's exposé of the Chicago stockyards, *The Jungle*, was turned down by five regular publishers (too much 'blood and guts'). Sinclair and some friends formed a syndicate to publish the novel, raising $4,000 on pre-publication subscription. Jack London wrote a pamphlet in support of the work. It so happened that a commercial publisher appeared at the last minute and engaged to bring out a simultaneous edition, but Sinclair continued through his life to publish work independently when commerce boycotted his controversial writing. (He also had work unacceptable to American houses published by the State Press in the USSR.) Lawrence was forced into self publication in America (*Women in Love*) as were, for different reasons, the lesser American novelists Zane Grey and Edgar Rice Burroughs. (In financial terms Burroughs is probably the most successful self-publisher ever; see the editor's opening chapter in Bill Henderson's *The Publish-it-Yourself Handbook*, New York, 1973, from which the above material is taken.)

American habits of independence were exported to Paris in the 1920s and 1930s with spectacular success. Paris between the wars is, in fact, the golden age of the unprofessional publisher. Although British writers and publishers were also involved, the expatriate literary renaissance in between-wars Paris is primarily an American affair, dominated by Sylvia Beach, Robert McAlmon, Harry Crosby, Ezra Pound, Hemingway, Gertrude Stein, Henry Miller. In this way one of the richest sections of American literature came into being independent of any contribution from conventional American publishers. (For the full account of this episode see Hugh Ford, *Published in Paris*, London, 1975.)

Americans were directed to Paris in the first place by prohibitions, literary and alcoholic and by the highly beneficial exchange rates in a war-exhausted Europe. This did not just mean cheap wine, but a relatively painless way of financing the production of literature—especially its more expensive varieties like avant garde fiction. In France the expatriate found a mature tradition of simply hiring a master printer and an artist friend for limited editions, thus short-circuiting the orthodox publishing process and liberating the writer from both employer's control and reader's censoriousness. A whole generation of writers was thus subsidised by the franc-dollar rate and emancipated from a temporarily puritanical America. For the first time, almost, fiction could be easily produced by the self-publisher or the independent publisher, and so could long, novel-length poetry, the imaginatively illustrated book and the distinguished translation.

Arguably this was one of the largest disinhibitions of modern times.

There is an amateurish quality about some of the operations of the Paris publishers. Nonetheless in terms of other kinds of expertise the activities of these independents and self-publishers surpassed anything that orthodox business publishers of the English speaking world could manage. This is not simply the case with such *editions de luxe* as came from Harrison of Paris. On a purely functional level the Paris publishers were admirably expeditious. *Ulysses*, the first major production of the era, is a case in point. Sylvia Beach was quite inexperienced and unqualified when she offered to publish Joyce's rejected and morally persecuted manuscript. Her Shakespeare and Co bookshop was barely profitable on a smallish turnover (1921 figures: expenditure 24,858,000 fr. income 25,738,550 fr. Ford, *Published in Paris*, p. 12). Yet she contrived a first edition of 1,000, eventually producing some 28,000 copies of the novel before the copyright was transferred. Her inevitable and initial problem was finance, which she solved by the antique method of subscription pre-payment (always a favourite mode of raising funds by independent publishers). Most important of all, Beach contracted a French printer, Darantière, who was infinitely patient with Joyce's massive proof alterations, allowing him up to five stages with which to continue composition (Ford, pp. 16–17). It is fair to say that Joyce was allowed far more latitude in this than any commercial house could have justified to itself (not that they would have handled such inflammatory material anyway in 1922). The success of the by no means inconsiderable first edition was assured in advance, guaranteeing Joyce a reasonable royalty. In all these respects it is hard to see how Random House or Bodley Head (the eventual commercial publishers) could have improved on the American amateur.

Obviously the pent-up feelings of the Great War helped create a wandering of genius to Paris which had, anyway, become more than ever an international city during 1914–18. And liberal French attitudes attracted advanced artists, many of whose books were unpublishable in the UK and US, and in some cases were to remain so for thirty years. Careers like Hemingway's, Miller's, Durrell's or Joyce's could not have worked themselves out as they did but for the Parisian license. Paris still serves something of the same function as a literary open market. Sinyavsky, Nabokov and Donleavy all required the facilities of Paris to escape the different repressions of their respective countries. ('I love it,' said one American publisher about *Lolita*, 'It's a great book. Nabokov's a great writer. But I can't print it. You think I'm crazy?' Obs 30.6.76.) For those resident there Paris has always encouraged café society, the formation of coteries and artistic colonies. Indeed, in its heyday it may be thought to have almost suffocated in its own success, and the hordes of imitative second-raters it attracted. George Orwell writes in *Inside the Whale* (an essay on Henry Miller):

During the boom years, when dollars were plentiful and the exchange value of the franc was low, Paris was invaded by such a swarm of artists, writers, students, dilettanti, sight seers, debauchees and plain idlers as the world has never seen. In some quarters of the town the so called artists must actually have outnumbered the working population. (*The Collected Essays, Journalism and Letters of George Orwell*, ed. I Angus and S. Orwell, London, 1968, 1, 493)

Periodically, at times of high prosperity and peace, such migrations, particularly of American artists and their camp-followers, occur—the latest was to the West Coast in the 1960s. They are a familiar feature of the sociology of American literature. But what one sees most clearly in the Parisian-American episode is the repudiation of the institutional publisher. A large section of the American writing community always struggles to eliminate the redundant middle man, to write directly for the reader. For once, and gloriously, this was achieved.

Paris was unique, an unparalleled florescence of a national literary ideal outside of its national territory. But the independent tradition continues undiminished among the publishing 'collectives' and the various small press ventures which flourish within America to the present day. According to Bill Henderson, self appointed publicist of contemporary do-it-yourself publishers, and proprietor of the Push-cart Press, self-publishing is as essentially American as the right to bear arms: 'Publishing-it-yourself is in the individualistic tradition of the American Dream . . . publishing has been and remains one of our most democratic institutions' (Bill Henderson *Publish-it-Yourself Handbook*, p. 36).

Self-publishing thrives in the US with its 2,000-odd small presses. And many acts of American self-publishing transcend what one would think of as 'small' press activity in the British context. *The*

Whole Earth Catalog, a huge bestseller, is one of many similar highly profitable do-it-yourself and politically engaged works. It remains the case, however, that fiction is difficult for alternative publishing systems to handle. It is not, however, impossible. A notable splash was made in 1974 by the New York based Fiction Collective. This outfit advertised itself with flair and was written up in mass circulation journals like *Newsweek* ('An idea whose time has come'). The Fiction Collective was never short of self-confidence and, borrowing rhetoric from the *Whole Earth* crew, proclaimed itself a 'non commercial writers' co-operative for the protection of an endangered species—innovative quality fiction'. It was brought together, according to its founders, 'by a deep concern for the future of the novel'. Taken at their own valuation FC represented a major effort to wrench the novel away from increasingly ruthless commercial producers. It was not, however, a valuation universally shared.

Collectives are fairly common in the US. In 1976 there were five reported as operating at a level significant enough to be compared with orthodox publishers (NYT 29.8.76). Of these five, however, four were concerned solely with poetry (Alicejames Books, The Inwood Press Collective, The Minnesota Writers' Co-operative Publishing House, Berkeley Poets Co-operative). All these manifest the classic 'peddling' or 'pushcart' sales pattern of the independent publisher. The Fiction Collective (which is the fifth of the above collectives) makes some adjustments to the venerable techniques of pavement selling, which are definitely not suitable for editions of many thousands of full-length novels. The Fiction Collective, therefore, arranged to have its books issued through the distributive chain of the commercial publisher, George Braziller Inc., who took 25 per cent of the gross income and subsidiary payments. Other arrangements show a similar hard-headedness and practical commonsense. The Fiction Collective agreed to make its selection on the basis of a 50 per cent affirmative vote by members. Its printers in Michigan produced a uniform 500 hard and 1,500 soft-back copies of each novel accepted. Only members' works were eligible for selection. The Collective needed, according to its 1975 estimate, 400 hard and 1,200 soft-back sales, at $3.95 and $7.95, to break even. Finance, however, was its most controversial feature. Every accepted author was obliged to 'loan' $3,000 for the production of his novel. As soon as the author's investment (or 'reverse advance') was repaid him, he would split with the FC, and get 60 per cent of all other rights. According to the FC manifesto:

The Fiction Collective offers recognition by one's peers. This clear insistence on the standards of those who, finally, know what the art is about, opens a path towards the maturity of the American novel, as well as a way for American novelists to assume their full prerogatives and responsibilities. (NYTBR 15.9.74)

Having made their practical arrangements, the Fiction Collective got themselves in proper artistic shape 'by consciousness raising sessions designed to eliminate the counterproductive addiction [to] the dream of "success"' (*New Writers* Feb. 75). Reduced expectation of success was necessary if one works out a few primitive sums as to the likely revenue from a combined edition of 2,000 at $3.95 and $7.95.

For all its radical idealism there were a number of other recognisably 'orthodox' features of the FC, apart from its marketing subcontract with Braziller. It was, for example, based on a university with a 'writing program'. CUNY's Brooklyn College supplied office space, services and teaching employment for FC personnel. As such it could be seen as an annexe to the American Creative Writing course, and the creative writer in CUNY. Two of the founders and first writers on the list, Baumbach and Spielberg, were based in Brooklyn. Other academic connections and previous experiments had laid the ground for FC, which was by no means the spontaneous growth that some commentators took it for. A number of FC's members had been associated with *Partisan Review* and an earlier dry run for the FC, the 50 cent tabloid *Fiction*, founded in 1972 which was also co-operative. Many FC authors were far from being novices or literary innocents. Ronald Sukenick, for example, was forty-two in 1975, had two novels already published, entitled prepositionally *Up* (Dial, 1968) and *Out* (Swallow, 1973) plus a collection of short stories, *The Death of the Novel* (Dial, 1969), a critical monograph on Wallace Stevens (NYUP, 1967) and contributions to *The New York Times Book Review* and *Village Voice*. Cynics might say that his recantations of the success ethic had come rather late in the day, for an author who was well into a conventional writing career.

Superficially the FC seems a variation on the state-publishing theme—the political associations of 'collective' suggesting idealised versions of communist organisation and bright young novelists in Mao tunics. The connection this suggests with radicalised American youth of the late 1960s is further reinforced by the anti-capitalist consciousness-raising sessions and the dedication to 'ecological' publishing. At a deeper level, however, the FC is obviously in the individualistic tradition of American independent publishing and, by the standards of that tradition, is a somewhat conservative operation. One notes, for example, that the key factor in the production sequence is that the author loans the initiating $3,000; a demand that no commercial publisher—outside a vanity press—would make (and even a vanity press would only try to extort a thousand or less). Working in batches of six novels, as it did, what the FC represented was an accumulation of working capital ($18,000), capital which would not be dissipated since they enjoyed unpaid editorial assistance and an overhead contribution donated by Brooklyn College (which enhanced the value of the $18,000 by about another 40 per cent). In short, stripped of the fancily political name, the Fiction Collective is an old-fashioned self-help club or syndicate, no different from that which helped Sinclair publish *The Jungle*. This orthodox aspect of the FC was confirmed by their delegating marketing arrangements (the most difficult and technical of the problems facing the independent publisher) to a commercial firm, and by the highly conventional advertising they took out.

In most independent publishing experiments there is a sad disparity between the manifesto and performance. FC was no exception. Although it garnered sufficient good notices to decorate its advertisements (e.g. 'intellectually stimulating . . .' *New York Times*), the FC was excoriated by many reviewers whose opinion it must have held to be most weighty. It was, for example, roundly disowned by hard-line literary radicals like Richard Kostelanetz, who saw the FC as a 'tribe of . . . full time university professors'. Their true title should be, he suggested, not 'a fiction collective but a fiction academic . . . pumping for promotion points' (Marg 25/26 1975). 'Vanity press' was an accusation made by other commentators, who observed that even RCA-Random House did not squeeze $3,000 from its authors.

If it got little comfort underground, above the ground the reception was also hard. *The New York Times Book Review* (whose Navasky had originally suggested the venture) carried a particularly severe review by Michael Mewshaw (NYTBR 13.10.74, 12.12.74). Mewshaw's material points were:

1. The FC books were 'shot through with grammatical mistakes, misspellings, typos, cliches and stylistic inferiorities'. They were, in short, shoddily edited.

2. There were no price benefits in works selling at $7.95 and $3.95; indeed in a number of cases FC offered positively bad value for the purchaser. *Museum*, for example, had 156 pages, 14 of which were blank.

3. Even if, as FC member Sukenick claimed, the first editions were 'sold out', this only meant a miniscule 2,000 combined sales. Some if not many of these would, in the nature of the American sale or return system, come back.

4. The FC offerings were not very good as novels, suggesting that the organisation existed only to publish their own, otherwise unpublishable, works.

The Mewshaw argument from quality suggested a disabling lack of proper editorial skills. The argument from price and low production suggested that the venture lacked the necessary capital resources to survive, and that it had no competitive edge with which to establish itself in a cut-throat marketplace. Inherent in Mewshaw's whole line of argument was the conviction that the FC lacked necessary capacities which only commerce could supply for the production of novels. In the absence of these it could enjoy only the temporary success of a fad and should be put down as such.

With hindsight one can see that the FC had no right to expect any welcome from anyone. It had disobeyed the first rule of the American alternative press—'no compromise'. In adopting professional and commercial aids and methods it laid itself open to the two-pronged charge of disgraceful amateurism from its commercial rivals and of treachery from its fellow independents. Literary radicals are unrelentingly savage against those of their number, like Erica Jong, Robert Stone or Ginsberg, who make it. For the purist the market must be boycotted, with a sense of grim, self-justifying satisfaction. I quote a representative expression of this philosophy from Tom Montag, editor of *Margins*:

Creative literature is vital to American culture(s), yet it has not been able to compete in the marketplace with the commercialized literature New York publishers are programming via marketing research. . . . Literature is not beefsteak. We are compromised by treating it as such. . . . We ought to realise by now that if we're intent on *selling* books, we're in the wrong part of the book 'business'. If you want to sell books, sign a contract with the next Harold Robbins and promote him. Or get into porno and get distributed by the Mafia. But don't publish *literature*. The stuff just don't sell. Sometimes you can't even give it away. No small press publisher, I submit, can or should hope to become commercially viable. (Marg. 25/26.75)

Montag's corollary is that literature can only survive and retain its integrity by being resolutely uncommercial, by not selling. Sales failure is positive proof of artistic virtue:

The integrity of the small-press editor-publisher, in some part at least, seems dependent on the fact that each book he or she produces will lose money out of pocket, will take groceries off the table . . . I think, in this context, of Russian Samizdat literature; the only manuscript I would risk Siberia for, the only one I'd spend endless hours typing, would be one I believed in. (Marg 25/26 1975)

Such theorists take their role seriously, and the heroic extreme of the samizdat is often invoked.

The most fevered exponent of radical literary politics today is Richard Kostelanetz, whose views may be briefly surveyed here for the light they throw on the American ideal of literary independence which, allegedly, the FC prostituted. Kostelanetz is convinced that things have reached an interestingly terminal stage: 'As far as commercial publishing is concerned, the *end* has come and gone; that world has passed beyond hell' (Marg. 25/26 1975). Kostelanetz loosed off a maddened series of articles in the 1970s, culminating in the apocalyptic book, *The End of Intelligent Writing: Literary Politics in America* (a book which, unsurprisingly, he found difficulty in persuading any commercial publisher to accept). Kostelanetz's thesis is that a literary fascism, made up of 'complexes' and 'establishments' has recently attained totalitarian power. He defies this oppression in a rabid jargon, which equates commercial publishing with industry and industry with organised crime. Literary America, if we credit *The End*, is a world of 'literary industrial complexes', 'New York Literary mobs', 'literary gangsters', 'professional violence'. New York, particularly, is a cauldron of intrigue, espionage and vengeance. ('Positions of cultural power', Kostelanetz notes meaningfully, 'tend to attract people prone to vengeance.') He suggests that the National Endowment for the Arts literary fellowships are deliberately awarded to bad writers, to starve out any lingering independent talents. Kostelanetz points to the presence of big publishers and *New York Review of Books* contributors (whom he particularly loathes) on the literary panel as proof enough of his dark accusations. There is also, he asserts, a clandestine blacklist passed among commercial publishers. Everywhere he sees suppression: 'the situation now could be characterized as rampant censorship prior to publication of works of literature and art. We are living in cultural jails.'

II

Kostelanetz's assault on the reader is so violent that one is liable to be rushed into equally violent assent or dissent. A usefully objective way to regard such extremity is as an index of the cultural pressure in America (and by analogy in the USSR, where a similarly fierce polarisation has taken place between state-approved and samizdat literature). Turning to the English scene the pressure is lower. Indeed, by comparison the English literary world may seem so low pressured as to be extinct. Part of this is to the credit (or discredit) of institutions like the Arts Council, which is forever mediating (busybodying) and making peace (papering cracks) between the avant garde and the cultured mass of readers. But partly it must be that Britain is, in terms of cultural climate, cooler, more diverse and loosely knit.

Surveying what has happened in America in the 1960s and after, many an English author must have felt that he inhabited an almost embarrassingly tame and nerveless literary world. There are self and independently-published novels in English literary history, from Richardson, through Charles Reade and Samuel Butler, to the Woolfs. There have also been theorists like Herbert Read who in the 1930s advocated that authors take over the means of production and distribution and run them on anarchist-syndicalist lines. But invariably there has been an accommodation and an absorption into orthodox practice. (The Hogarth Press becomes a straight publisher. Herbert Read joins the board of Faber's. Faber's itself, with Eliot as poetry director, becomes a conventional publisher.) It is hard to point to anything recent in the independent publishing of novels which has had even the dubious success of the American Fiction Collective.

The lack of results is not for want of projections or prophetic vision. The novelist B. S. Johnson made the following diagnosis and recommendations in 1969. It reads like a blueprint for the later Fiction Collective:

After all the explanations of and excuses for the present system have been made, one hard and indisputable fact still remains: everyone else engaged in the publishing of books makes a living out of it, and the vast majority of writers don't. Here's a way they might make that living from their work which those in any way engaged in almost every other trade take for granted. A group of (say) ten established writers could form themselves into what, for want of a less emotive word, must be called a co-operative. This group would themselves pay directly for the production of their books: buy their own paper from the mills, pay the printer for setting up and machining the sheets, and the binder for completing the job. In fact production would be very similar to that of commercial publishers now. But the first difference would be in the way the finished copies would be sold. The chief selling method would be advertisements published in the press announcing: THE ONLY WAY YOU CAN READ SO AND SO'S BESTSELLER IS BY SENDING 25s TO THE ADDRESS BELOW. Since it has been calculated that the majority of the bookbuying public can be reached by advertising in four key papers, advertisements in these would clearly be the most economical way of making the book known to the maximum number of potential readers. The second difference would be in the ... price. (NSoc 9.1.69)

In his visionary enthusiasm Johnson reckoned that a 40–60 per cent price reduction would be possible, largely by cutting out the middleman bookseller—the 'avaricious' bookseller as he called him: 'Does any bookseller really think his part is more than twice as important as Graham Greene's?' (N Soc 9.1.69).

Members of the booktrade were quick to point to flaws in Johnson's utopian scheme. First: in order to get the scheme going he needed a 'bestseller'. What bestselling author would donate his work? Secondly, as Johnson noted, some £200–£300 would be required from each of the ten participating members. Thirdly, it was pointed out that he had overlooked the importance of the publisher as financier who takes all the author's 'risk', for the very good reason that in most cases the author is too insolvent to take it himself.

Despite the evident flaws in such schemes as Johnson's the co-operative venture still lures British novelists who can see it elsewhere coming tantalisingly near a kind of success which could transform the literary scene. There is, for example, the West German 'Verlag der Autoren', formed in April 1969. Neil Jordan, writing in October 1976, gives an account of a more *ad hoc* Irish collective:

In Ireland for some years now it has been almost impossible to publish a novel through the normal channels. Publishers wouldn't touch fiction, saying it doesn't sell etc. So several of us younger writers here got together about a year ago, and formed the Irish Writers' Co-operative. We have published one book since, *The Ikon Maker*, a novel by Desmond Hogan. We did it in paperback, publicised it as brashly as possible and it was sold out within two months. It held second in the bestseller paperback lists for almost four weeks.... The success of it amazed us, and enabled us to get the backing for another title, due out in November, and for probably four more titles next year. (NF Oct. 76)

One can scent a revolution in bookselling and publishing in examples such as this; though Jordan is at pains to point out that Ireland, like the US, is different from Britain: 'Ireland is a small country, of course, where small voices find it easier to be heard, but the success of that novel proved something about the possibilities over here [i.e. the UK] of fiction in general.' One cannot help feeling, like Jordan, that all that is needed is the extra touch which, say, Allen Lane brought to the mass market paperback in 1935, for a whole new era to open up whose influence would quickly spread over the English-speaking world. On the other hand there is a law of literary inertia which almost guarantees that authors would be unable to sustain the extraordinary energy and community spirit to keep a collective going for as long as even the most rickety publishing houses.

One cohesive force which could keep a co-operative together is shared political idealism (in the long run this is probably more durable than the idealism of, say, the Fiction Collective). It will be interesting in this respect to see how the Writers and Readers Publishing Co-operative, formed in 1975, develops. This British outfit, dedicated to 'mass publishing on a non-commercial basis', claims sales of 5,000–10,000 for its volumes and has elected to distribute its books through commercially orthodox channels. Authors are given a conventional royalty. W & R has a radical flavour in all its list; it does publish novelists—but only apparently novelists with some congenial political flavour to their work (John

Berger and Chris Searle, for example). One is inclined to think that W & R has a better than normal chance of survival, for two reasons. Political zeal coheres the co-operative membership; political affiliation identifies a definite and predictably book-buying market. To this extent the name is apt—the readers are co-operative, in a way that Fiction Collective readers are not. FC merely wants to take a slice of the current fiction reading public, to squeeze into the existing market, not to make a new market for itself. Its readers are essentially a selection of those catered for by the orthodox publisher. W & R can legitimately claim that it is supplying a hitherto unsupplied readership—the young New Left, for whom no other publishing house wholeheartedly caters.

III

It is, of course, open to any novelist to go it alone, whether in Britain or America. That is to say an author can commission a printer to produce his work, and undertake to market it himself. It makes for quite dramatic gestures of independence. Orwell, for example, proposed to do this with *Animal Farm* when he despaired of finding a publisher courageous enough to take the work. His plan was to issue the book as a 2s pamphlet. (The fact that it came out as a commercially produced novelette at four times the price is itself a comment on literary economics.) In the abstract, going it alone has attractions; in the working out, however, there are major problems which render it unattractive to any but the most dogged writer. These problems are clearly shown in the case of a British novelist who recently took on the system, single handed, with only a very limited degree of success.

By summer 1971 Trevor Hoyle's novel, *The Relatively Constant Copywriter*, had been rejected by eighteen publishers. Four of them, however, had thought the work to have real value and prospects. All four were publishers whose opinion any writer would respect. Secker and Warburg found *The Relatively Constant Copywriter* well written and felt 'it certainly has enough merit to warrant your offering it to other publishers'. Gollancz turned it down 'reluctantly', saying, 'we would be extremely interested to consider the next novel you write'. Allison and Busby 'chewed it over a great deal' and hoped he would resubmit the book next year. Michael Joseph echoed Gollancz in wanting 'to consider anything else you may write'.

Joseph also gave what was the universal reason for declining: 'I am afraid I shall just have to be frank and say that it is an uncommercial novel.' There was, of course, the other factor that Hoyle was unknown. Novelists should wait till their third or fourth novel before being experimental.

Hoyle, who was thirty-one, had been trying to get into print for ten years. He was, as he says, 'near the end of his tether.' He decided therefore to form his own imprint, Northern Writers, and publish his novel in a limited edition of 1,000 copies. The book would appear as a midway, costing 65p, (not a profit-making price, even if all 1,000 sold). The total production cost came to between £600 and £700, and £100 worth of review copies were sent out. Bookshops were Hoyle's first major problem:

Distribution is where the difficulties begin: this was slow, painful, and in some places non-existent. I placed copies on sale or return through the North West, mainly in Manchester, and an independent book salesman filed orders from London the major cities and some of the university towns. But British booksellers must be the most conservative species on earth. (NF Oct. 75)

Hoyle had flair and great energy. As a result he got publicity and the book was fairly widely reviewed. He sold his edition, showing, as he claimed, 'a market for original fiction does exist, if only British publishers will wake up to the fact'. On the credit side, Hoyle sees himself as having defied the philistine commercialism of general publishing:

The truth is that many publishers aren't in books at all; they're in packaged consumer durables—which might just as well be tubes of toothpaste or cans of beans.... Nowadays the question directed by editorial policy is not: 'is this a good book?' but 'will it sell?' And rather than becoming more adventurous, publishers are tending to draw in their horns, and more and more shy away from work that doesn't hold any immediate commercial rewards. (NF Oct. 75)

Nonetheless Hoyle is not optimistic about self-publishing as a widespread remedy; it remains a defiant gesture, not a blueprint for future pioneers:

Several writers have written asking whether they ought to publish their own book. I advise them not to. Until the archaic machinery of British publishing, distribution and bookselling is radically overhauled, nobody—

from the big prestigious houses to the lone self-publishing writer—has the slightest hope of bringing serious modern fiction to a wider audience and making it a paying proposition. (NF Oct. 75)

One may follow Hoyle's career onto his second novel. This was published as an original paperback by Futura. Hoyle evidently had trouble again in getting his novel placed ('about time too!' runs the dedication). As is usual with paperbacks, *Rule of Night* received virtually no reviews. A tough book in the American naturalist vein, though with a British provincial setting (a kind of *Last Exit to Rochdale*), it has as much interest as any other of the grab-bag selection of works with nothing to recommend them but their hard covers, which are reviewed in the Sundays and weeklies. In this respect the second novel confirms Hoyle's earlier claim that some major overhauling changes are needed, before any specific improvements to the system can be expected. What is required, particularly, is the discovery of new markets for cheaper new fiction. Hoyle sees possibilities as yet unexploited in the higher education public, which is interested in 'serious modern fiction' but can't afford it at current prices:

Consider this: sales of the average novel are between 800 and 1,100 copies, which is nowhere near a commercially viable proposition. Yet because only hardbacks get reviewed, publishers cling to this outmoded practice and hope to recoup on the paperback rights—thus completing the vicious circle. The trouble, as we all know, lies with the market: those who can afford £2.50 aren't interested in serious modern fiction, and those who are interested can't afford £2.50. (NF Oct. 75)

Alternative and self-publishing remains a field full of fascinating possibilities, but without any clearly defined success to base a convincing argument on. It is not clear, for example, to what extent one should regard alternative and orthodox publishing as sealed off from each other, in a state of self-sustaining contradiction. Or are they better considered as assemblages of component parts which can be effectively interchanged? This has a close bearing on such cases as the Fiction Collective and *The Relatively Constant Copywriter*. What these two operations did was to mix those parts of the alternative system which pleased their authors (independence from dictation by commercial authorities) with parts of the commercial system (efficient sales and distribution, profitable sales to the general public, attention in opinion-forming journals). Critics of the FC and Hoyle himself condemn the hybridisation as futile and dishonest—but is it? Could not the right combination or compromise be struck by writer-publishers more gifted, more dedicated or simply luckier? One cannot help feeling that the self-publishing of fiction, which has had its *Ulysses*, awaits its Allen Lane or its Robert de Graff.

12 The Telenovel

The most convenient way of communicating to a large number of people now is through television. If we were working in the second half of the nineteenth century we might be writing serialised novels.
Tony Garnett, *The Listener*, 29 October 1970

I get my money from TV.
Simon Raven

The various deviations of literary genius caused by commercial incentives and inhibitions are usually too fine to trace, except in those large drifts which one can see, for example, towards drama in the seventeenth century, lyric poetry in the early-nineteenth or fiction in the late-nineteenth century. In the 1960s one main drift has been that which draws creative writers out of fiction and into television. Roughly speaking the authors so affected fall into two categories. There are those who are primarily novelists, like Kingsley Amis, William Trevor or Malcolm Bradbury who lend their talents to the other medium in the more or less mercenary spirit of Simon Raven, quoted above, on the grounds that it pays 'fifteen times' as well as fiction (NF Apr. 76). And there are those other, and usually younger, writers who transfer wholeheartedly, deserting the novel (although we may suspect that in happier circumstances they would certainly have stayed with the form). A good example of the second kind is Simon Gray (b. 1936), author of *Butley* (1971) and *Otherwise Engaged* (1975) for the stage, of *Plaintiffs and Defendants* and *Two Sundays* for television and, originally, of the novels *Colmain* (1963), *Simple People* (1965), *Little Portia* (1968), *A Comeback for Stark* (1969). Gray describes how he first became involved with broadcasting and theatre:

Q. You began your writing career as a novelist but you are probably better known as a playwright. Why did you give up writing novels?
SG: It wasn't a conscious choice. It was a matter of accident. I'd written a short story published in a collection which was seen by the script editor for 30 minute theatre. [This was apparently Kenith Trodd, see T. 26.7.75]. He offered to buy the rights and I asked him who was going to do the adaptation and how much he would be paid for this and discovered that whoever did the adaptation would get more than I did for

the story. As the story was virtually written in dialogue I insisted on doing it myself. While I was doing that they commissioned me to write a play for what was then The Wednesday Play [*The Caramel Crisis*]. I wrote a couple more for them and then I wrote one that was totally unacceptable because they thought it was too involved—in too delicate an area. That was *Wise Child* and so I sent a draft to Codron who then commissioned it as a stage play. (JAM King's College London, 2, 1976)

Elsewhere Gray has ruefully commented: 'I can think of at least one novel which is infinitely better than anything I've written for stage or screen but that's still not sold 2,000 copies' (RT 11–17. 10.75). He probably has around 5m viewers for each of his television plays, and *Butley* and *Otherwise Engaged* must have reached over a million people in their London runs alone.

The financial inducement around the time Gray made the switch in his career was about £1,000 for an original work from a writer 'at the very top of the scale'. Lesser writers would get the best they could, starting from a basic fee of £300. For a thirty-minute radio play in the mid-1960s the rate was 45 guineas. One has no way of knowing, but from what he says it is doubtful if Gray had more than £100–£200 for his novels. 'Accident' then is a somewhat neutral term for the economic suction force which brought him into broadcast media. One can see other talented young writers drawn in the same direction. Ian McEwan and Peter Prince, for example, had television plays produced in 1976 (though McEwan, at least, claimed to dislike the medium; RT 10–16.4.76). It will be interesting to see how their careers move in the future. Prince, at going rates, must have received two or three times as much for his televised as for his printed *Playthings* (Gollancz, £1.60, winner of the 1973 Somerset Maugham award; the play was broadcast 6 May 1976). McEwan calculated in 1975 that a short story which would take four to eight weeks to write would earn him only between £10 and £75 in the British literary market (NF July 75).

The disparity in audience size is clearly not lost on such writers. As William Trevor says: 'every play I write is adapted from one of my old stories, something that's been read by—at the most—a few thousand people. On television the audience is instantly multiplied by millions. It's a bit mystifying' (ST. 20.6.76). Trevor, who is forty-eight, seems set in his ways and determined to remain primarily a novelist and short-story writer; younger and more impressionable writers might well be inclined to follow their major audience and their major source of income. Nor would it be a simple case of novelists taking television money and running. In an interesting broadcast conversation with Margaret Forster on 31 May 1977 Melvyn Bragg gave three reasons for his being a 'teleperson': (1) 'You can't live off fiction.' (2) television work offers a 'world—a society to which the writer can belong' (3) television offers an outlet for the writer's evangelical desire to instruct a large audience on the value of fiction.

II

There have in the past been highly paid alternatives for novelists. A whole generation of American (and some British) writers sacrificed their best years in Hollywood. To what extent they were badly done by is a matter of recent dispute. (See e.g. Tom Dardis, *Some Time in the Sun*, New York, 1976). But there is little doubt that Fitzgerald, say, could have been better employed than on *Winter Carnival*. In 1976 one could still find a novelist as brilliant as Anthony Burgess lurking in the credits of *Moses*. ('Lew Grade presents MOSES', as the posters modestly put it. The film wasn't around very long to embarrass its scriptwriter; but it returned, inflated, as a London Weekend Television serial, and sparked off some hostile correspondence between Burgess and his critics.)

The distinction of British television drama in the 1960s and 1970s was that it offered a thoroughly respectable alternative, intellectually, aesthetically and, above all, economically. This was the result of the courageous policy of the BBC in the 1960s. One may quote the account of the dominant producer of the period, Tony Garnett:

> Some time before I joined the BBC David Mercer wrote a television play called *A Suitable Case for Treatment.* That play was put out and it had a very mixed response, and got a very low audience figure. But fortunately in the BBC, when the BBC is feeling in a good state, one has the right to fail. And when I got to the BBC there were plays coming on my desk that could never have been written if David's play hadn't been transmitted. And one or two of these were put on and were received very favourably. (List 29.10.70)

The effect was to put the creative writer in touch with a potentially maximum audience, much larger than he could ever hope for from the circulation of his books. There was, of course, some unwelcome interposition of producer and director, and occasional censorship. But enough freedom remained to preserve artistic dignity. No one need feel prostituted. And with television fully operational the audience was virtually the whole nation. On average during 1975, the British watched television nearly eighteen hours a week. The 'A' class socio-economic adult—representing the top 6 per cent of the population, and the principal consumers of quality fiction—averaged two hours of television time each day. The 'Play for Today' enjoyed audiences which amount to sizeable fractions of the total British population. 'The danger is,' said the outgoing head of drama at the BBC, Christopher Morahan, 'that you get disappointed at a mere 8½ million' (Grd 12.4.76).

It is not entirely a question of crocks of gold and audiences of millions. In an unspectacular way Samuel Beckett illustrates how purely literary genius can be formatively pushed and pulled by a medium which is commercially dominant but not exploitative. Beckett, born in 1906, wrote no significant drama until the early 1950s, some twenty-five years after his literary debut. The stage success of *Waiting for Godot* in 1953 promoted him to world-wide fame. Association with a BBC producer on *Endgame* led on to work specifically designed for the BBC Third Programme: *All that Fall: A Play for Radio* (1957), *Embers* (1959) and, for television, *Eh Joe* (1966). *Molloy*, *Malone Dies* and *The Unnamable* were all given performance as dramatic monologues on the Third Programme in the late 1950s, at a period of openness and receptivity to experimental theatre.

It is fair to say that insofar as Beckett now has a mass public (and few writers as advanced can claim to have enjoyed such wide performance in their lifetimes) it is because of: first, the success of *Godot*; second, his Nobel Prize; third, and by no means least, the efforts of BBC radio and latterly TV. The distinguished critic and former head of BBC radio drama, Martin Esslin, has gone so far as to suggest that radio is in some sense Beckett's 'true' genre, allowing him a fulfilment denied, for example, his technologically prehistoric mentor, James Joyce: '[Beckett] welcomes a medium in which the voice is supreme. And it is a matter of immense pride for radio that he has acknowledged it as a medium, writing some of his best work for it' (RT 10–16.4.76). This is as may be; but one can suspect that it is less the peculiar felicities of the broadcast media than their ability to pay handsomely which has recruited much recent talent, initially directed towards purely literary expression. As the publisher Anthony Blond observes, in a somewhat injured spirit:

> Bright British novelists like Simon Raven, the late James Kennaway, Frederic Raphael, Margaret Forster, both the Drabbles and Melvyn Bragg, not to speak of Len Deighton, can make a thousand pounds or more for a television play . . . which renders them less attentive to the demands of their publishers. (*The Publishing Game*, London, 1971, p. 25)

This state of affairs seems likely to continue. The BBC, alone, spends as much on arts patronage as the Arts Council. As a casual employer of writers its bounty is unequalled, with between seventy and eighty new television plays a year, something like two hundred episodes of specially written drama series and six hundred original radio plays. There is much more work than the small corps of dramatists proper can handle. What these impressive figures add up to is employment for all moderately versatile writers. As the producer Irene Shubik recalls in her book *Play for Today* (London, 1975), one of the first tasks of producers in the 1960s was to go out and actually look for likely novelists to write plays. (She, incidentally, takes the credit for recruiting William Trevor as a television playwright.)

III

Television drama is a subject on its own, and not my subject. Nor, though one can point to its existence, is it necessary to go into some of the usefully incidental employments for writers which the broadcast media offer (Ian McEwan's features in *The Radio Times*, Melvyn Bragg's assignments on 'Read All About It', George MacBeth's long-held post as director of poetry, Kingsley Amis's television reviewing). What is to the point is the variety of television drama which in 1975 came to be known as telefiction or the telenovel.

The term telenovel was, I believe, first used in America to describe the major networks' showing of large blockbuster features like Paramount's awful *QB VII*, or NBC's series of 'television novels' (including, among other carefully selected best-sellers, Alison Lurie's *War Between the Tates*) and, particularly, ABC's hugely successful seven-part adaptation of Irwin Shaw's *Rich Man Poor Man*, which was shown from February 1976 onwards and its follow-ups, *Rich Man Poor Man II* and *Gibbsville* (from John O'Hara's saga). Properly speaking these were television adaptations of novels, in which transcription played a dominant part. Televised performance was equivalent to paperback or movie tie-ins. As the term telenovel came to be used in Britain in 1975–6, it meant something more complex. It implied a degree of intermediate conception—a novelist thinking primarily in terms of televisual realisation of his work. It was not fiction which would go through a secondary stage of televising, but television from the first. A critic in *Time Out* describes the genre well:

The telenovel is a relatively recent form. A group of writers, or increasingly and more logically, one writer, develops a set of themes over a linked and finite number of episodes. The appearance of the work in regular instalments is analogous to the mode of Victorian publishing whereby novels appeared part by part in magazines. With 'The Glittering Prizes' the telenovel reaches a watershed—either it goes on to become the dominant dramatic form of television, kicking the one off play when it's down and gradually easing out the serialised adaptation and the historical or thematic anthology, or it withers once the present commitments (Trevor Griffiths' 'Bill Brand' and Howard Schuman's 'Rock Follies' lead the imminent pack) are worked out. (TO 16–22.1.76)

At the same time Philip Purser, in *The Daily Telegraph*, noted a spate of 'television novels' (*The Glittering Prizes*, *Bouquet of Barbed Wire*, *When the Boat Comes In*) and, reading Andrea Newman's determination henceforth to prepare her 'novels' directly for the screen, bypassing the printed page, observed: 'Given the present plight of printed fiction, this attitude is understandable.' (DT. 8.2.76. In fact, after a second series of *Barbed Wire*, Newman returned to fiction with her 1977 novel, *An Evil Streak*).

Other notable telenovels of the period were Arthur Hopcraft's *The Nearly Man*, Mervyn Jones's *Holding On*, and in 1977 *Fathers and Families* by John Hopkins. Certain producers were particularly associated with the new genre; and indeed, since so much of the telenovel's success depended on the telenovelist's autonomy, it was essential that there should be nothing like the American 'executive producer' intruding on the composition of the work. Nor should formula or running-situations cramp the writer's imagination. A large measure of authorial freedom was essential; and this was by no means automatic in an art form where executive decisions are made by accountant heads of departments and committees. Producer forbearance seems to be acknowledged in the dedication of the book version of *The Glittering Prizes* to Stella Richman—a neat variation on the traditional publisher dedicatee (Richman and Mark Shivas took credit for the two best received telenovels, *Glittering Prizes* and *Brand*). In this respect it is significant that the initiator of the vogue was probably Ingmar Bergman's six-part *Scenes from a Marriage*. Bergman brought to his telenovel all the authority of the 'auteur' director-cum-writer.

In the remainder of this section I want to concentrate on the pre-eminent telenovel of this period, Frederic Raphael's *The Glittering Prizes*. This six-part series was transmitted on BBC 2, January–February 1976, and on BBC 1 in November–December of the same year. To coincide with the second screening Penguin brought out a double edition of the 'novelised' *Glittering Prizes*, simultaneously in paperback at 80p and Allen Lane hardback at £3.75. In winter 1976 the work thus existed as a 'new' television serial, a 'new' hardback, and a 'new' paperback. This must have been a unique concatenation. And Penguin presumably used the book as a trial for the new Penguin–Viking operation, for which they would henceforth be purchasing hard and paperback rights.

Raphael, like his hero Adam Morris, is primarily a novelist (though of novels hitherto very different to *Glittering Prizes*). 'What he really sees himself as—and he didn't hesitate when the question was put—is a novelist,' declared one profile (Grd 28.1.76). Up to 1975 he had written thirteen, all of which lay in that inert band of respectably highbrow fiction which is well reviewed but never sells enough to get into the mass-market paperback. ('He does rather wish his publishers would put him in paperback,' ran the same publicity profile). Raphael's previous novel to *Glittering Prizes*, *California Time*, published by Cape, plunged into the literary world with scarcely a ripple of interest. It was an unusually complex and artful novel, and Raphael complained bitterly about the 'brainless' quality of the English literary-critical establishment in the face of such fiction.

Raphael would have had a mean sort of life had he depended on his novel writing. He had, however, other cards to play. He had written plays for radio and television a decade earlier and, most remuneratively, like Morris again, had done film work. Raphael did screen plays for *Nothing but the Best* (an offshoot of the Cambridge satirists in the 1960s, a group with whom Raphael has strong links), *Darling*, *Two for the Road* (1967), *Far from the Madding Crowd* (1967), *How About Us?* (1971), *A Severed Head* (1971—unreleased), and lastly, Bogdanovich's ill-fated *Daisy Miller* (1974). It was estimated that Raphael's earnings could reach £50,000 a year from this source, and even before *The Glittering Prizes* he could afford to live abroad and send his children to English public schools. His life-style resembles somewhat those of Maugham, whose biography he has written, and Huxley, a writer with whose intellectual brilliance he has other strong affinities.

Despite its evident generosity to him, Raphael bears the film industry no love: 'I thank God English television absorbed the film industry . . . the vulgarity of the British cinema is really sickening. If that's the only way the industry can survive then frankly I think the funeral would be preferable to the visits to the hospital' (S 21.2.76). Judging from his statements in the welter of publicity which surrounded *The Glittering Prizes* one can discern a number of sources of discontent in Raphael. First, it may be assumed, he resented the comparative neglect of the fiction into which he put his best efforts. On the other hand, he disdained the vulgarity of the film world, whose fame was worse than neglect. He disliked the necessity of having to subordinate his sensibility to other novelists (Hardy, James, Murdoch), and to the strong directors with whom he was habitually teamed. In 1976 he was quoted as saying: 'I'm not about to disrupt my personal life and my professional life in order to prove John Schlesinger right not to work with me again' (S 21.2.76). Of Bogdanovich's *Daisy Miller* Raphael said: 'he made it as badly as anyone could possibly have made a film. Next to it . . . a home movie looks like Eisenstein' (S 21.2.76). And despite the success of his 1960s films, Raphael would seem to have recently had an unhappy knack of investing his talents in box office failures. We shall probably never know what his screenplay for *The Severed Head* was like. His career in the 1970s was, it would seem, littered with film scripts for which, presumably, he was well paid but which never made general release or—in the case of *Daisy Miller*—did so only to flop.

Television, especially in collaboration with a sympathetic producer, was clearly an attractive compromise between the dusty neglect of the literary world, and the neon vulgarity of Hollywood, with its mechanical exploitation of the writer. The point was made in a number of the profile comments in 1976:

What he likes about television is the opportunity to address people directly, without needing reviewers and the machinery of publishing, the cinema industry and publicity to find the audience. (Grd 28.1.76)

In television, ***the writer's involvement continues into production*** and Raphael worked closely with the actors and directors [of *Glittering Prizes*] throughout. 'Problems of discipline and position weigh more heavily on film directors. They are more concerned if some bloody writer hangs around the place.' (S 21.2.76, my italics)

Yet television, Raphael agrees, is a writer's medium—at least in Britain . . . being a co-operative medium, the writer can work on the characters with the actors. In the movies it's somewhow never the right moment to tell the director he's got something wrong. (RT 17–23.1.76)

One should emphasise that the freedom which Raphael enjoyed is not a 'given' aspect of television. It was awarded in this case by the producers and the culturally responsible executive of the BBC. It was also, probably, earned by Raphael's undeniable stature and egotism as an author. One of the great dangers in this kind of venture is that the television producer has not, like the publisher, had centuries during which to develop a professional 'code' which guarantees the artist's freedom. It is a feature of television drama generally, and in the US particularly, that the writer is at the mercy of the television producer who straddles the worlds of finance and art. Television plays are expensive, in the way that a modestly ambitious novel is not. (About ten times as expensive, if we compare a £50,000 production like *The Glittering Prizes* with the probable investment in *California Time* by Cape). The television producer may be enlightened. But even an enlightened producer like Richard Bates of LWT (producer of *A Man of Our Times*, and *Helen A Woman of Today*) can be found saying: 'The advantages of television are that I have total creative freedom. I'm my own boss. I'm well paid, and I've got all the money I need for production. What's more I can choose what creative people I like' (Vogue 15.4.75). People thus chosen must, of course, enjoy that much less 'total creative freedom'.

IV

Raphael has excelled in many literary parts. The theme of *The Glittering Prizes* seems to have come to him in his fortieth year, the time when, traditionally, mid-life assessments are made and personal achievements rapped for hollowness. Given the retrospection and introspection of the theme, one naturally sees *The Glittering Prizes* as an *apologia pro vita sua*. Raphael, however, was at pains to emphasise that it was no act of confession or cathartic (indeed, he is on record as rejecting 'the concept that an author can achieve some kind of catharsis by writing round his own career', Grd 28.1.76). The series ends with an elegant Bluebeard reference to the author's 'one chamber locked . . . and its contents safe from scrutiny'. Nonetheless the vulgar interpretation of the series was too tempting for the BBC to overlook and their cover-page illustration for the series on *The Radio Times* (17–23.1.76) carried a caption which deliberately and tantalisingly confused life and art:

GOING UP AND COMING DOWN
Out of the Cambridge of the 50s sprang a whole generation who today dominate the arts and the media. Tom Conti plays Adam Morris (BA Cantab), the aspiring writer in *The Glittering Prizes*, Wednesday BBC2. Back feature: Novelist and scriptwriter Frederic Raphael, 20 years on from Cambridge.

Whether or not Raphael intended it, *Glittering Prizes* was taken to analyse a whole brilliant generation and the nature of their brilliance. The period 1950–70, which it covers, has peculiar significance in that during it the mass media were fully developed. The scheme of the work is an investigation of how a 'celebrity' evolves, and how modern celebrity, boosted by the media, is to be measured against the ideals of fame and achievement embodied in the Cambridge tradition. Success is analysed in terms of the mid-points of illustrious careers, from Cambridge glimmerings to metropolitan blaze (or in one interesting case, neurotic rural obscurity among maladjusted children). The main characters are variously, novelist-screenwriter, dramatist-impressario, academic highflyer, media interviewer, actress-novelist (artfully hinted at are Raphael himself, Frost, Cook, Nunn, Hall, Bakewell, the Drabbles, Clive Swift, et al). *The Radio Times*, as we have seen, stressed the *roman à clef* side of the work as hard as they could, and probably to the point of the publicity vulgarity which Raphael himself scorns: 'he expects certain people to be watching with typical thruster's schizophrenia. To be *in*, savaged by Raphael's wit, will be pretty bad; but to be *out* will be much worse. It may mean that they have not got nearly such glittering prizes as they like to think' (RT 17–23.1.76).

The Glittering Prizes apparently originated in January 1972, when Raphael told Shivas that he wanted to do eight plays about people in Cambridge in the mid-1950s. The 8 × 50 minutes idea was later cut down to 6 × 75; at the same time some of Raphael's extravagant set requirements were pared. Mark Shivas recalls: 'The first play arrived at the start of April and fell open at the last page. 'Scene 76. Interior, St Peter's Rome. Day.' I shut it again fast, gulped, then began reading from page one' (SS Winter 75–6). Raphael was allowed this epilogue to the lavish first number; but it is noticeable that as the series advances the settings become progressively more austere. We are told that the writer acquiesced in apparatus, 'more containable in financial terms' (SS Winter 75–6). The costing of the series was, apparently, tight for a conception of such scale: £40,000 per episode with a ceiling of £210,000. (Though as Shivas pointed out in a later letter to *Screen International*, salary and equipment costs which did not appear in the budget brought the cost up to a true figure of £58,000 per episode.) The figure comes out as something absurdly cheap for a feature film, unthinkably expensive for a novel.

Two directors were given three plays each. From what Shivas writes it seems that some politicking was needed to ensure the series' viability; at a delicate mid-point stage Gerald Savory who had originally 'liked the plan very much' (SS Winter 75–6) was replaced by Christopher Morahan as Head of Plays: 'it was important that he should have enthusiasm for the project, too, if it was ever to get on the screen' (SS Winter 75–6). Morahan's assent was forthcoming, though whether his enthusiasm as well is not entirely clear. His real approval seems to have been reserved for more socially relevant drama than Raphael's ironic and, to some eyes, nihilistic confections. According to Shivas, Morahan insisted after a 'heavy meeting . . . I was not to exceed the budget by one penny' (SS Winter 75–6).

Whatever anxiety there was for the success of *The Glittering Prizes* must have been quickly eased by the unprecedented amount of interest and publicity it inspired. Not all was favourable. Clive

James was repeatedly sarcastic in *The Observer* about the self-regarding quality of the work. Peter Lennon took the same line in *The Sunday Times*: '*Glittering Prizes* is nothing more than an exercise in narcissism' (ST 8.2.76). Alan Coren in *The Times* used the series as a pretext for a dismissive and facetious comic essay, concluding: 'I wept, I laughed, I went out and bought a radio' (T 26.2.76). Valerie Jenkins adopted a pose of proletarian disdain for the series' 'élitism' in *The Evening Standard* (ES 22.1.76). Generally, however, the series was acclaimed: 'a sumptuous series' (Grd 22.1.76), 'a rich and rewarding sequence' (T 22.1.76), 'Clever novelist hero bowls out opposition' (DT 26.1.76).

A pretty necklace of blurb tags could have been made up from the critics' plaudits. Nor was reference restricted to the normal television reviewing bodies. John Sullivan reviewed the series in a feature article in *The Times Higher Education Supplement* (12.3.76), noting the author's clever use of peripety and *coups de ciné*—learned presumably in his other trade. *The Times Literary Supplement*, which only very rarely notices television, gave *The Glittering Prizes* a review after three episodes, as did *New Society* after five. Nonetheless the very extensiveness of the coverage of the series showed up how inadequate is the television reviewing establishment, and how incapable of the concentration needed to assess anything as new, complex and sustained as *The Glittering Prizes*. Television criticism vies with its object in disposable ephemerality. It exists only to give flash impressions, selected on the most random principles. Often television is less reviewed than viewed, and the best received critics are those who make apropos columns out of their newspaper space. The point was forcefully made by Julian Mitchell, himself at work on a historical telenovel, *Jennie*. (Produced by Stella Richman, this was in some ways even more successful than *Glittering Prizes*. It was, for example, sold to twenty-four countries. Mitchell himself is a prime case of the young writer who transfers his allegiance from fiction to television. An original Hutchinson's 'New Authors' discovery, he wrote five novels between 1961–68. Since 1968, when he was thirty-three, he has produced no fiction.) Mitchell's complaints, which stirred up controversy, were made in an article in *The Radio Times* entitled 'Larger than Realism', which concluded that the television reviewing establishment was utterly incompetent to deal with a work as unprecedented as *Glittering*

Prizes. What notices there were simply demonstrated 'the pathetic level at which television drama is discussed' (13–19.3.76).

It is not merely a matter of critical appreciation. Writers like to think of themselves living 'for all time', earning a place in history by their literary efforts. Literature's achievements are symbolised by monuments to permanence—the book and the library. Television is 'consumed', massively and absolutely, leaving no residue. Christopher Morahan, otherwise enlightened, is represented as 'not minding' (the journalist's own views come through as somewhat astonished by the indifference):

He believes that if a play speaks to a particular audience on a particular night, around 12m for two 'Plays for Today' this season, it has done its job. He is content that a production, which has involved its makers in months of work, should be regarded as ephemeral. He can think of it like today's newspaper which tomorrow only has value as history. (DT 19.4.76)

This is not how ambitious writers like to think of their work. Against Morahan's—which is the realistic view, and one which clearly reflects official policy—one can cite the case of Simon Gray, again, as recounted in *The New Review*:

One of producer Kenith Trodd's projects for this summer was to have been a 'retrospective' of early plays by Simon Gray—plays like *Death of a Teddy Bear*, *Sleeping Dog* and *Spoiled*. It was a nice idea. Gray's *Otherwise Engaged* was probably the most successful stage play of 1975 and his work as a whole was beginning to get heavyweight critical attention. It would have been a good moment to let people take another look at this emerging author's early television work. Anyway, Gray liked the idea and Trodd went off to set it up. Both of them were appalled to find that all Gray's early work had been wiped from the tapes. (NR June 76)

In effect, this is equivalent to the disappearance of the backlist, discussed in the second chapter. The offensive consequences to the traditional notions of authorship are self-evident. Gray himself indignantly demanded 'that the name of the BBC vandal who ordered the destruction of all the tapes of all my plays be made public; and that he then be made to make public a list of all the plays by all the other writers he has destroyed.' He didn't get the name, though a committee was set up in January 1976 to review the BBC archives (T 2.6.76). Their regretful conclusion seemed to be that it was nobody's fault and nothing could be done. Archiving television material on the lines of 'copyright' libraries was just too difficult in view of its mass, Equity awkwardness and problems of 'creator's' ownership.

It is not just a case of being unable to judge television offerings after the event, as one can re-read a book or make a second visit to a theatre. For some baffling reason the television work is normally denied the privileged inspection by accredited critics which is normal in other fields. Take the following *Evening Standard* notice, advertising one of Gray's plays in October 1975, on the evening of its first showing:

> *Plaintiffs and Defendants* is a play by Simon Gray in which he and Alan Bates bring to the small screen the partnership which has been celebrated since the stage play *Butley*. Bates plays a lawyer beset by a demanding girl friend (Georgina Hale) a preoccupied wife (Rosemary McHale), a daunting son and a no-hope client. As it is not the BBC's policy to preview plays I can't tell you much more than that. This is the first of two Simon Gray plays which open a new season of Plays for Today. (ES 14.10.75)

Probably the most acute danger, however, is that to the autonomy which the novelist, after centuries of struggle, now enjoys. Publishers know their place and respect authorial freedom. The same cannot always be said of those concerned with television production. In the mid-1970s there were a number of cautionary cases of censorship by executives on creative writers. One was Quentin Crisp's *The Naked Civil Servant* which the BBC (against Morahan's wishes, apparently) declined. It went to commercial television, where it had a huge success of esteem, and went on to win prizes. Morahan's aim, according to one commentator, 'was always to bring back social relevance to a medium that had got a bit frightened of it' (Grd 12.4.76). That he had not succeeded in dispelling this fright was clearly indicated by the subsequent dropping, after an estimated £70,000 production cost (NS 23.4.76), of Dennis Potter's *Brimstone and Treacle* (which, again, Morahan and producer Kenith Trodd fought for), in the face of possible blasphemy writs from Mrs Whitehouse and disapproval by the Director of Programmes ('I found the play brilliantly written and made, but nauseating'; NS 23.4.76). Trodd was reported as having come under the scrutiny of MI5's 'men in black raincoats', for political reasons (ES 9.9.76). The reports were confidently repudiated (ST 12.9.76), but the affair indicated the climate of inhibition with which any engaged, or unconventional spirit might have to contend. A month after the Trodd affair there were further complaints at the BBC's alleged interference with the production of *When the Boat Comes In*. The President of the Association of Directors and Producers, Piers Haggard, wrote in complaint to *The Guardian*: 'the television service was not always so heavy handed. The tremendous achievements of the last fifteen years were built on artistic freedom, moral concern and flair; not interference, censoring and strong-arm tactics. The BBC is not only betraying its own best traditions; it is sabotaging its creative future as well' (Grd 6.10.76).

The frontal assault by the heavy hand of censorship is probably less significant in the long run than the gradual erosions of authorial privileges by inbuilt features of television production and consumption: story-editors, producers, directors, apparatchiks, agents, captious reviewers, 'concerned' audience pressure groups, busybodies of all persuasions.

The telenovel, then, has a future beset with difficulty. It is hard to see how authorial freedom can be guaranteed for extended and involved television work. To be fully successful the telenovelist needs to have some of the important privileges of producer and director; these will not be surrendered easily. It is possible that the telenovel will not develop as a genre; that television's appeal will be exercised more by recruiting writing talent directly for drama, where the writer works more like an artisan, producing a commodity for others to deal with as they wish. Reviewing no less than twelve 'novelisations' of television series in *The Listener* (List 9.12.76), Neil Hepburn concluded that *The Glittering Prizes* was 'the only one of the dozen with serious pretensions to literary excellence'. Assuming the telenovel does have a future it would seem to lie with myriad hacks and very occasional writers of Raphaelesque skill and will.

Postscript

In September 1977 David Holbrook, a professional writer of many parts, initiated a spirited correspondence in *The Times* on the subject of authors' miserable earnings. Holbrook's complaints provoked a large postbag. Among the predictably philistine responses ('authors get what they are worth') was the now familiar plea for Public Lending Right—though its proponents were noticeably lamed by the defeat of the measure in parliament a few months earlier. At the conclusion of the correspondence the former chairman of W. H. Allen, Mark Goulden, wrote in with his remedy:

> I suggest the time is ripe to revive and develop a nation-wide service that has prematurely and regrettably sunk into desuetude—the private lending library... As a senior British publisher with over 50 years' experience in catering for 'the reading public' I believe the resuscitation of the private lending library... would be welcomed by the majority of readers; it would assuredly result in more books being sold (giving joy to booksellers and publishers) and above all it would give authors the square deal they so avidly seek and so richly deserve. I further believe it to be eminently practical, timely and potentially profitable. (T 19.9.77)

This correspondence neatly formulated the question of how literature and its producers were best to be served: by forward-looking measures such as PLR, or by a return to the 1930s and the commercial rental library? On the whole the retrogressive party seemed to have the better of it. Among the booktrade, in fact, there were advocates for going even further back, to before 1900 and the net book agreement. In the same week as Goulden's letter to *The Times* Max Harris contributed a pugnacious piece to *The Spectator*, rejoicing in the imminent decontrolling of the British retail booktrade: 'The "net book agreement" in Britain is going to be destroyed by silent if not legislated consent' (Sp 17.9.77) he prophesied. In his Australian zeal Harris may have jumped the gun somewhat, but a new era of *laissez aller* was clearly signalled. Certainly the mood of the time seems to have turned against some of the kinds of cultural interventionism discussed in this book—PLR and the New Fiction Society, for example. (The Arts Council Literature department was also suffering a bad press, following the resignation of Roy Fuller as chairman of the Literature Panel, and his public attack on its activities.) Meanwhile a sense of confident self-sufficiency is exuded by the British booktrade. It has weathered the recession, apparently, and in its recovered buoyancy can be left to solve its problems (and the novel's problems) without outside assistance and by recourse to the most robust forms of free enterprise.

In retrospect the crisis might well appear to be no more than an economic hiccup, a brief intermission of otherwise sustained post-war prosperity. But it is not entirely a case of change merely delivering the same thing. Certain things do seem radically altered as regards the publishing and patronage of fiction. The public libraries have not enjoyed a complete recovery, nor will Goulden's private libraries fill the gap in the immediate future, if indeed they ever do. A theme of this book has been that the cost of producing a novel will ultimately condition the kind of fiction which is produced. And the economics of fiction have changed—put bluntly novels are more expensive investments for the producer, distributor and seller. Together with the cutback in enlightened institutional purchase, the expansion of the mass-paperback sector, the industrialisation of publishing, all trends would seem inescapably towards the 'American future' described in chapter 3. Of necessity this will entail a harsher climate for the creation of new and ambitious fiction. On present evidence legislation and state patronage can do little to mitigate this inclemency.

Seriousness is in order, but one should not be too gloomy about such developments. Per Gedin, for example, in his recent *Literature in the Market Place* (London, 1977) seems to me to be extravagantly pessimistic when he foresees the end of the 'literary novel' and takes it to be symptomatic of a general cultural collapse in Europe:

Even though the novel no longer occupies the same central position in our culture it is an irreplaceable part of it. But the novel can only survive and flourish with a reasonably broad offering, if it is to reach its public in a natural way. To keep it from being isolated it must be given powerful support by society. No section of the cultivated circuit will in the future have the potential to give the novel the support it requires, neither writers, publishers nor booksellers. It is perhaps logical, but hardly satisfactory, that those cultural forms such as the theatre and films, which are better suited to the mass society, have already received considerable government aid in many countries while the book has so far had to go without. An immediate and sizeable contribution by society is needed in order to preserve and continue the literary book—as much for the sake of society itself as for the book. (p. 195. Gedin's injunction gains force from this being the last paragraph in the book.)

That Western society should mend itself by looking to the season's novels is an odd prescription. One feels like answering it with the purgative Marxism of Walter Benjamin, concerned about the survival of a more obviously threatened Europe in 1934 and relatively nonchalant about the survival of its fiction:

Novels did not always exist in the past, nor must they necessarily always exist in the future; nor, always, tragedies; nor great epics; literary forms such as the commentary, the translation, yes, even the pastiche, have not always existed merely as minor exercises in the margin of literature, but have had a place, not only in the philosophical but also the literary traditions of Arabia or China. ('The Author as Producer,' *Understanding Brecht*, London, 1973, p. 89)

One need not, however, adopt Benjamin's world-historical scale in order to contradict Gedin's alarmism. His over-valuation of the novel as intrinsically humane and culturally necessary accompanies a questionable post-war analysis. Gedin discerns a critical shift ('decline') from bourgeois to mass culture in Western democracies over this relatively short period. The approved bourgeois culture was broad, uncoerced and diverse—tolerating even creative antagonism in the shape of avant garde art. The disapproved mass democracy is uniform and commercially exploitative. America precedes Europe in the trend towards mass democracy and denatured literature not because it is more advanced, but because 'Americans have never had a bourgeois class with homogeneous reading habits' (p. 186). The novel is a prime casualty in this calamitous shift and in mass culture's mature phase 'it no longer has a crucial or central function in literature' (p. 153).

Gedin's Spenglerian thesis begs larger questions than can be answered here. But a somewhat sceptical perspective can be given it by reminding ourselves that the same gloomily terminal views have been delivered authoritatively any time this last hundred years (by Ruskin, Henry James and Q. D. Leavis, among many others).

Gedin's argument also suffers a self-inflicted wound by the examples with which he chooses to clinch it. Apropos of quality novelists who have allegedly become isolated in our mass culture he tells us:

There are already a number of very good writers who receive excellent reviews, but whose books are confined to a closed system with few readers, and they have virtually no hope of a breakthrough in the future. In the USA, for instance, there are Walker Percy, William Gass, John Cheever, John Barth, or in England Margaret Drabble, Brigid Brophy, Penelope Mortimer and Colin Wilson. (pp. 184–5).

In the year of *Falconer* and *The Ice Age* this commiseration reads peculiarly hollowly. (Nor would one despise the royalties of *The Sot-Weed Factor*, *Ritual in the Dark* or *The Pumpkin Eater*; at least half of this list may be said to have been bestsellers at some stage of their career.)

Gedin's jeremiad indicates the risk of using booktrade evidence to bolster tendentious historical theses. Clearly there may have been transforming influences on the production of fiction recently. None-the less we do not yet face Benjamin's future without novels, nor even Gedin's displacement of the literary novel to peripheral inconsequence. Transforming influences will transform—but such influences are frequent in the evolution of the novel over the past two hundred and fifty years. The crisis of the 1970s will probably take its place in a long series of critical episodes in the production of fiction none of which has yet proved final, however painful they seemed at the time.

www.ingramcontent.com/pod-product-compliance
Ingram Content Group UK Ltd.
Pitfield, Milton Keynes, MK11 3LW, UK
UKHW021908150926
475560UK00003B/255

9 781472 513151